Beginning PowerShell for SharePoint 2013

Nikolas Charlebois-Laprade

Apress·

Beginning PowerShell for SharePoint 2013

Copyright © 2014 by Nikolas Charlebois-Laprade

ISBN-13 (pbk): 978-1-4302-6472-9

ISBN-13 (electronic): 978-1-4302-6473-6

President and Publisher: Paul Manning
Lead Editor: Jonathan Hassell
Development Editor: Chris Nelson
Technical Reviewer: Mathieu Desmarais
Editorial Board: Steve Anglin, Mark Beckner, Ewan Buckingham, Gary Cornell, Louise Corrigan, Jim DeWolf, Jonathan Gennick, Jonathan Hassell, Robert Hutchinson, Michelle Lowman, James Markham, Matthew Moodie, Jeff Olson, Jeffrey Pepper, Douglas Pundick, Ben Renow-Clarke, Dominic Shakeshaft, Gwenan Spearing, Matt Wade, Steve Weiss
Coordinating Editor: Mark Powers
Copy Editor: Laura Lawrie
Compositor: SPi Global
Indexer: SPi Global
Artist: SPi Global
Cover Designer: Anna Ishchenko

Distributed to the book trade worldwide by Springer Science+Business Media New York, 233 Spring Street, 6th Floor, New York, NY 10013. Phone 1-800-SPRINGER, fax (201) 348-4505, e-mail orders-ny@springer-sbm.com, or visit www.springeronline.com. Apress Media, LLC is a California LLC and the sole member (owner) is Springer Science + Business Media Finance Inc (SSBM Finance Inc). SSBM Finance Inc is a Delaware corporation.

For information on translations, please e-mail rights@apress.com, or visit www.apress.com.

Apress and friends of ED books may be purchased in bulk for academic, corporate, or promotional use. eBook versions and licenses are also available for most titles. For more information, reference our Special Bulk Sales–eBook Licensing web page at www.apress.com/bulk-sales.

Any source code or other supplementary material referenced by the author in this text is available to readers at www.apress.com/9781430264729. For detailed information about how to locate your book's source code, go to www.apress.com/source-code.

To my wife Krystel, who doesn't always love this incredibly busy life I live, but who's always there to support me in all my crazy projects: Je t'aime.

Contents at a Glance

Contents

About the Author

Nikolas Charlebois-Laprade is an early adopter of anything worth a try, and he's always trying to think outside the box. He is a software engineer based in Gatineau, Québec, where he manages several technical project teams. An active blogger, Nik also speaks at several technology-focused conferences every year. Nik is also the owner of IgniteSoft, a startup that specializes in custom web deployment and cloud hosting.

Nik is a geek with people skills. He often is thought of as only being a SharePoint guy. However, as SharePoint is an integration technology forcing experts to learn an incredible variety of different web technologies, Nik prefers to think of himself as a software generalist. Always trying to innovate, his favorite quote is from George Bernard Shaw: "You see things; and you say, 'Why?' But I dream things that never were; and I say, 'Why not?'" This quote summarizes Nik perfectly! His wife and kids are what motivates him to always push the boundaries of what is possible to achieve.

About the Technical Reviewer

Mathieu Desmarais is an independent consultant, SharePoint architect, and developer, certified as MCPD and MCTS. IIe has worked with SharePoint for the past 9 years on multiple projects for a wide range of sectors and has over 13 years' experience in the IT industry. Blogger and speaker, Mathieu loves to share his passion and knowledge for SharePoint and other cool technology with the world. When he is not learning or coding, he spends his time with his wife and five amazing kids.

Acknowledgments

There are many people to thank for the successful completion of this book, starting with my wife, Krystel, who's been putting up with my crazy working hours for the past few years. If it wasn't for her, I would have never been able to pull out enough time in my schedule to write this book. I always have these crazy new projects popping up in my head when I'm not even done with the previous ones. Just wait until I retire; I have many more in store just for you and me!

Next on the list are my two wonderful children, Eloïk and Emy, who I need to thank for motivating me in writing this book. I wished to show you both that nothing is impossible if you really put your heart into it. This book is a real proof of this, and I love you with all my heart.

I also would like to take the opportunity to thank my mother for guiding me throughout the various choices I made earlier on in my career and in my life. You really did an awesome job making something out of this hyperactive son of yours.

I have always strongly believed in associating oneself with a mentor if you wish to become better in life: socially and in your career. I have been extremely lucky in my career to always work with somebody who I can look up to. All of you have contributed to the professional I have become.

To Anne Latreille, thanks for giving a chance to the 17-year-old student you interviewed a decade ago. Thanks for teaching me your professional ethic for dealing with clients, and thank you for always trying to push me to move forward in my career.

To Sean Kibbee, thanks for making me realize that there is an application for everything I had learned in school. This book is a technical one, and, to me, I owe all of the technical skills that I now possess to that sense of curiosity for technology that you passed on to me. Thanks for everything you taught me, and for the fun I had learning it with you. I truly hope our professional paths cross again in the near future.

To Pat Liston, thanks for seeing potential in me. If it wasn't for you, I believe I would still be writing static HTML websites and would have never had the chance to fully leverage my potential. You have given me the strength to always challenge someone when they say something is not feasible. You really did a lot for me and I am forever in your debt for this.

To Peter Kusovac, thanks for that chance to play in your lab, dude; I had a blast. You taught me not to be afraid to break outside of the tradition, and to study a problem from new angles that nobody ever thought of before. It is because of you, and you only, if I am now drenched in the wonderful world of SharePoint, and I could never be too much grateful for this.

To Charles Davis, thanks for giving me such a great platform to innovate within your team. You have a contagious passion about the work you do and the business you serve.

Thanks to Mathieu Desmarais and Chris Nelson, my technical reviewer and editor for this book. It was a pleasure working with you both, and thanks for saving my skin on more than one occasion throughout these chapters.

Finally, a huge thank you to all of the SharePoint community. You guys are the best. To all the people mentionned above, I hope that you can all have an impact on someone else's professional life as big as the one you all have had on mine.

CHAPTER 1

■ ■ ■

Introduction

The concept behind *Beginning PowerShell for SharePoint 2013* is an idea I've been holding on to for a few years now. In every technology stream you look at, there's always a clear distinction between administrators, referred to as IT Pros in the Microsoft world, and developers. Administrators often think of developers as taking too many risks and not considering the overall impact that their solutions may have on the system as a whole. They also don't like the fact that they don't have control over what is being executed by the code provided. I can't tell you how often I've seen developers provide administrators with command line executables for them to run on SharePoint servers in order to fix some issues with the SharePoint farm. On the other end, developers tend to think of administrators as being too restrictive and always trying to put sticks in their wheels. I've seen this everywhere I've worked in the past, and I'm sure most readers can picture themselves in this situation.

PowerShell brings the best of both worlds, allowing administrators to view in clear text what is being executed as part of a script, and letting developers reuse their knowledge of the SharePoint object model by writing reusable modules and methods. It doesn't require users to compile any code, and it is leveraging all of the power of the Microsoft .NET framework. The goal of this book is to try to bridge the gap that exists between SharePoint IT Pros and developers by giving users tools to be able to deploy, manage, and monitor their SharePoint environment themselves. At the end of the book, users will be able to perform most operations that are available through the Central Administration interface or through the SharePoint object model, by developing their own flexible and reusable PowerShell scripts.

The SharePoint Challenges

In every IT organization, it is very common to find a clear distinction between the developers and the administrators. Developers create new modules and functionalities for systems, and administrators are responsible for implementing and deploying them to production environments. Administrators are also normally in charge of configuring and maintaining the environments where these solutions have been deployed. In many cases, developers are creating solutions without really getting a grasp of what their solution will imply from a configuration perspective. They give the administrators the instructions to implement their product and off they go. Even in the SharePoint world, this is often the case.

I've worked in several different IT organizations that have been dealing with the technology, and I've seen many cases in which administrators have to perform hours of manual intervention to properly configure solutions across all sites in a SharePoint environment. To give you a concrete example, think of a scenario in which a development team creates a new web part that needs to be added to all existing webs in an environment. This is a typical scenario, but what if the environment includes 10,000 webs spread across multiple site collections? To think that someone is going to go through each of these and manually add the web part is pure craziness. This type of situation highlights the need for a solution that would let administrators responsible for implementing solutions automate tasks in a repeatable fashion.

I remember my first ever SharePoint-related assignment. I was then responsible for my organization's internal SharePoint 2003 environment. We had well over 25,000 webs across various site collections. My job was to activate the French language in the regional settings in each of them. My team and I ended up creating a custom console application that was using the SharePoint 2003 object model to loop through each site collection, go into every web and activate the language setting. This console application was being compiled as an executable file (.exe) and had to be executed directly on the SharePoint server for it to be able to properly communicate with the various components. My job as a developer was to produce this executable file, and to hand it over to the environment's administrators, who had no clue what my executable really was doing in the backend. They had to trust me that it did exactly what I said it would, and that it wouldn't impact servers for which they were accountable. It was like a black box; you couldn't view what was in it. Double-clicking these executable files to initiate the processes was always a very stressful process. Administrators like to be in control and know what is going on. That is just the nature of the beast. At the time, we implemented all of our "repetitive" configuration processes using this methodology. We ended up with over 20 such executable files, and nobody knew for sure exactly what each of them were doing without opening their code in Visual Studio and figure out the execution flow. What a mess that was. Other than the fact that this process made it tough on the administrators to identify what was being done to their environments by an obscure piece of software, the only way you could create such a repetitive configuration task was to know how to code. You had to be a .NET developer in order to find your way through the object model.

When PowerShell came around, near the end of SharePoint 2007 product's life, it was like a revelation. Now, we could have the same repetitive configuration tasks being executed against the server, but they were no longer contained in these black boxes that were the console applications. They were now stored as plain text PowerShell scripts that administrators could open to take a peek at the logic they contained. For the record, PowerShell scripts are stored as .ps1 files and can be edited using any text editor software. I personally use Notepad for all my scripts, but there are some other good free alternatives that offer advanced features such as the automatic completion of commands' names after a few characters to help speed the writing process. The problem, however, was that if you didn't know your way in the .NET programming world, chances were that you would be totally lost in the code. SharePoint 2007 did not provide any PowerShell methods to interact with its components. You had to load the SharePoint assemblies in your PowerShell sessions and interact with the .NET objects directly. It was basically the same as writing your code in Visual Studio.

SharePoint 2010 then came to the rescue. It offered what we can call shortcut methods, or cmdlets (pronounced command-lets), that allowed users to interact with various SharePoint artifacts in a very straightforward and easy way. For example, assume that you are trying to get the title of a specific SharePoint web in your environment. In the SharePoint 2007 world, this had to be achieved using the something similar to the following lines of PowerShell:

```
[System.Reflection.Assembly]::LoadWithPartialName("Microsoft.SharePoint")
$site = New-Object Microsoft.SharePoint.SPSite("http://localhost")
$web = $site.RootWeb
$title = $web.Title
```

Using PowerShell with SharePoint, the same operation can now be achieved using the following two lines of PowerShell:

```
$web = Get-SPWeb http://localhost
$title = $web.Title
```

This new way of using PowerShell to interact with SharePoint not only made the scripts simpler, it also made them more readable. Administrators wanting to write scripts no longer had to know the SharePoint object model inside-out in order to build powerful PowerShell scripts (although it definitively helped).

PowerShell is not just for administrators, however. Complex scripts might still require some level of programming skills in order to be completed. In many organizations, developers are still responsible for writing the PowerShell scripts for maintenance tasks. This is an interesting paradigm, because it forces them to be aware of how the administration modules of SharePoint actually work. If you want to have a PowerShell script developed for your organization that automates the creation of hundreds of crawled properties for your SharePoint search engine, the developer writing the script will need to understand the various search administrative components in order to properly develop his script. This means that, on one end, we need administrators to start understanding some high-level programming concept and understand the SharePoint object model to some level, and, on the other end, we have developers that need to be more open-minded about the administration aspect and learn how to properly configure administrative components of SharePoint. Figure 1-1 illustrates this concept.

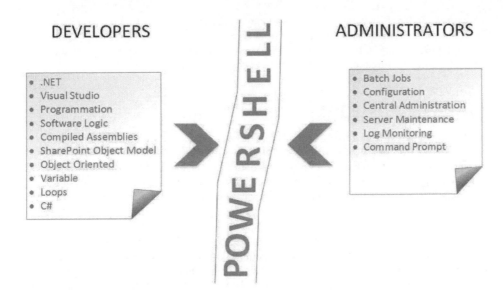

Figure 1-1. *Traditional developers versus trditional administrators*

Throughout this book, we will cover material that in a traditional mind-set would be specific to SharePoint administrators, such as timer jobs, health monitors, and backups, but we will also touch on topics that developers would normally be more familiar with such as lists and list items. By writing this book, my goal was to try to bring traditional SharePoint developers to learn more on the administration aspect of the product, and for administrators to learn more about how the various artifacts are organized in the SharePoint object model. Therefore, by the end of this reading, I hope to bring you out of your comfort zone by opening your horizons and making you understand the possibilities to bring as many developers and administrators on par with regard to their SharePoint skillsets.

History of PowerShell

Microsoft's latest scripting language, PowerShell, was first released back in fall of 2006, just a few months before the release of SharePoint 2007. Because of the parallel development schedule for the two products, SharePoint 2007 never really had any integration points with PowerShell. Sure, you could interact with your environment using PowerShell and by making direct calls to objects inside the SharePoint assemblies, but that was never really publicized or even recommended by Microsoft as an official way of managing your systems. SharePoint administrators had to manage their environments using a legacy command line tool called Stsadm that was first introduced with the original release of SharePoint, then called SharePoint Team Sites (STS).

A few years after came SharePoint 2010, and the story changed completely. Microsoft finally came out and announced that PowerShell was now an official contender on the SharePoint administration scene. In this version, administrators were now officially allowed to choose between the old Stsadmway of managing SharePoint environments or to use this new technology called PowerShell and be part of the cool kids. Microsoft also announced that they were investing a lot in the technology, and that they were making over 400 methods available to administrators to help them better manage their farms. Not only is PowerShell more powerful in terms of the type of scripts you can produce using it, but it is also more performant in most cases, compared to its Stsadm equivalent. The technology allows you to directly interact with any .NET entity and to declare custom ones if need be, placing it somewhere between a pure development language, and a traditional sequential scripting one.

When SharePoint 2013 was released in the spring of 2013, Microsoft announced that they had made several new methods available through PowerShell to interact with the new platform's features. Nowadays, PowerShell has definitively become the standard tool for SharePoint administrators to use when managing their farms. It is important to note, however, that the Stsadm command line tool is still available to people that are feeling nostalgic.

So, What Is PowerShell Anyway?

Without giving away too much information about what PowerShell truly is under the hood (this will be covered in detail in Chapter 4), I'll try to give a 1,000-foot overview of what it really is about. First, PowerShell is a scripting language. It is not a tool, nor is it framework; it's just a plain human-readable language you can use to write your scripts. PowerShell scripts are in many ways similar to batch jobs, in that they are simply plain text files that you execute through a console application to achieve the automation of certain administrative tasks on a machine. The scripts are now compiled, and can be written using any good old text editor software. I write all of my PowerShell scripts using Notepad (I love living on the edge).

A PowerShell script can contain logic loops, variables, methods, and other entities from the programming world. When you write a PowerShell script, you normally save it as a plain text file having a .ps1 extension. You are then required to initiate a PowerShell console session to execute your script. The PowerShell console looks in every aspect similar to the plain and old boring command line console we all know and love, with the exception that it has a blue background with white text. Everything that you can do in a command line console can be done in a PowerShell console session—and more. You do not even need to write scripts in PowerShell to execute a sequence of logical operations. The console keeps the various variable declarations in memory for the entire duration of the PowerShell session. Figure 1-2 shows you a fairly simple PowerShell session in which variables have been declared and are remembered throughout the execution of the various commands. It starts by declaring two variables, `variableA` and `variableB`, and later their values will be reused to perform mathematical operations. You then continue by changing the value of one of the two variables that you already declared and by rerunning the same addition operation to get a different result based on the new value entered.

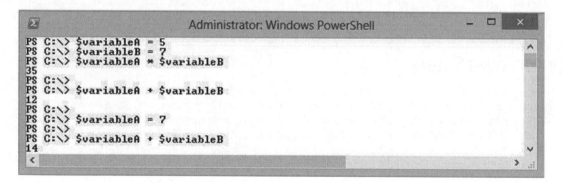

Figure 1-2. *Using variables in a PowerShell console session*

PowerShell scripts can also make use of external .NET assemblies, which, in my mind, is what really brings the scripting tool to the next level. Imagine that developers in your organization have developed a .NET utility that exposes a bunch of methods that are to be used by various .NET applications and services in your organization. If the methods contained in the resulting assemblies are publicly exposed, meaning that any external process can access them, then PowerShell can leverage the functionality inside of these utilities for scripting purpose.

Take the following example, in which you have developed a .NET application that has an graphical interface that lets the users view and interact with an interactive bedtime story, say *Snow White* (yes, I have a young daughter). Now, pretend that your developers have exposed a method called `MirrorMirror` that, when called by the graphical interface, returns the name of the person who's the fairest of them all. Well, you could use PowerShell to import a reference to this functionality and have it used in your script for other purposes. Figure 1-3 shows that this fictive scenario is easily achievable with the PowerShell technology.

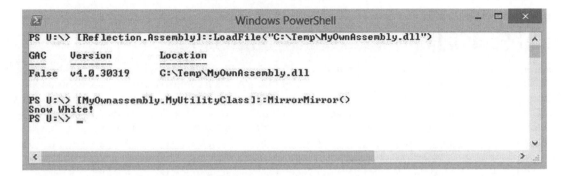

Figure 1-3. *Using PowerShell to interact with external .NET assemblies*

Another very interesting thing to note from PowerShell is that because it is built on top of the Microsoft .NET stack, it can also reuse any graphical interface component.NET has to offer. Although you could argue why you would ever need to build a graphical user interface using PowerShell, this highlights the fundamentals of reusing various building blocks that are made available through existing components to come up with interesting solutions. For instance, you could reuse a combination of .NET libraries and the SharePoint Client Object Model to build interactive graphical applications that can interact remotely with a SharePoint environment. An example of such an application can be found on my blog at http://www.nikcharlebois.com/Lists/Posts/Post.aspx?ID=53. Figure 1-4 shows a graphical interface generated by PowerShell.

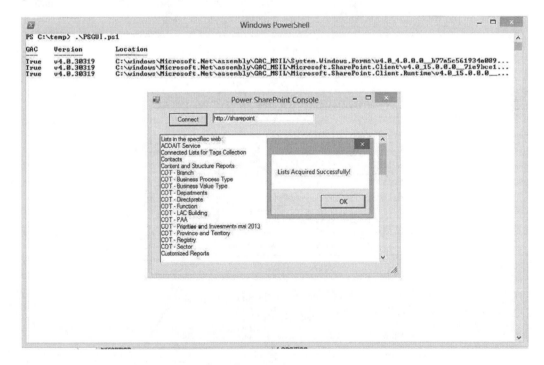

Figure 1-4. *A graphical interface generated by PowerShell*

During the process of writing this book, Microsoft officially announced the general availability of Windows Server 2012 R2 in October 2013. This release of Microsoft's latest server operating system also introduced the latest version of the PowerShell scripting engine, version 4.0. There are a few new goodies included in this latest release, but I won't be covering those in details in this book.

SharePoint Foundation versus SharePoint Server

One of the questionsthat you may ask yourself when you first start playing with PowerShell is what is different between the SharePoint 2013 Server and the SharePoint Foundation 2013 editions. As we'll come to learn later on in this book, the component responsible for all the PowerShell goodness in SharePoint 2013 is in the `Microsoft.SharePoint.PowerShell` definition file contained in the ISAPI folder of the SharePoint's 15 hive. This file existswhether you'd be running SharePoint 2013 Foundation, SharePoint 2013 Standard Edition, or SharePoint Server 2013. In theory, this would mean that all the PowerShell components are the same for all three editions wouldn't it? The answers to that question is no, even if the file exists for all of them, because they each have restrictions on the methods you can use. For example, SharePoint 2013 Foundation RTM exposes about 600 PowerShell methods, whereas SharePoint Server Enterprise and SharePoint Server Standard both have around 700. This makes sense, given the number of features that are available in SharePoint Server but not in the Foundationedition.

If you take a closer look at the list of available methods for each edition, you will realize that the set of available methods is incremental, starting with SharePoint 2013 Foundation as being the edition with the least available, and the Enterprise edition having the most (which makes total sense). If you compare the Foundation edition with the Standard edition, you will see that the latter adds methods such as those to create a new instance of the Metadata Service Application. This service application is only made available in the SharePoint 2013 Standard and Enterprise editions; therefore, it is not part of the available methods for the Foundation edition. Comparing the Standard and Enterprise editions, you will see that there are several new methods that deal with components such as the Machine Translation Service, Excel Services, and others that have been introduced in the Enterprise edition of the product. Figure 1-5 illustrates some of the available PowerShell methods available by edition. We can clearly see in this figure that the more you go up in the pyramid, the more available PowerShell options are available.

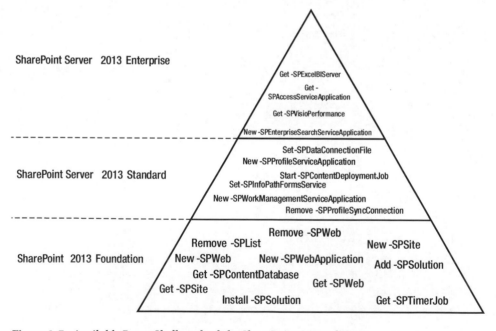

Figure 1-5. *Available PowerShell methods by SharePoint 2013 editions*

If you take a closer look at the available methods for each edition of the SharePoint 2013 product, one of the surprises is to see the PowerShell methods that deal with the Enterprise Search components. For example, the `New-SPEnterpriseSearchServiceApplication` method, which creates a new instance of the SharePoint 2013 Enterprise Search Service Application, is made available in SharePoint 2013 Foundation. As surprising as this may be, you need to know that the Enterprise Search service application has always been available in the SharePoint Foundation. In fact, it is one of the very few service applications available in this edition. However, there is a caveat with the service application: only one instance of it can exist in SharePoint 2013 Foundation. By default, when you install SharePoint Foundation, a default instance of it is created. If you try to use PowerShell to instantiate a second one, you'll get an error similar to that shown in Figure 1-6. This simply means that it is not just because a PowerShell method is made available to us that it is officially supported for a given edition of the product.

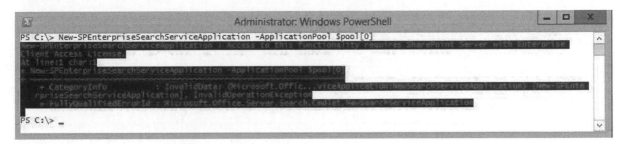

Figure 1-6. *PowerShell error when trying to provision a new search service application in SharePoint 2013 Foundation*

What You Will Learn in This Book

This book is all about bringing both the SharePoint developers and the SharePoint administrators to a level where they both understand how they can use PowerShell to help them in their daily jobs. It is not about teaching the internals of SharePoint, although we will take a brief look under the hood. I will be assuming through this book that readers have had some exposure to SharePoint 2013 but no exposure to the PowerShell technology whatsoever. I will be covering the basic concepts of PowerShell, and will slowly dive into the various aspects of SharePoint administration. There's one thing that readers need to keep in mind throughout this book: I am a developer, and my background is purely development. The ultimate goal of this book is to allow developers to slowly make a move toward the dark side of SharePoint administration, and for administrators to improve their development skills by developing dynamic PowerShell scripts.

Throughout this book, you will learn what is new in the latest version of SharePoint 2013 with PowerShell, learn how to configure your environment to use PowerShell, learn how to interact with the various components of SharePoint 2013 both onpremises and in the cloud, and also learn how to facilitate your SharePoint 2010 to 2013 migration using PowerShell. Special attention will be given to interacting with the new SharePoint 2013 app model. I will also be covering several real-life examples of scenarios in which you may want to consider writing a PowerShell script for your own organization.

Summary

Now that you've learned a bit more about what PowerShell is and how it can interact with your SharePoint environment, you are ready to move on to the next level and give you an overview of the different types of scenarios in which you can use PowerShell to assist you in your daily work. In the next chapter, we will give you an overview of the various sections of this book, as well as introduce you to the new features in PowerShell with SharePoint 2013. Remember that each chapter builds on the previous one to deliver new material. It is strongly recommended that you read carefully through each chapter to make sure that you grasp every concept. Whether you are a SharePoint administrator or a developer, I truly believe this book will help you grow as an Information Technology specialist, and I hope that you have as much fun reading the information it contains as I had writing it.

CHAPTER 2

■ ■ ■

What's New in PowerShell for SharePoint 2013

As the saying goes, with great power comes great responsibilities, and with every great version of SharePoint comes a great set of PowerShell features. Okay, that's a very cheesy joke, but on a serious note the PowerShell story with SharePoint 2013 just got better; a lot better! I remember when I first heard of using PowerShell to manage a SharePoint environment. That was back in 2009 while sitting in a session at the SharePoint Conference at which Microsoft first announced SharePoint 2010. Back in those days, people were using a command line tool called stsadm to manage their environments, and dinosaurs still walked the earth. The presenter had shown a demo in which an automated script using stsadm was creating 100,000 site collections. He had then compared the results with running the same type of logic, but this time using PowerShell. The results were just unbelievable: PowerShell was on average four times faster than the traditional command line way of doing things. With every major release since then, Microsoft just kept adding more and more new PowerShell methods to make our life as easy as possible.

Version 3.0 of PowerShell was released by Microsoft early fall 2012, and SharePoint 2013 has been made so that it can leverage its full power. Assuming that you have PowerShell version 3.0 installed on a SharePoint 2010 farm, you are still able to switch back to version 2.0 of the tool. SharePoint 2010 doesn't work with PowerShell version 3.0, which is why you may need to switch back to version 2.0. With SharePoint 2013, tons of new methods have been introduced. You will discover these new methods and features throughout this book. The focus of the present chapter is to highlight some of the new features that have been made available with the venue of PowerShell version 3.0 for managing SharePoint 2013. You will get an overview of some of the major new improvements to the tool in this chapter. Further details will be given in later chapters of this book.

SharePoint 2013 Apps

With SharePoint 2013, Microsoft introduced a new type of building block for custom business solutions, called SharePoint apps. These apps represent pieces of functionality that can run alongside or outside the SharePoint environment. Because these are brand new with SharePoint 2013, Microsoft introduced a full set of new PowerShell methods to help to install, deploy, manage, upgrade, and uninstall these apps in the SharePoint environment. For more details on how PowerShell can help you manage SharePoint 2013 apps in your environment, please refer to Chapter 7. Figure 2-1 shows the newly added Apps section in the SharePoint 2013 central administration web interface.

Apps
Manage App Catalog
Manage App Licenses
Monitor Apps

Figure 2-1. *The Apps feature set in Central Administration*

Service Applications

Back in the 2010 version of SharePoint, Microsoft introduced a new concept called *service applications*. These include the Search Service application, the Visio Graphics Service, the secure store, and the Business Connectivity Services, to name a few. In SharePoint 2007, these were called Shared Services Providers (SSPs) and were limited in terms of scalability and flexibility. The concept behind service applications was that they could be exposed and reused by other SharePoint farms.

In SharePoint 2013, there are several new service applications that have been introduced (Work Management, App Management, etc.). Because these are entirely new pieces of the SharePoint ecosystem, Microsoft introduced a large set of new PowerShell methods to allow to the creation, configuration, and management of these new service applications. For more details on how to use PowerShell to manage SharePoint 2013 service applications, please refer to Chapters 7 and 8. Figure 2-2 shows how to use PowerShell to list all of the available service applications in a SharePoint environment.

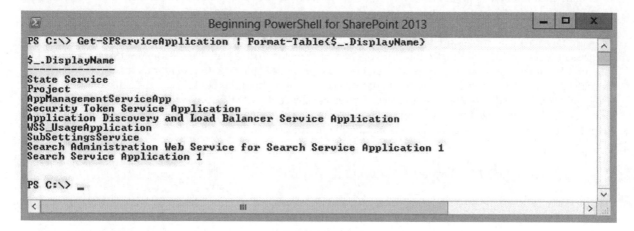

Figure 2-2. *Listing existing service applications in a SharePoint 2013 farm using PowerShell*

User License Enforcements

In previous versions of SharePoint, managing end-users' licenses has always been a real nightmare. With SharePoint 2013, it is now feasible for administrators to map users and security groups to specific licenses. It is now possible, for example, to assign basic SharePoint Server 2013 licenses to a certain set of users while assigning enterprise licenses to others. The type of license that is assigned to a user will decide what features the user is authorized to use and consume. Let's take, for example, the Excel Services feature, which is an enterprise feature. Assume that I'm assigned an enterprise license and that I build a page that has various images and blocks of text but that uses an Excel Services web part to expose data. A user who's only assigned a basic license comes to my page will be able to view the images and text; however, where the Excel Services web parts shows for me, the user will see an error message saying that a valid license to use this feature could not be found (see Figure 2-3). The set of new PowerShell features offered by SharePoint 2013 includes a dozen of user-license enforcement specific methods to help you manage the various types of licenses that you may have in your organization. To learn more about user-license enforcement, refer to Chapter 8 of this book.

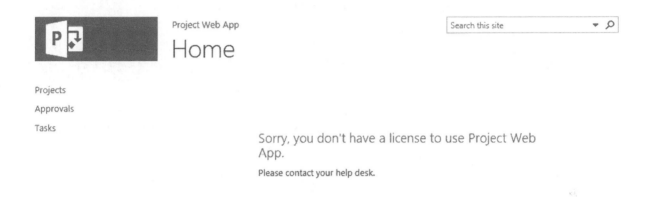

Figure 2-3. Error message when trying to use a SharePoint 2013 component for which you are not granted a valid license

PowerShell Web Access

Although this is not a SharePoint 2013 specific feature, it is nice to know that PowerShell Web Access (PWA) is something that could easily be implemented to ease your job as a SharePoint administrator. With version 3.0 of PowerShell, Microsoft introduced this new feature. As the name would indicate, it is a mechanism by which administrators can set up a web portal on the SharePoint server to allow remote authenticated users to run PowerShell commands at a distance. This can prove very useful in certain scenarios in which administrators having to execute an emergency script only have access to the web interface of the SharePoint environment. Maybe they don't have VPN support to instantiate a remote session on the server to allow them to run PowerShell on it directly. PowerShell Web Access would prove to be extremely useful in such scenarios. To learn more on how to properly install and deploy PowerShell Web Access within your environment, you can refer to Chapter 3 of this book. Figure 2-4 shows the main screen of a PowerShell Web Access session viewed through a web browser.

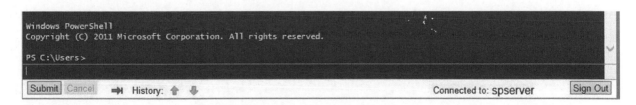

Figure 2-4. PowerShell Web Access main session window

Backups

The concept of backing up data and artifacts in SharePoint got a major overhaul in the 2010 version of the product. Microsoft continues to build on this very important aspect of SharePoint administration in their latest release of the product. They introduced the capability to back up the index generated by the newly redesigned Enterprise Search module. This can prove to be a valuable asset when dealing with multiple large indexes for your SharePoint Search environment. On top of this, Microsoft continues to offer to possibility to backup entire farms, site collections, and configuration databases using PowerShell (see Figure 2-5). To learn more about automating backups in SharePoint 2013 using PowerShell, refer to Chapter 8 of this book.

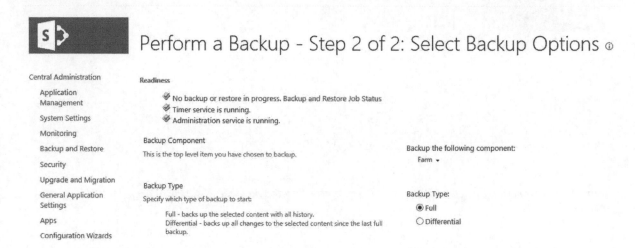

Figure 2-5. *SharePoint 2013 Backup Options screen from Central Administration*

Bing Maps

A great new addition to the SharePoint 2013 family is the integration of Bing Maps as part of the geolocation field types. It is now possible in SharePoint 2013 to use a new type of field called Geolocation, which lets you specify coordinates for a specific location as input (see Figure 2-6). You can then use Bing Maps to visualize this location on the item view form. All of these features are available out-of-the-box, but you must use PowerShell to activate it. For more details on using the Geolocation field in SharePoint 2013, you can refer to Microsoft's TechNet entry at http://msdn.microsoft.com/en-us/library/jj163135(v=office.15).aspx.

Figure 2-6. *Entering a new item that uses the new Geolocation field in SharePoint 2013*

■ **Note**   For more information on how to integrate the Geolocation field with your SharePoint 2013 environment, you can refer to Microsoft's article at `http://msdn.microsoft.com/en-us/library/jj163135.aspx`. Note, however, that in order for you to be able to visualize its data using Bing Maps, you'll need to configure it with your own personal key. Instructions to do so are provided in the series of articles mentioned earlier in this chapter.

Search

I have already covered to a certain level the Search aspect of SharePoint. However, I strongly believe it is important to put emphasis on the fact that Microsoft really outdid themselves with SharePoint 2013 to try to expose to PowerShell as many features as possible from their new Search infrastructure. Just by looking at the list of new PowerShell commands for SharePoint 2013 that Microsoft released back in July 2012, that's 51 new methods just for the search component. As you can see in Figure 2-7, this brings the total number of available PowerShell methods to manage search to close to 150 (depending on the platform version you are running). New methods are still being added every now and then as new cumulative updates to the product are released. Even though I won't be covering these 51 methods in depth throughout this book, you can refer to Chapter 8 to learn more about how to deploy and configure the SharePoint 2013 Search modules using PowerShell.

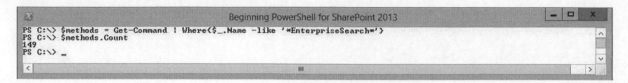

```
PS C:\> $methods = Get-Command | Where($_.Name -like '*EnterpriseSearch*')
PS C:\> $methods.Count
149
PS C:\> _
```

Figure 2-7. *Counting all available SharePoint 2013 search methods using PowerShell*

Tenants

When Microsoft built SharePoint 2013, they had one thing in mind: to build a product that would work well for on-premises deployments, and that would work equally well on cloud scenarios. Back in 2009, when the software giant announced their upcoming release of what they then called SharePoint Online, which eventually became known as Office 365, SharePoint 2013 was already well into its development phase. They knew that in order to make their online vision become a reality, some major changes in the way they allowed administrators to manage tenants environment had to be done. When I talk about multitenancy, you can think of it as hosting services. This is a concept that was officially introduced back with SharePoint 2010, which allows organizations to share a singular SharePoint farm with several different other organizations or governing bodies. It allows an organization to manage its own data, sites, and services while having them coexist in a secure way with other organizations on the same set of hardware.

SharePoint 2013 continues to build on the multitenancy features that were introduced by SharePoint 2010 by continuing to add additional support for new services and features. Office 365 is one of the best examples. When you register for an account on Microsoft's cloud platform, you are actually assigned SharePoint space on a server that cohosts several thousand other accounts. It wouldn't make sense for Microsoft to have to maintain a SharePoint farm for each of its Office 365 users. With SharePoint 2013, you now have a way of managing some newly added service applications and to partition them across different tenants. These new PowerShell features are what allowed Microsoft to expose the Search Administration pieces in SharePoint 2013 Online (Office 365), which is something that they never managed to do when the online platform was still running SharePoint 2010. The concept of multitenancy can easily become a very complex topic, and I won't be discussing it in this book. If you are interested, however, in getting more information on how you can use PowerShell to enable multitenancy in your on-premise SharePoint farms, you can refer to the following Microsoft TechNet article: http://technet.microsoft.com/en-us/library/ff652528(v=office.14).aspx. The content was released for SharePoint 2010, but the core of its content has not changed for SharePoint 2013. Figure 2-8 shows the administrative console of a SharePoint 2013 tenant site collection.

Figure 2-8. *Tenant Administration site created by PowerShell*

Office 365

Office 365 was first released to the public back in 2011. At that time, users were given the option to create various site collections based on SharePoint 2010. At first, the administrative option to manage our online SharePoint environments were very limited, but with every product update, Microsoft slowly added more and more capabilities. As an example, the ability to use the Business Connectivity services were made available in October 2011, giving users the ability to connect to external business data sources and expose them via SharePoint on Office 365. Something was still missing, however, to allow administrators to be able to automate tasks, and give them additional features than what was exposed through the web interface.

In July 2012, when Microsoft first announced SharePoint 2013, they also launched a beta preview of the new Office 365 environment. SharePoint sites in this environment were now running on SharePoint 2013. At the same time as the beta program was launched, Microsoft also released a preview version of a set of tools called the SharePoint Online Management Shell. These allowed SharePoint administrators to connect remotely to their SharePoint Online sites using PowerShell and to interact with them using a subset of the available PowerShell methods for SharePoint. During the fall of the year 2012, the final version of these tools were finally launched to the public. Over the first six months of 2013, Microsoft upgraded the existing SharePoint Online sites still on 2010 to the latest 2013 version of the platform.

Office 365 users running on SharePoint 2013 are now able to manage their SharePoint online environment remotely using PowerShell. The SharePoint Online Management Shell requires users to run PowerShell version 3.0, and requires users that use it to be granted the global administrator role on the SharePoint online environment to which they are trying to connect. As mentioned earlier, you are only given a subset of the available PowerShell commands that are available on premises, when using the Online Management shell. Microsoft continues to build on the existing list of available online PowerShell methods with every new product upgrade now scheduled for every three months. The current set of available methods include ways to create and delete SharePoint site collections and webs, manage apps and users, as well as some methods to manage security groups. At the time of writing this book, the total count of available SharePoint-specific PowerShell methods that are available online is 30. However, if you take into account the methods that are made available to maintain your overall Office 365 environment (Exchange, Outlook, Licenses, etc.), that's over 2,000 available methods to which you have access. To learn more about how you can use PowerShell to manage Office 365 accounts, please refer to Chapter 9 of this book. Figure 2-9 lists several PowerShell methods that are available with Office 365.

```
PS C:\> $items = Get-Command | Where($_.Name -like '*-SP*')
PS C:\> $items | Format-Table Name,ModuleName

Name                                  ModuleName
----                                  ----------
Add-SPOUser                           Microsoft.Online.SharePoint.PowerShell
Connect-SPOService                    Microsoft.Online.SharePoint.PowerShell
Disconnect-SPOService                 Microsoft.Online.SharePoint.PowerShell
Get-SPOAppErrors                      Microsoft.Online.SharePoint.PowerShell
Get-SPOAppInfo                        Microsoft.Online.SharePoint.PowerShell
Get-SPODeletedSite                    Microsoft.Online.SharePoint.PowerShell
Get-SPOExternalUser                   Microsoft.Online.SharePoint.PowerShell
Get-SPOSite                           Microsoft.Online.SharePoint.PowerShell
Get-SPOSiteGroup                      Microsoft.Online.SharePoint.PowerShell
Get-SPOTenant                         Microsoft.Online.SharePoint.PowerShell
Get-SPOTenantLogEntry                 Microsoft.Online.SharePoint.PowerShell
Get-SPOTenantLogLastAvailableTimeInUtc Microsoft.Online.SharePoint.PowerShell
Get-SPOUser                           Microsoft.Online.SharePoint.PowerShell
Get-SPOWebTemplate                    Microsoft.Online.SharePoint.PowerShell
New-SPOSite                           Microsoft.Online.SharePoint.PowerShell
New-SPOSiteGroup                      Microsoft.Online.SharePoint.PowerShell
Remove-SPODeletedSite                 Microsoft.Online.SharePoint.PowerShell
Remove-SPOExternalUser                Microsoft.Online.SharePoint.PowerShell
Remove-SPOSite                        Microsoft.Online.SharePoint.PowerShell
Remove-SPOSiteGroup                   Microsoft.Online.SharePoint.PowerShell
Remove-SPOUser                        Microsoft.Online.SharePoint.PowerShell
Repair-SPOSite                        Microsoft.Online.SharePoint.PowerShell
Request-SPOUpgradeEvaluationSite      Microsoft.Online.SharePoint.PowerShell
Restore-SPODeletedSite                Microsoft.Online.SharePoint.PowerShell
Set-SPOSite                           Microsoft.Online.SharePoint.PowerShell
Set-SPOSiteGroup                      Microsoft.Online.SharePoint.PowerShell
Set-SPOTenant                         Microsoft.Online.SharePoint.PowerShell
Set-SPOUser                           Microsoft.Online.SharePoint.PowerShell
Test-SPOSite                          Microsoft.Online.SharePoint.PowerShell
Upgrade-SPOSite                       Microsoft.Online.SharePoint.PowerShell

PS C:\>
```

Figure 2-9. Listing available PowerShell cmdlets using the SharePoint Online Management Shell

Site Upgrade

If you had to upgrade a SharePoint 2007 environment to SharePoint 2010, you probably remember the concept of visual upgrade that was introduced by Microsoft to create a temporary preview of what an upgraded SharePoint 2007 site collection would look like using the 2010 interface. This process was basically taking the existing site collection and applying the new SharePoint 2010 master page on top of it and updating the UIVersion property of the collection from 3 to 4 (SharePoint Foundation is version 4, whereas in the 2007 days it was called Windows SharePoint Services 3.0). The upgrade process wasn't always as straightforward as Microsoft had described it, and very often features that were working well when running on SharePoint 2007 were broken when upgrading to 2010, even if the 2007 look was still being applied. In SharePoint 2013, the story changed entirely.

Before I go further, I need to take a step back and discuss the internals of the platform. When you install SharePoint locally on a machine, it creates a folder hidden deep in the program files directory structure (normally at C:\Program Files\Common Files\Microsoft Shared\Web Server Extension\<SharePoint Version>). The cool kids normally refer to this folder as the "hive" (the 14 hive for SharePoint 2010 and the 15 hive for 2013). This folder is where SharePoint will store all of its goodies: features, web services, resources files, images, style sheets, master pages, and so on is stored in there. When you install SharePoint 2013, it actually created both hives, the 14 one and the 15 one. This ensures full fidelity for sites that run in SharePoint 2010, but on an infrastructure that is on SharePoint 2013. This means that you basically have both SharePoint 2010 and SharePoint 2013 installed in parallel and you are able to run both versions at the same time in your environment. When you create a new site collection in SharePoint 2013, you are even given the choice to create one using the SharePoint 2010 mode.

Because you have the two hives on our server, you can now be almost certain that you won't break a SharePoint site by simply upgrading its platform to SharePoint 2013 in the back end. You may see issues, however, when you upgrade a site collection from SharePoint 2010 to SharePoint 2013. When viewing a SharePoint 2010 site that is hosted on a SharePoint 2013 environment, you will get a notification message telling you that you have the option to upgrade (see Figure 2-10).

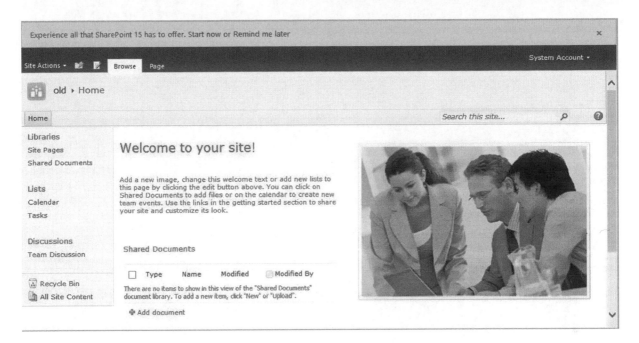

Figure 2-10. *Notification to upgrade a SharePoint 2010 site collection to SharePoint 2013*

Assuming that you are ready to upgrade your site collection to SharePoint 2013, you have the ability to create what Microsoft calls an Upgrade Evaluation Site Collection. This is a temporary copy of an existing site collection, which will be upgraded to SharePoint 2013 and that will allow you to test you upgrade. Once you are satisfy with the end result, you can officially upgrade the existing site collection, at which point the evaluation site collection will be deleted permanently. PowerShell provides various methods to allow you to control how and when to create evaluation site collection. By interacting with the SharePoint timer jobs, you can force a preview site collection to be created on the fly instead of waiting in queue for several hours before being processed. You are also provided with methods to allow you to monitor site collection upgrades while they are happening, and you have the option of controlling the automated expiration of evaluation site collections in your environment. For more information on how to perform upgrades to SharePoint 2013 using PowerShell, please refer to Chapter 10 of this book.

Summary

In this chapter you've learned about several new features that have been introduced in PowerShell version 3 that allow you to better interact and manage your SharePoint 2013 environments as a SharePoint administrator. This chapter focused on the new material for SharePoint 2013. However, if you are not familiar with the concepts of managing your SharePoint environment that have been in existence since the first release of PowerShell, the next chapters will help you learn a great deal. Because Microsoft keeps updating the platform, especially its cloud version, it is very possible that new features not discussed in the present chapter will get introduced as time goes. In the next chapter I will go over the steps required to properly configure your environment to start using PowerShell to its full potential.

CHAPTER 3

■ ■ ■

Configuring Your Environment for PowerShell

We are now ready to get our hands dirty, and start playing with PowerShell. Throughout the following pages, you will learn the fundamentals of how you should be configuring your environment to allow you to leverage the full power of PowerShell. At the end of it, you should be able to understand how to set up and configure your own environment to allow you to create, test, and execute your own scripts.

In this chapter, you will be writing and deploying your scripts locally on the SharePoint server. However, I am well aware that this scenario does not reflect the normal Lifecycle Management of PowerShell scripts that enterprises will normally follow. This chapter will provide guidance on how you can set up your scripting environment to be on a separate client operating system. It will act as a foundation to all other topics covered in the other chapters of this book. You should make sure to read all of the details carefully, and ensure that you have a stable environment to help guide you through the rest of the material covered.

In the pre–Windows Server 2008 world, you had to go on Microsoft's site and download installer files in order to have PowerShell installed on your server. With the release of Windows Server 2008, Microsoft has included the technology directly into the product, but you still have to go and activate it as a server feature in the Server Manager Console. Starting with Windows 2008 R2, PowerShell comes preinstalled with the server's operating system, which gives us a good indication of how more and more important the tool has become over the years.

After completing this chapter, you will be able to:

- Understand how to prepare your environment to use PowerShell

- Manage scripts permissions

- Setup your scripting environment

Getting Started with the Integrated Scripting Environment (ISE)

Realistically, all you need to write a PowerShell script is a text editor such as Notepad, but since version 2.0 of its PowerShell technology, Microsoft has introduced its own integrated scripting environment (ISE) to help simplify scripts development.

Windows Server 2008 R2

By default, the Scripting Environment doesn't come preinstalled, even though the core bits of the PowerShell technology are all there from the start. You will need to go in the Server Manager's console, and manually add it as a feature of your environment (see Figure 3-1). The Server Manager console can be launched by running the command ServerManager.exe from the command prompt.

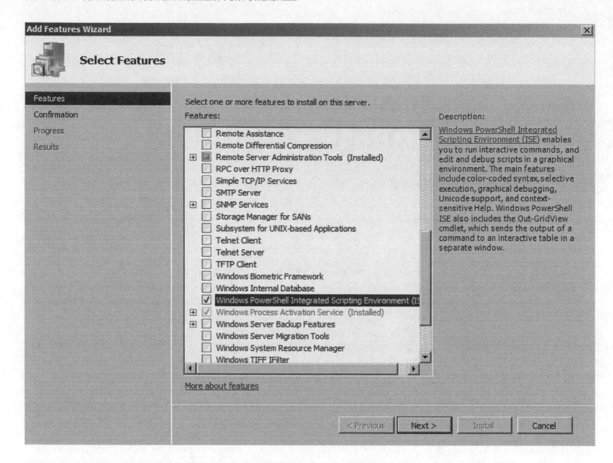

Figure 3-1. *Adding the PowerShell ISE feature in Windows Server 2008 R2*

The feature should only take a few seconds to install. Once the installation is completed, you will be able to launch the Windows PowerShell Integrated Scripting Environment (ISE) program from the Windows Run box by typing in powershell_ise (see Figure 3-2).

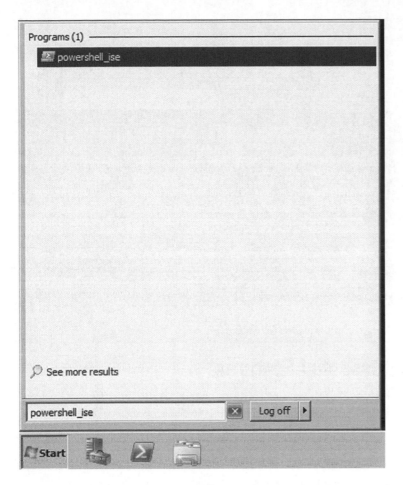

***Figure 3-2.** Launching the PowerShell ISE v2 from Windows Server 2008 R2*

It is very important to note that doing this will actually install version 2.0 of the PowerShell ISE, because, by default, Windows Server 2008 R2 has PowerShell 2.0 preinstalled. In order for you to get the v3.0 bits, you will need to go to Microsoft's site and download the Windows Management Framework 3.0 installer (www.microsoft.com/en-us/download/details.aspx?34595). There is nothing preventing you from writing your scripts for SharePoint 2013 using the v2.0 ISE; your scripts will always execute against the version of PowerShell installed on the server on which it is run, unless otherwise specified. Installing SharePoint 2013 on your Windows Server 2008 R2 environment will automatically install the Windows Management Framework 3.0. So if you are writing your scripts directly on your SharePoint box, you'll automatically get the latest version of the ISE. The latest version of the ISE is actually called Windows PowerShell ISE, so make sure that you search for that term when trying to launch the program from the Run box. It is my recommendation that you always write your scripts against the v3.0 Framework as it offers more flexibility and robustness than its predecessors.

Windows Server 2012

Good news! If you're running Windows Server 2012, the Management Framework 3.0 is already installed on your server, and so is the Windows PowerShell Integrated Scripting Environment. You will be able to launch it from the modern UI screen by searching for "Windows PowerShell ISE" (see Figure 3-3).

Figure 3-3. Launching the Windows PowerShell ISE from Windows Server 2012

Windows PowerShell ISE Essential Features

Microsoft really outdid themselves for this release of their PowerShell ISE. Tons of new features have been introduced, and many have been improved compared to its predecessors. This section will give you an overview of some of the essential features offered in the tool.

IntelliSense

This is something that all developers use on a daily basis. IntelliSense offers you suggestions as you type, and gives you intuitive descriptions of what the various methods (cmdlets) are expecting as parameters (see Figure 3-4). This is something that was missed by many in the earlier version of the product. Many third-party vendors added this as part of their offering in order to attract more customers. Now, however, this is built in and is an out-of-the-box feature.

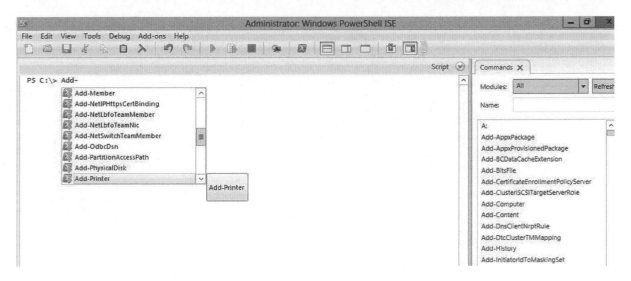

Figure 3-4. *IntelliSense in Windows PowerShell ISE*

Snippets

Think of snippets as being reusable patterns of code that are likely to be used more than once in your scripts. Snippets allow you to easily add a reusable pattern of code to your script with a single click—for example, a try-catch or a try-finally clause that prevents your script from crashing in case of errors, and that allows you to handle the exceptions in a managed way. This is something that I encourage every PowerShell developer to use. In order to add this to your code, simply right-click anywhere in the console pane, and pick Start Snippets (Ctrl+J also does the trick). You will then be presented with a list of all available snippets that you can add to your code. Simply double-click on one of them to have it inserted where your cursor is positioned (see Figure 3-5).

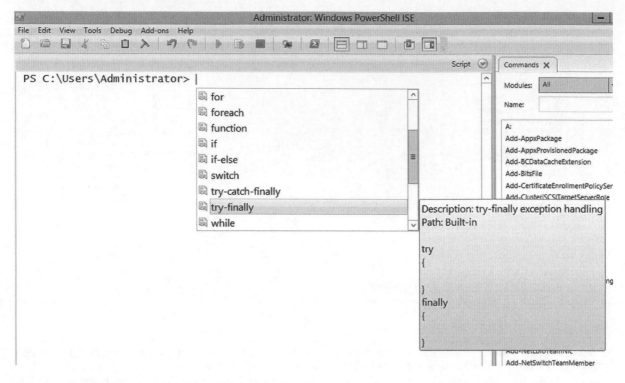

Figure 3-5. *Snippets in Windows PowerShell ISE*

New snippets can be added to the Windows PowerShell ISE by using the New-ISESnippet cmdlet from within the ISE. In the following example, I've created a new snippet that simply prints out a dashed line to the console. I've created the new snippet by using the following line of code. In order for this to execute properly, you will need to set the execution policy to Unrestricted (see "Execution Policy"):

```
New-IseESnippet –Title "Print Dashed Line" –Description "Prints a line on screen" –Author "Nik"
–Text "write-host '-------------------------'"
```

Once created, your new snippet will be accessible in the snippet gallery for you to use, as shown in Figure 3-6.

	foreach
	function
	if
	if-else
Description: Prints a line on screen **Path: C:\Users\Administrator\Documents\WindowsPowerShell\Snippets\Print Dashed** **Line.snippets.ps1xml** **write-host '----------------'**	**Print Dashed Line**
	switch
	try-catch-finally
	try-finally
	while

Figure 3-6. *My custom Print Dashed Line Snippet*

Commands Explorer

Another great addition to the Integrated Scripting Environment is the Commands Explorer panel on the right-hand side of the interface, which allows you to quickly browse through all the cmdlets that are available in the current session. By default, the SharePoint cmdlets are not listed. In order for them to show up, you need to add the SharePoint snap-in to the current session. Type in the following line in the console pane, and run (press Enter) your code. This will automatically import all SharePoint related operations in your current PowerShell session.

```
Add-PSSnapin Microsoft.SharePoint.PowerShell
```

Once added, simply click on the Refresh button at the top of the Commands Explorer panel to have all the SharePoint related cmdlets appear in the list (see Figure 3-7).

Figure 3-7. Commands Explorer in Windows PowerShell ISE

■ **Did you know?** The PowerShell executables and libraries are all stored in the
`c:\Windows\System32\WindowsPowerShell\v1.0` folder, even in version 3.0.

Execution Policy

PowerShell has its own set of mechanisms to prevent any harm from being done to the server without proper approval from the server's administrator. One of these mechanisms is what we refer to as *execution policies*, which determine what types of PowerShell scripts are allowed to be run on the server. There are a few execution policy levels. Here is a description of the four main types that you will encounter and that you can use to specify what type of scripts you want to allow to run on the server:

- `AllSigned`. This policy only allows scripts that have been signed by a trusted publisher to be run.

- `RemoteSigned`. This policy forces all scripts downloaded from the internet to be signed by a trusted publisher before being run.

- `Restricted`. This policy means that no scripts can be run. Administrators can only use PowerShell in interactive mode (typing in commands one at a time in the console).

- `Unrestricted`. This policy allows all scripts to be run without description.

Execution policies can be set on the server by running the `Set-ExecutionPolicy` cmdlet. What this does in the backend is update a registry key to contain the name of the effective policy (`\HKEY_LOCAL_MACHINE\SOFTWARE\Microsoft\PowerShell\1\Shellds\Microsoft.PowerShell`). On running the cmdlet, as in the following line, you will be asked to confirm the change:

```
Set-ExecutionPolicy AllSigned
```

■ **Did you know?** PowerShell looks at a script's property to determine if it was downloaded from an external source or not. It checks the file's `ZoneId` property. If its value is greater than or equal to 3, it will automatically treat it as being a remote script. You can view the value of this property by using the Streams tool (http://technet.microsoft.com/en-ca/sysinternals/bb897440.aspx).

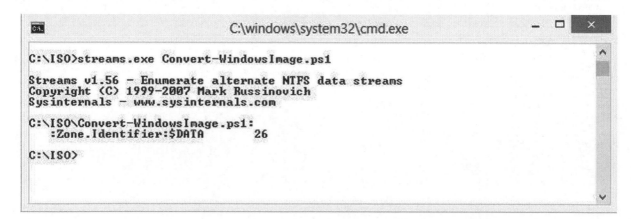

PowerShell Web Access (PWA)

This PWA feature requires you to have Windows Server 2012 installed as the server operating system for your SharePoint farm. It acts as a gateway to provide you with a web-based interface representing Windows PowerShell console. That's right, as you've probably figured it out by now, this allows users to run PowerShell scripts remotely on servers. You can probably already imagine all of the red flags that this will trigger with your security folks. Don't you worry, though; Microsoft thought of this, too, and they introduced many mechanisms to allow you and your team to control the access to this feature.

Requirements

In order for you to be able to run PowerShell Web Access, you need to ensure that the following components are installed and configured on your destination server:

- IIS Web Server
- .NET Framework 4.5 or greater
- Windows Management Framework 3.0 or greater
- Windows Server 2012 or Windows Server 2012 R2

Installing PWA

PowerShell Web Access is considered a server feature in Windows Server 2012; therefore, you can either activate it by going in the Server Manager Console, and adding it as a feature, or by using the following PowerShell cmdlets:

```
Install-WindowsFeature –Name WindowsPowerShellWebAccess –ComputerName <computer_name>
-IncludeManagementTools –Restart
```

On executing these cmdlets, you should see a teal-colored bar appear in your PowerShell console, and the status of your installation should be displayed. The installation should take about a minute to complete, and PowerShell should display the installation results in a tabular format such as the one illustrated in Figure 3-8. Once the installation is completed, your machine will automatically be restarted.

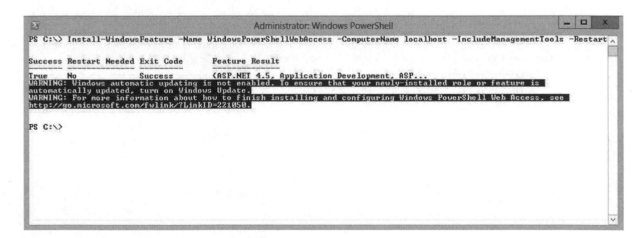

Figure 3-8. *Output of the PowerShell Web Access installation*

Configuring the Gateway

I am no expert when it comes to network configuration, and I've never tried to pretend otherwise. Luckily for me, Microsoft made it as simple as possible to configure the PowerShell Web Access Gateway. All you have to do is to run the following cmdlet. For advanced users, there is a way for you to specify a genuine signed SSL certificate, but in this case, I will simply have PowerShell generate a test certificate by using the –useTestCertificate switch:

```
Install-PSWAWebApplication -UseTestCertificate
```

When you run this cmdlet, what PowerShell actually does is create a new web application and its associated Application Pool entity in IIS. The physical path of the newly created web application is located at C:\Windows\Web\ PowerShellWebAccess\wwwroot. By default, PowerShell names the web application pswa, but you are allowed to name it whatever you see fit by using the –WebApplicationName parameter and specifying your own name. I used the default web application name. Open the Internet Information Service Manager console, and ensure that the Default Web site is started. If it is not, click on it and choose Start from the right-hand Actions panel:

```
Install-PSWAWebApplication –UseTestCertificate –WebApplicationName "MyCustomPSWAName"
```

Once you have PowerShell Web Access configured, you are ready to hit the road and try out the Web console. You can navigate to it by typing in https://<server name>/<Web application name>. I am accessing it at https://spps. contoso.com/pswa/. Once you have accessed the web application, you'll be presented with a login screen. By default, nobody is allowed access to the PowerShell Web Access Gateway. You will need to manually grant users access using PowerShell, by creating what we refer to as an *authorization rule*. An authorization rule allows specific users to access a computer on the network, granting them access to a special PowerShell session that is configured to include the list of cmdlets that they normally use. New authorization rules can be created by using:

```
Add-PSWAAuthorizationRule –username domain\username –ComputerName computerName
–ConfigurationName Admins
```

The next step is to register a new session configuration with the environment. The session configuration is where we will specify which cmdlets and modules should be loaded by default in the PowerShell Web Access session when a specific user connects. New session configurations are created by calling the following cmdlet:

```
Register-pssessionconfiguration –Name Admins –RunAsCredential domain\username
```

Next, you will be prompted to enter the credentials for the account specified. Enter the requested password and click OK. The system will then ask you to confirm a series of operations, involving restarting certain services. You'll need to input "Y" for yes to each of these questions and press Enter. At one point, the system will ask you to confirm the specified accounts rights on the remote PowerShell service. Simply keep the default options recommended by the system, such as those shown in Figure 3-9, and click OK.

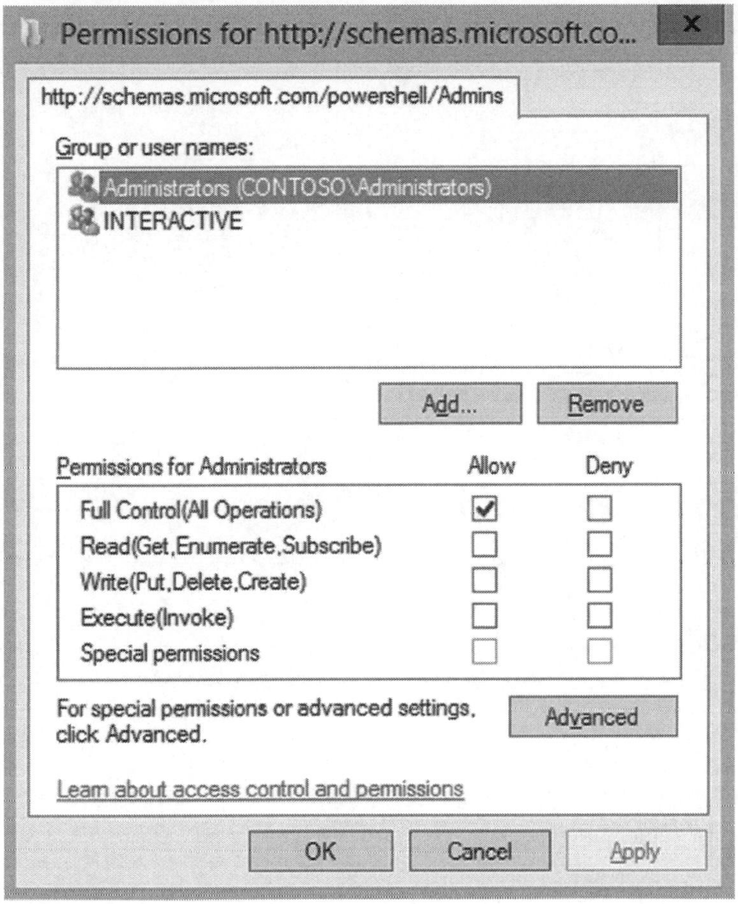

Figure 3-9. Setting default permissions for the remote PowerShell Service

The session configuration object that we created will include all basic cmdlets that a PowerShell session will have the first time you initialize it after installing the operating system. Adding additional cmdlets and modules to session configuration objects is outside the scope of this book. We are now ready to connect to the Web interface:

1. Navigate to your PowerShell Web Access Gateway page in a new Internet Explorer window. The login screen should look similar to the one in Figure 3-10.

Figure 3-10. *PowerShell Web Access Login Screen*

2. Fill in all required information, and expand the optional connection settings panel.

3. In the Configuration Name box, simply enter Admins as this is how we called our new configuration object.

4. Click Sign In.

After a few seconds, you should see what looks similar to a desktop PowerShell session inside your web browser. We are now connected to the Windows PowerShell Web Access application and can use it to run commands just like we would within a normal desktop PowerShell session. In order to prove that it is working, you could run the following command to change the date and see it reflected live on the machine. Please note that changing the date of a system is not something that you should try on a production server, as it may have unexpected results on your applications. In the session console, type in the following:

```
Set-data –date '08/09/1985'
```

Press Enter to submit your command to the console, and pay close attention to the date at the bottom right of your screen to see it flash.

Summary

In this chapter, you have learned how to configure your environment to be able to leverage PowerShell to its full potential. What you've accomplished throughout the previous sections will act as a building block for the chapters to come. If you are using a virtual machine to follow along, it might be a good idea for you to create a snapshot of your machine at this point. This will allow you to go back to a clean installation of your environment, and it could be used as a template for building additional servers in the future.

CHAPTER 4

■ ■ ■

PowerShell Basics

Throughout this book, it is assumed that readers have had some level of exposure with SharePoint but no experience with the PowerShell technology whatsoever. The content of this chapter will help readers get familiar with the core elements of PowerShell. Here is a summary of what you will learn in the current chapter:

- Understand how PowerShell sessions work

- Learn about the common PowerShell operators

- Learn about customization of your PowerShell sessions

- Learn how to extend the list of default available methods (cmdlets)

- Understand the difference between a PowerShell snap-in and a PowerShell module

Terminology

Before diving any further into the core of what PowerShell really is, there are several terms and expressions that I need to define for you so that you will better understand all the elements I will be discussing in this chapter.

Session

Think of a PowerShell session as being the current PowerShell window in which you are working. PowerShell resembles the default command line in many aspects. However, it is important to remember that PowerShell is built on top of the .NET Framework. You can therefore use it to access and manipulate any .NET object loaded in memory. Normal command-line methods and operations will still work inside of PowerShell (e.g. `dir`, `copy`, etc.). Objects and variables declared in a PowerShell session will continue to exist and to be accessible throughout the lifetime of the session. Closing the Windows PowerShell window will automatically terminate the session.

Cmdlets

Pronounced "command-lets," these represent the set of methods that are available in the current session. They are normally written in the form of verb-object (e.g., `Get-SPSite`, `Set-ExecutionPolicy`, `Delete-SPListItem`, etc.). As you will learn later in this chapter, it is possible for you to extend the default set of available cmdlets by adding your own to the PowerShell ecosystem.

Profile

A PowerShell profile is a script that gets executed every time that a PowerShell session is initialized. It allows users to modify their global settings for all PowerShell sessions and to instantiate global objects and variables by default. The PowerShell profile is where you'll need to start looking if you'd like to personalize and customize your PowerShell environment.

Snap-In

Snap-ins in the PowerShell world are sets of methods and objects that can be imported in a session. Think of themas being .NET namespaces that would be imported at the beginning of your classes by calling the using statement. When you launch the SharePoint Management Shell, all you are really doing in the background is starting a new PowerShell session and importing the SharePoint packages in the current session by calling Add-PSSnapin Microsoft. SharePoint.PowerShell. Snap-ins only contains PowerShell cmdlets and nothing else. All PowerShell snap-ins have to have been written in .NET and have been compiled as assemblies. Snap-ins are by default saved in the registry under \HKEY_LOCAL_MACHINE\SOFTWARE\Microsoft\PowerShell\1\PowerShellSnap-ins\. You can get a list of all registered PowerShell snap-ins for the current session by using the Get-PSSnapin -Registeredcmdlet. Figure 4-1 gives you an overview of how you can use thiscmdlet to get the list of registered cmdlet in a PowerShell session in which we have registered the SharePoint snap-ins.

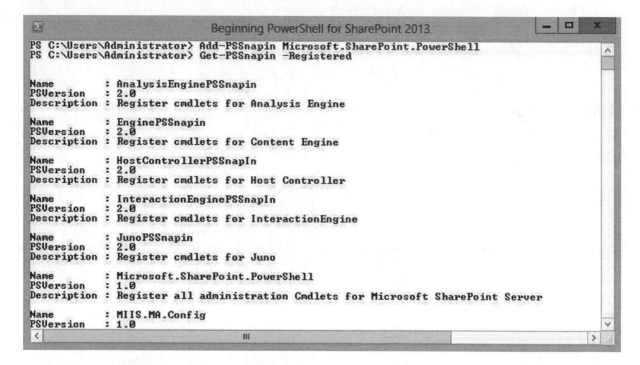

Figure 4-1. *Listing all registered snap-ins with PowerShell*

Module

The concept of modules was introduced in PowerShell version 2.0. A module represents a set of PowerShell functionalities that can be added to a PowerShell session. It can contain cmdlets, functions, variables, and so on. In comparison to PowerShell snap-ins, modules don't have to be compiled assemblies; they could be, for example, external PowerShell scripts that are referenced by the current session. For example, assume that you are writing a new script that simply contains a set of mathematical functions, say, Add, Subtract, Multiply, and Divide. This script is simply a text file saved on disk as a custom PowerShell extension (.psd1 or .psm1). By importing it as a module in your current session, you will be able to access all of its declared mathematical function as if they were part of the script that you were currently writing. For this to have been achievable with snap-ins, your functions would have needed to have been compiled as a .NET assembly (.dll file), which would have made it harder for you to make any modifications to your functions.

By default, when trying to import a module, PowerShell looks in the `%windir%\System32\WindowsPowerShell\v1.0\Modules` directory. It is possible to list all available PowerShell modules in your environment by using the `Get-Module -ListAvailable`cmdlet (see Figure 4-2).

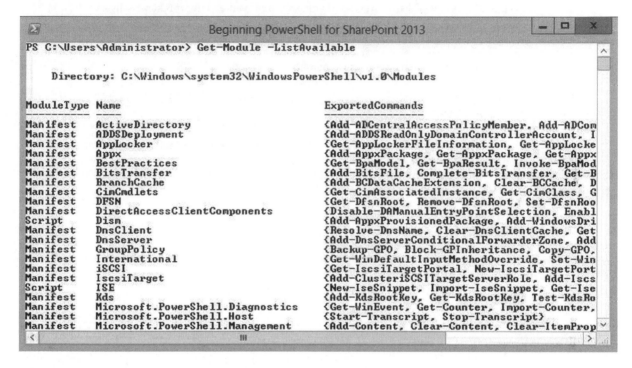

Figure 4-2. *Listing all available modules in PowerShell*

As you can see in Figure 4-2, there are several different types of modules that can exist. There are currently five types of supported modules in PowerShell v3.0:

Binary (.dll): Module that is defined in an assembly. This type includes snap-ins and class libraries that contain cmdlet classes.

Cim (.cdxml): Called cmdlets-over-objects. These are saved in a file format referred to as cmdlet Definition XML. They define a mapping between Windows PowerShell cmdlets and CIM class operations or methods. Think of using them as being a way to make calls into external APIs as if their methods were accessible as PowerShell cmdlets.

Manifest (.psd1): Windows PowerShell data file that is used to describe and define how a module is being processed. Module manifest files contain a hash table with keys and values. These are not required, but they can help describing existing modules by providing information about the author and givingmore details about what the specified module actually does.

Script (.psm1): Module having its members declared in an external script. Script modules normally contain cmdlets definitions. For example, if we take a look at the Script module for the Integrated Scripting Environment (ISE), we see that it contains several cmdlets definition, such as New-IseSnippet, Import-IseSnipper, and Get-IseSnippet.

Workflow (.xaml): Some of you probably recognize the extension associated with this type of PowerShell modules. Pronounced "zammel," XAML stands for Extensible Application Markup Language, and it is Microsoft's XML-based markup language behind the Windows Presentation Framework (WPF). It is used to abstract the visual presentation layer of applications from their actual logic. However, in this case, the Windows Workflow Foundation (WWF) is the one responsible for executing our workflow's logic. A workflow module is basically a special script structure that PowerShell is able to interpret and convert into Windows Workflow Foundation code. The WWF engine is then called to execute the workflow's activities. PowerShell workflow methods are identified by using the keyword workflow instead of function. Code inside a workflow method is able to fork its logic, meaning that several activities can execute in parallel.

PowerShell Operators and Common Operations

For every new language you learn, there is a new syntax to get familiar with and PowerShell is no different. The beauty of it, however, is that if you are familiar with the C# syntax, you'll find lots of commonalities with the scripting language. The following section gives you an overview of the various PowerShell operators that you will need to master in order to become a skilled SharePoint administrator.

Printing Values on Screen

During a script execution, you'll want to interact with the user. The two main methods you'll need to remember are the write-host cmdlet to print a string on screen, and the read-host cmdlet to capture a user's input from the console. Both cmdlets are shown in use in Figure 4-3.

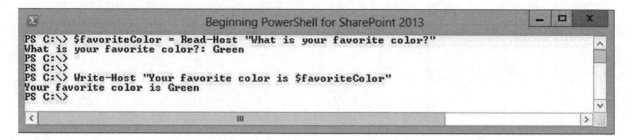

Figure 4-3. Usage of write-host and read-host cmdlets

Console Colors

One of the great advantages of PowerShell over its command-prompt predecessor, is its ability to interact with the graphical interface. This allows users to use visual cues in their scripts to help identify different information elements that you normally would have to spend time figuring out manually otherwise. Within your PowerShell session, you have the option of specifying the colors to use for both the text's background and foreground. The following line will print a line of red text on a yellow background:

```
write-host "See how cool this is?" -backgroundcolor yellow -foregroundcolor red
```

This can prove to be very useful when displaying lots of information on screen. Imagine, for example, a PowerShell script that will loop through all sub sites on a SharePoint site collection that has over 1,000 sites. Let's suppose that the purpose of this script is to identify subsites that have unique permissions but that you still want to obtain a full list of all sites. Your script could introduce some conditional logic that would display the URL of all sites that inherit permissions from the parent with a green background, and the URLs of all subsites that have unique permissions with a red background. This would achieve both goals, providing you with a full list of the URLs for all subsites as well as giving you an easy visual cue to identify subsites that don't inherit permissions from their parents.

Variables

Variables in PowerShell are declared and referenced using the '$' operator. As seen in the earlier example, when capturing the user's input for their favorite color, youassign the value to a variable. This value is later reused to print out a confirmation message to the users,as seen in this example:

```
$myVariableText = "My favorite number is:"
$myVariableNumber = 7
Write-Host $myVariable $myVariableNumber
```

Executing this code will print the following message on the PowerShell console: "My favorite number is: 7."

Comments

What would be a good piece of code without proper comments to describe what it is actually doing? Commenting the logic of a piece of code or script is something every good IT professional should discipline himself to do. Comments in PowerShell are preceded with the '#' symbol. It is possible to create comments blocks by enclosing them inside of "<# #>" tags.This example gives you an example of how comments could be used to describe a script to help future users understand its logic:

```
# The following variable contains the number of Days in the week
$numDaysInWeek = 7
<# The following lines of code does two things:
1 - Reads the answer  to the question from the user;
2 - Validate the answer #>
$answer = Read-Host "How many days in a week?"
if($answer -eq 7)
{
    Write-Host "You are correct"
}
else
{
Write-Host "Wrong answer!"
}
```

Casting

This is the process of converting an object from one type to another. Casting operations are represented by an object declaration between square brackets ([]) followed by the object to convert. For example, converting a string to an integer could be done,as shown in Figure 4-4.

```
$stringValue = "12"
Write-Host ([int] $stringValue +13)
Write-Host $stringValue + 13
```

```
┌──────────────────────────────────────────────────────────────────────────────┐
│ ⚫              Beginning PowerShell for SharePoint 2013        [─][□][ x ]      │
├──────────────────────────────────────────────────────────────────────────────┤
│ PS C:\> $stringValue = "12"                                              [∧]   │
│ PS C:\> Write-Host ([int]$stringValue + 13>                                    │
│ 25                                                                             │
│ PS C:\> Write-Host $stringValue + 13                                           │
│ 12 + 13                                                                        │
│ PS C:\> _                                                                [∨]   │
│ [<]                        III                              [>]                 │
└──────────────────────────────────────────────────────────────────────────────┘
```

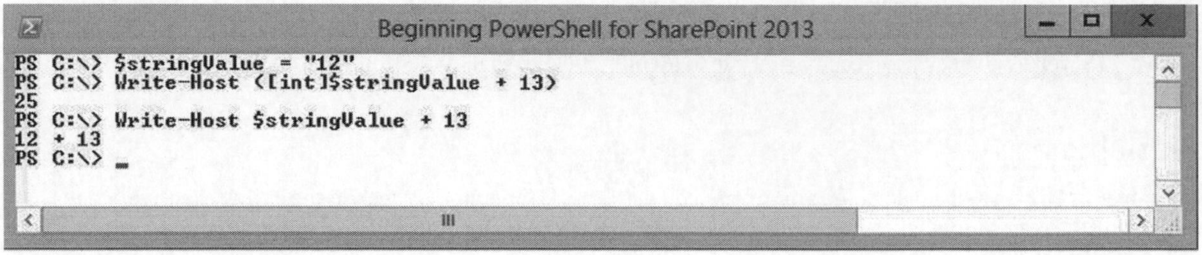

Figure 4-4. *Converting a string into an integer*

In this demo, you can see that the first statement casts the string value of variable $stringValue into a number and then adds 13 units to it. The resulting value, 25 in this case, is of type integer. The second statement doesn't cast the variable's value as a number, and considers it to be a string. The write-host then treats the entire statement as a string and print out the operation in a textual fashion.

Conditional Logic

In many cases, you'll need to gate your logic and branch your code's logic in one direction or another based on a decision. PowerShell includes its own set of operators just like any other good programming language.

Decisions

Decisions in the context of PowerShell are expressed by using if and else statements. These allow your script to make a decision based on values you wish to evaluate against a specific condition. It allows the code to execute only if specific conditions are met. Otherwise, the script proceeds with the code contained in the else statement. For example, assume you are writing a very simple script to teach math to young kids in school. The script will ask the students to input any positive number, and will print out a message stating if the number is even or odd. The following lines of script represent how you could create such a script using PowerShell:

```
$number = Read-Host "Please enter a positive number:"
<# Use the modulo operation to divide the number by 2. Module returns the remainder of a division
operation. If the result is 0 then the number is even, otherwise it is odd. #>
$result = $number % 2
if($result -eq 0)
{
Write-Host "The number is even!"
}
else
{
Write-Host "The number is odd!"
}
```

Comparison

Table 4-1 lists the different comparisons operators that can be used to validate conditional statements.

Table 4-1. *Comparison operators*

Operator	Meaning
-ge	Greater-than or equal to $\geq$
-gl	Greater than $>$
-le	Less-than or equal to $\leq$
-lt	Less than $<$
-eq	Equal to $=$
-ne	Not equal $\neq$
-like	Wildcard %word%
-notlike	Not matching wildcard

In addition to the operators mentioned in Table 4-1, there are additional operators that enforce case-sensitivity. Simply prefix operators in Table 4-1 with a 'c' (e.g. -ceq, -clike, etc.). Figures 4-5 and 4-6 show examples of how to use some of the comparison operators.

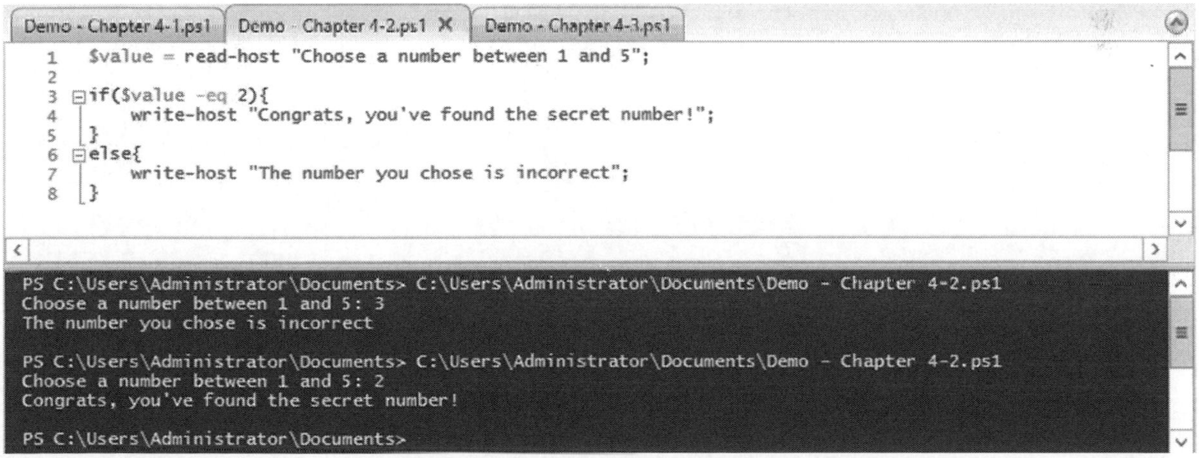

Figure 4-5. *Comparing numbers*

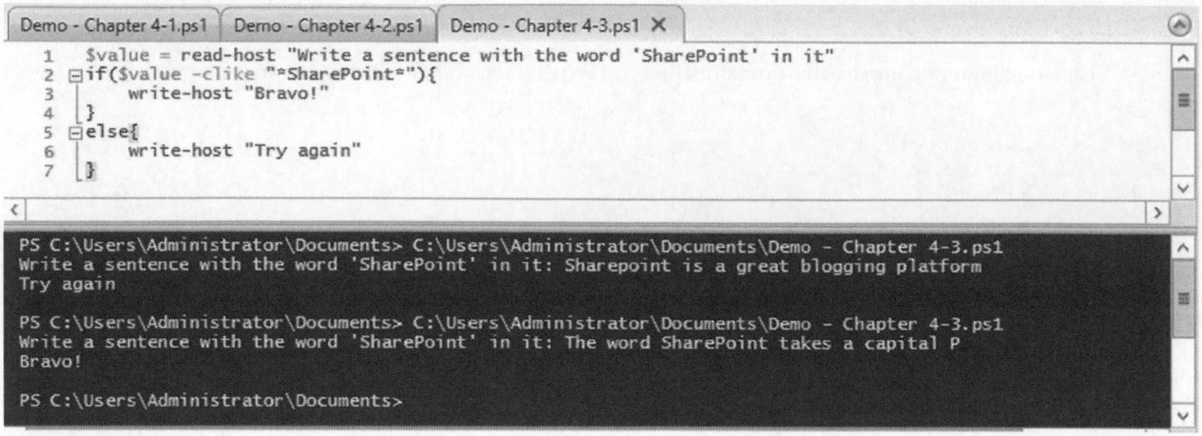

```
Demo - Chapter 4-1.ps1    Demo - Chapter 4-2.ps1    Demo - Chapter 4-3.ps1  X
1    $value = read-host "Write a sentence with the word 'SharePoint' in it"
2  ⊟if($value -clike "*SharePoint*"){
3  │     write-host "Bravo!"
4  └}
5  ⊟else{
6  │     write-host "Try again"
7  └}
```

```
PS C:\Users\Administrator\Documents> C:\Users\Administrator\Documents\Demo - Chapter 4-3.ps1
Write a sentence with the word 'SharePoint' in it: Sharepoint is a great blogging platform
Try again

PS C:\Users\Administrator\Documents> C:\Users\Administrator\Documents\Demo - Chapter 4-3.ps1
Write a sentence with the word 'SharePoint' in it: The word SharePoint takes a capital P
Bravo!

PS C:\Users\Administrator\Documents>
```

Figure 4-6. *Comparing strings*

Logical Operators

Table 4-2 lists the different logical operators that can be used to make up conditional statements.

Table 4-2. *Logical operators*

Operator	Meaning
-not	Does not meet the following condition
!	Same as -not
-and	Meets both statements
-or	Meets one of the two statements

Figure 4-7 shows you an example of how you can use the logical operators in conjunction with the comparison operators to create powerful logic in your PowerShell scripts.

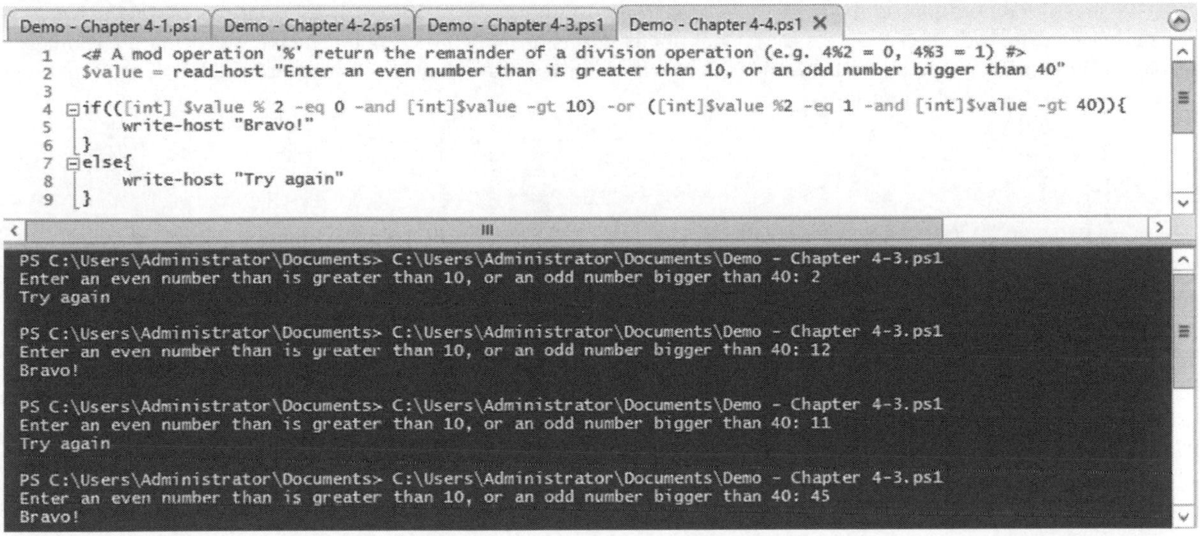

```
Demo - Chapter 4-1.ps1   Demo - Chapter 4-2.ps1   Demo - Chapter 4-3.ps1   Demo - Chapter 4-4.ps1 X

1   <# A mod operation '%' return the remainder of a division operation (e.g. 4%2 = 0, 4%3 = 1) #>
2   $value = read-host "Enter an even number than is greater than 10, or an odd number bigger than 40"
3
4   if((([int] $value % 2 -eq 0 -and [int]$value -gt 10) -or ([int]$value %2 -eq 1 -and [int]$value -gt 40)){
5       write-host "Bravo!"
6   }
7   else{
8       write-host "Try again"
9   }
```

```
PS C:\Users\Administrator\Documents> C:\Users\Administrator\Documents\Demo - Chapter 4-3.ps1
Enter an even number than is greater than 10, or an odd number bigger than 40: 2
Try again

PS C:\Users\Administrator\Documents> C:\Users\Administrator\Documents\Demo - Chapter 4-3.ps1
Enter an even number than is greater than 10, or an odd number bigger than 40: 12
Bravo!

PS C:\Users\Administrator\Documents> C:\Users\Administrator\Documents\Demo - Chapter 4-3.ps1
Enter an even number than is greater than 10, or an odd number bigger than 40: 11
Try again

PS C:\Users\Administrator\Documents> C:\Users\Administrator\Documents\Demo - Chapter 4-3.ps1
Enter an even number than is greater than 10, or an odd number bigger than 40: 45
Bravo!
```

Figure 4-7. *Demo 4-4—Multiple logical operators*

Function

A function is a reusable block of code that can receive parameters and return a specific output. Think of it as being a black box in which you input something, and something else comes out of it. A function normally takes in a set of parameters, and often returns a very specific value back. Some functions don't return any value; these are called void methods. These functionswill normally perform an operation or a modification on an existing object but do not need to return the value back to the main portion of the script. PowerShell functions are declared using the function keyword and don't require you to specify a return type. In that fashion,they are closer to JavaScript functions than to actual C# methods. Variables declared inside a method are said to belocal, meaning it only exists within its context. To illustrate what we mean by local variable, let's take a look at the demo in Figure 4-8.

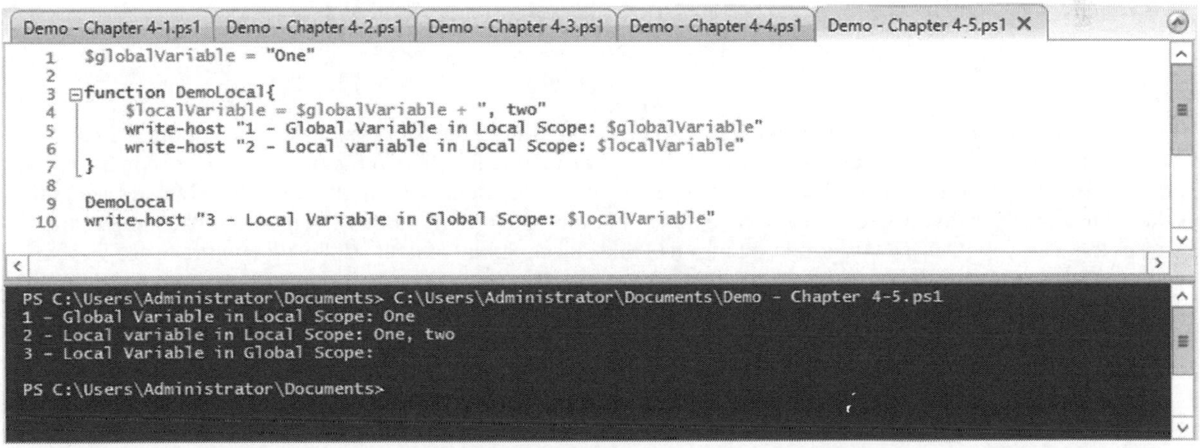

```
Demo - Chapter 4-1.ps1   Demo - Chapter 4-2.ps1   Demo - Chapter 4-3.ps1   Demo - Chapter 4-4.ps1   Demo - Chapter 4-5.ps1 X

1   $globalVariable = "One"
2
3   function DemoLocal{
4       $localVariable = $globalVariable + ", two"
5       write-host "1 - Global Variable in Local Scope: $globalVariable"
6       write-host "2 - Local variable in Local Scope: $localVariable"
7   }
8
9   DemoLocal
10  write-host "3 - Local Variable in Global Scope: $localVariable"
```

```
PS C:\Users\Administrator\Documents> C:\Users\Administrator\Documents\Demo - Chapter 4-5.ps1
1 - Global Variable in Local Scope: One
2 - Local variable in Local Scope: One, two
3 - Local Variable in Global Scope:

PS C:\Users\Administrator\Documents>
```

Figure 4-8. *Demo 4-5—Usage of local variables*

We see from the script's output in Figure 4-8 that the host's output from line 10 is not printing out anything. This is because the variable `$localVariable` does not exist outside of the function in which it was declared. Globally declared variables,by contrast, are accessible through the script because they have been declared outside of functions in what we call the global scope.

Loops

There are two types of loops in PowerShell, `for` loops and `while` loops. The first type normally has a very specific number of iterations specified, whereas the second one tends to run indefinitely until a certain condition is met. The condition for a `while` loop is evaluated before beginning the execution of each loop. There is also another type of loop called the `do-while` loop, but it is basically a `while` loop for which you evaluate the condition to continue execution after each loop has completed. In the example in Figure 4-9, the two loops are equivalent.

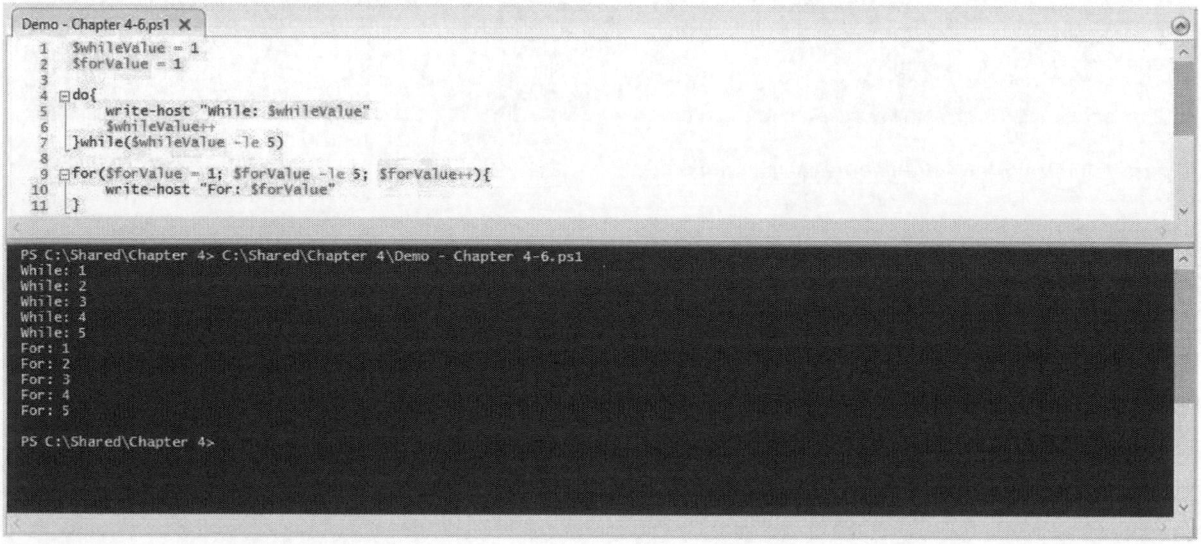

```
Demo - Chapter 4-6.ps1  ✕
1    $whileValue = 1
2    $forValue = 1
3
4  ⊟ do{
5        write-host "While: $whileValue"
6        $whileValue++
7    }while($whileValue -le 5)
8
9  ⊟ for($forValue = 1; $forValue -le 5; $forValue++){
10       write-host "For: $forValue"
11   }
```

```
PS C:\Shared\Chapter 4> C:\Shared\Chapter 4\Demo - Chapter 4-6.ps1
While: 1
While: 2
While: 3
While: 4
While: 5
For: 1
For: 2
For: 3
For: 4
For: 5

PS C:\Shared\Chapter 4>
```

Figure 4-9. *Forloop and whileloop*

Piping

The concept of piping is not something new, and it's been around since the old days of MS-DOS. Piping is the idea of taking an object or a result of a function, and sending it out to another function. A piping operation is represented by the '|' (pipe) symbol, and the flow of action is from left to right. A very important tip that you should always remember is that piping an object to the `get-member` cmdlet allows you to display all properties and methods of an object and exposes them for you to use. For example, piping an SPSite object (SharePoint Site Collection) with the `get-member` cmdlet will return all properties of the SPSite object (e.g., Title, URL, UIVersion, etc.), as well as all methods that can be called on that object (e.g.,`Update()`, `Delete()`, etc.). Think of this as being a reflection mechanism to get some insights into external objects. The example in Figure 4-10 illustrates how parameters and values are passed through the piping operation.

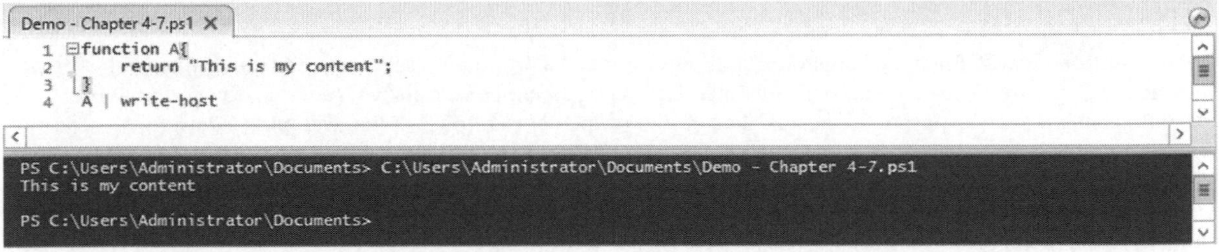

```
Demo - Chapter 4-7.ps1 ×
1  ⊟function A{
2  |      return "This is my content";
3  └}
4   A | write-host
```

```
PS C:\Users\Administrator\Documents> C:\Users\Administrator\Documents\Demo - Chapter 4-7.ps1
This is my content

PS C:\Users\Administrator\Documents>
```

Figure 4-10. *Demo 4-7—Using the piping operation*

In this example, we start off by calling the function A, which simply returns a string. We then pipe the returned string into the `write-host` cmdlet that prints it to screen. This example is equivalent to having typed `write-host` A. It simply helps you understand the mechanisms behind the pipe operation.

Instance Referrer

As in every other modern programming language, there is a way to access the current instance of an enumeration in PowerShell. The operator `$_` ensures that you always get access to the value of the current instance in a loop. C# developers will recognize this concept from the `this` operator.The `$_` operator always refers to the current instance that is being accessed in the context of the pipeline execution. The results of a piping operation will almost always result in a loop in the logic where PowerShell will iterate through a list of objects. This parameter represents the current instance inside the context of an iteration. It is a very hard concept to explain in words, soI'm better off showing you some examples. For instance, assume the following line of PowerShell:

```
"a","b","c","d" | %{write-host $_}
```

In this example, the '%' operator is used as a shortcut to the `ForEach-Object` operator that loops through objects in a collection. This line will loop through each value of the string array, and pass it on to the `write-host` cmdlet. Notice that the value we're trying to print is the instance referrer operator, meaning that for each value in the array, we will be printing the currently accessed value on to the screen. The result of this line of code will be the following:

```
a
b
c
d
```

Another useful way to use this operator is to query large lists of objects. Assume that we are trying to list every single command that is available to us in the current PowerShell session using the `Get-Command` cmdlet. Just running this command will return over 2,000 various cmdlets available in PowerShell 3.0. What if we only wanted to list the cmdlets that alow us to interact with group policies for example? Using the pipe operator in conjunction with the instance referrer, we could build a select statement that would filter the list of all available cmdlets, and only return those that apply to group policy object. Let's have a look at the following line of PowerShell:

```
$gpCmdlets = Get-Command | Where{$_.ModuleName -eq "GroupPolicy"}
```

This line of code will only return the list of cmdlets that belong to the `GroupPolicy` module and assign them to the gpCmdlets variable. The way it works is that PowerShell will start by looping through each cmdlet returned by the `Get-Command` call and will pass it to our query selector through the pipe operator. The `Where` statement will then examine each cmdlet received by getting its instance using the instance referrer. It will then take a decision to add the current cmdlet to the results based on whether or not it meets the condition in which its module name has to be equal to `GroupPolicy`.

Error Handling

There is nothing scarier for an administrator running a script on a production server than to see a bunch of red error messages being printed on screen. There are times when even the best of scripts will generate exceptions. Some exceptions might even be part of the normal flow of your script. For example, when developing a PowerShell script that automatically uninstalls a SharePoint solution from a server and redeploys it, you'll get an exception the first time you run your script, because the solution you're trying to uninstall doesn't already exist on the destination server. If you leave your script as is, administrators will get several lines in red, and will probably freak out. To solve this issue, there are two possible solutions. One would be to override the default PowerShell color scheme to display error messages in another color, but that won't do anygood (smell the sarcasm?). The other option would be to trap the exception within a try/catch block.

Error handling in PowerShell works just like it does in C#. Code inside the try statement will execute, and if any error is encountered, the execution flow of your script will be passed down to the catch statement along with the exception's related information. You will then be able to handle the exception thrown and decide what to do with it. You also have the option of adding an optional finally block to your try/catch statement. Code in the finally statement will always get executed, doesn't matter if an exception is thrown or not. It is normally a best practice to include in your finally statement the codethatensures you dispose of any objects that have been instantiated within the try statement to ensure that memory taken by these objects is freed even in case of errors.

You can specify what type of exception to look for in your statement by specifying the exception's type as a declaration in your code's block. Remember that every exception thrown is inheriting the System.Exception class, which means that specifying [System.Exception] as a type of exception to catch comes back to not specifying any type of exception whatsoever. In this case, every exception thrown will be handled by this error handling declaration. The example shown in Figure 4-11 shows how to catch different exception thrown by your PowerShell code.

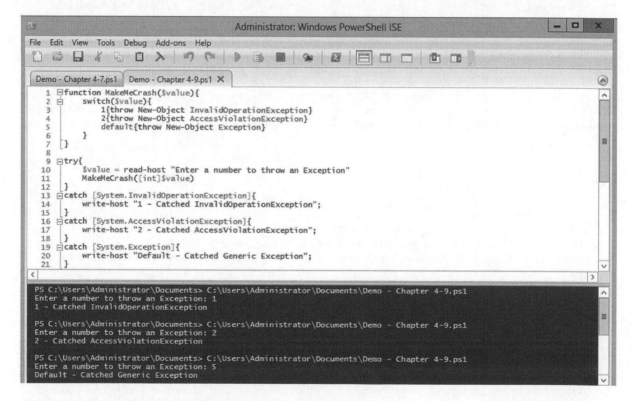

Figure 4-11. *Error handling with multiple types of exceptions*

Enumerations

Just like in any good programming language, PowerShell allows you to declare enumerations objects. You can think of an enumeration as being a list of keys with predefined constant values that can be referenced by your script. Enumerations in PowerShell are accessed by making calls to the object in the following fashion [*Enumeration Object's Name*]::[*Key Name*]. A good example of this is the DayOfWeek property of the .NET DateTime object. It is possible for you to get a reference to the week's day enumeration by calling the following:

```
[Enum]::GetNames([System.DayOfWeek])
```

Figure 4-12 shows the onscreen result.

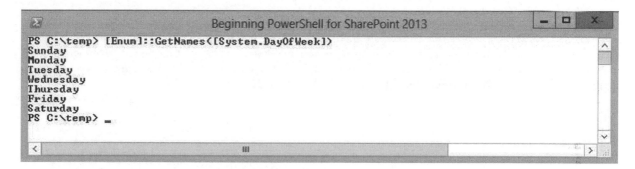

Figure 4-12. *Enumeration of the days of the week*

You could also get a reference to a specific day by calling an element directly:

```
[System.DayOfWeek]::Thursday
```

Arrays

In many scenarios, arrays will play an important part of your scripts. They represent a list of values that can be accessed using an integer index. In PowerShell, arrays are declared by using the @ symbol followed by the list of values you wish to declare in between parentheses:

```
$myArray = @('Red', 'Green', 'Blue')
```

In order to access a specific element of the array, you need to specify its index position in between square brackets. Remember, the first element of an array is always located at position 0. For example, calling:

```
$myArray[1]
```

willreturn element 'Green' from the declared array. Arrays in PowerShell behave like dynamic vectors, meaning that you can add additional elements and remove others as you wish. The following line of code will insert a new value 'Yellow' at the end of your array:

```
$myArray += 'Yellow'
```

To verify that the command worked, and that it did in fact append the new value to the existing array, you can print out the length of your array variable to ensure that it now contains four values.

```
$myArray.Length
```

The line of script should write the value '4' on screen. It is also possible for you to combine two arrays of different types in PowerShell. Assume that you declare a new array that only contains numbers:

```
$myArray2 = @(1, 2, 3)
```

It is possible for you to combine the two arrays, even if the first one contains a list of string values and the second one contains a list of integers. To combine arrays, you simply need to use the + operand:

```
$combinedArray = $myArray + $myArray2
```

In our example, the newly declared variable $combinedArray will now contain seven elements, where the first four are strings, and the last three are integers. In order to prove to you that elements in combined arrays keep their original object type, we'll create the following script:

```
$words = @('My', 'is ' , ' favorite number ')
$numbers = @(2,3,2)
$combined = $words + $numbers

# Array now looks like ('My ', ' is ', ' favorite number ', 2, 3, 2)
$fav = $combined[3] + $combined[5]
$sentence = $combined[0] + $combined[2] + $combined[1]

$sentence + $fav
```

Running this script will result in a message being printed onscreen that will display the 'My favorite number is 4,' as shown in Figure 4-13.

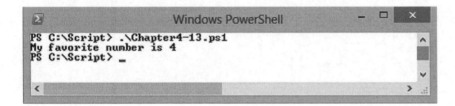

Figure 4-13. *Result of combining arrays with different types*

Environment Variables

It is possible for you to get direct access to all global environment variables declared on a machine. By default, PowerShell declares the following global variable:$env. You can access different information regarding your current environment by calling $env:[*Variable Name*]. For example, if you want to get the current computer name, you can simply call:

```
$env:computername
```

WhatIf Rollback

Those familiar with the Transact SQL syntax will recognize this neat little feature that allows you to run a command that tries to modify or delete existing content, that displays the end result but that never actually commits the transaction. This comes in very handy when you want to test a script or procedure against production data that continuously changes, and that can't be accurately replicated in a dev environment. In order to use the PowerShell rollback features, simply include the -WhatIf switch after your actual command. You will be presented with the results of your query on screen, if you are satisfied with the results, all you'll need to do is remove the switch and run the command again to have it committed.

Graphical User Interface

Guess what? You can build interactive user experiences with a PowerShell script. Remember, PowerShell is .NET in the backend, so it is possible for us to reuse the control libraries exposed by the framework to create a visual interface for our scripts. For example, assume you are writing a script that simply asks for a user's name, and displays a greeting message on screen. Instead of simply using the default write-host cmdlet to display the greeting message, you could build a graphic form displays the welcome text in a visual fashion. The following lines of code take you through the process of creating such a script:

```
Add-Type -AssemblyName System.Windows.Forms
$form = New-Object Windows.Forms.Form
$form.Height = 100

$name = read-host "What is your name?"

$lblWelcome = New-Object System.Windows.Forms.Label
$lblWelcome.Text = "Welcome $name !"

$form.Controls.Add($lblWelcome)
$form.ShowDialog()
```

The resulting script will prompt the user for their name in the PowerShell console, and once the user has entered the information, a Windows form will be displayed with the greeting message appearing in a text label (see Figure 4-14).

Figure 4-14. *Result of the graphical interface script*

Demo Project—Selective Deletion of Files in a Folder

In the following demo, you will learn how you can use PowerShell to interact with files stored on your machine, and I will illustrate how you can use the -WhatIf switch to test the execution of your script before committing any changes. Assume the following scenario in which you are asked to develop a PowerShell script that will loop through all the files in a specified folder, and that will only delete files that have the extension .txt. The script will need to prompt the user to enter the path for the folder containing the files. Your script should also prompt the user to choose to run the script in "test" mode, which will implement the -WhatIf switch, and not commit the changes directly. Figure 4-15 shows the files that exist in the folder against which you will execute your script.

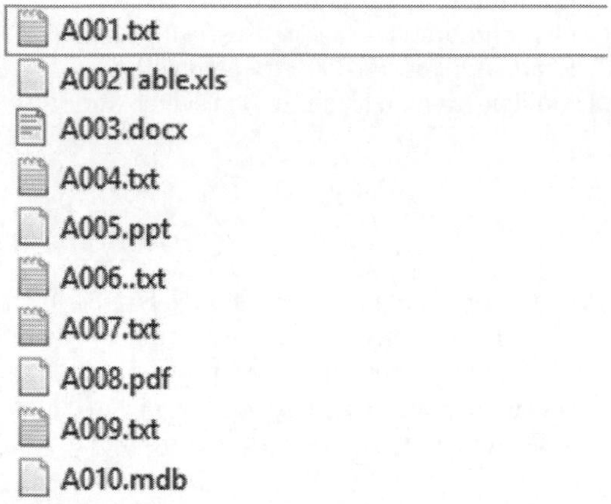

📄 A001.txt

📄 A002Table.xls

📄 A003.docx

📄 A004.txt

📄 A005.ppt

📄 A006..txt

📄 A007.txt

📄 A008.pdf

📄 A009.txt

📄 A010.mdb

Figure 4-15. *Files listing of folder*

The script that you will be developing will need to capture two inputs from the user: a value, 'y' or 'n', that will identify if the user wants to run the script in "test" mode or not, and the location of the folder containing the files, in this case C:\Demo 1\Files. The script will then need to loop through all files in that folder and check their extension. Whenever you encounter a file with the .txt extension, you will need to decide, based on the user's input, if you call the method that will delete the current file with the rollback switch (-WhatIf) or not. The resulting script and result will look like the following:

```
$rollback = read-host "Run in Test mode? (Y/N)"

# Get path the the folder
$folderPath = read-host "Folder Path"

# Get all files in specified folder and loop through each;
$files = Get-ChildItem $folderPath
foreach($file in $files)
{
    if($file.Extension -eq ".txt") # Check for files with the TXT extension
    {
        if($rollback.ToLower() -eq "y")
        {
            Remove-Item $file.FullName -WhatIf
        }
        elseif($rollback.ToLower() -eq "n") #Notice how elseif is spelled in one word in PowerShell
        {
            Remove-Item $file.FullName
        }
    }
}
```

Figure 4-16 shows the execution of this script against your folder.

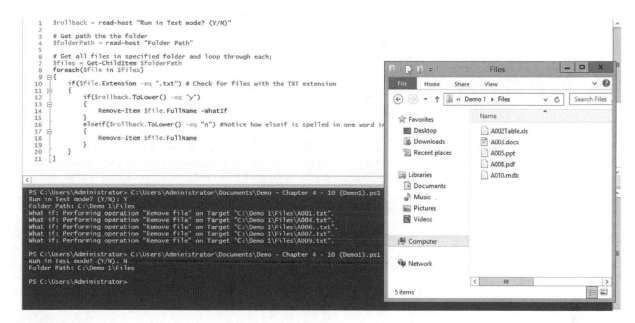

Figure 4-16. *Result of script deleting text files only*

Customization

Another nice feature of PowerShell is its ability to create predefined customized sessions for different users. For example, I'm a SharePoint developer, so almost any PowerShell script that I write and execute will be committed against a SharePoint environment. Therefore, it would be nice if, by default, every time I open a new PowerShell session window, the Microsoft.SharePoint.PowerShell snap-in be registered, instead of having to manually register it every time. Also, some people may have preferences as to how the text and background of the PowerShell window should look like by default. These are only a few scenarios that led the PowerShell team to come up with something called PowerShell profiles. These allow you to save various configuration and artifacts such as custom modules in a separate file that will automatically be preloaded everytime you launch a new PowerShell session.

Profiles are simply .ps1 files that are stored on disk. These profile files are stored in each user's personal documents folder. You can view where your current profile is stored at by calling the following variable:

$profile

In this case, the profile on your server is located at:

c:\Users\Administrator\Documents\WindowsPowerShell\Microsoft.PowerShell_profile.ps1

Every time a new session is launched, this .ps1 PowerShell script will try to get executed. By default, the file does not exist; this is very important to remember. If the file does not exist, PowerShell will simply continue its normal execution flow. You should also pay special attention to the various PowerShell environments that can coexist on the machine. For example, the PowerShell profile associated with a session running in the integrated scripting environment is different than the one running directly on the desktop. Remember to also use the $profile call to see what profile the current PowerShell environment is using.

My Profile

Modifying the default profile for a specific user is as simple as modifying the .ps1 file associated with its profile. Remember, however, that the file does not exist by default, so to begin modifying your profile, you'll first need to go and create the associated .ps1 file. By default, PowerShell declares a default variable named $profile that contains a reference to the path where PowerShell is looking for the current user's profile file. The easiest way for you to create the file if it doesn't already exist is to call the Notepad application, passing it the path to where your profile should be located. This will automatically create the profile file and let you edit it using the text editor tool.

```
Notepad $profile
```

Calling this operation will automatically launch Notepad and prompt you to save the file. After the file is created, simply open it and add the operations that you want to have executed at the beginning of each session. It is important to take note that adding too many operations by default could very well slow down the launch of every new PowerShell window in your environment. It is recommended to keep the preloaded commands to a minimum, and to abstain from calling operation that take a long time to load. For example, the default SharePoint PowerShell console tries to load all SharePoint modules every time you launch it. You will most likely observe a delay of a few seconds every time you launch a new instance of it, because PowerShell snap-ins take a long time to load.

Let us now go in and modify the profile script so that it prints off a nice greeting message every time we launch a new PowerShell session. Open the profile file associated with your profile, and add the following line to it, replacing the {Your Name} value:

```
Write-host "Welcome {Your Name}!"
```

Save your changes, and launch a new PowerShell session. If everything worked, you should now see your greeting message being displayed as the first line after the PowerShell copyright information.

Other types of customization that you may want to apply could be related to the visual aspect of you default PowerShell windows. For example, because the illustrations in the current book are in black and white, I'll want to change the default background color of the sessions to white and the default foreground to black. In order to achieve this, I'll add the following lines of code in my default PowerShell profile's script:

```
$console = Get-Host
$console.UI.RawUI.BackgroundColor = "White"
$console.UI.RawUI.ForegroundColor = "Black"

# Need to call Clear-Host to wipe out the navy blue color that has already been put on screen.
Clear-Host
```

Save your modified profile file, and launch a new PowerShell session window. You should see it flash on hitting the Clear-Host command, and then the entire PowerShell window should be in black and white.

Custom Modules

In some cases, you may have developed useful methods that are generic enough that you would like to have them included in every PowerShell session so that you can call them as you want, just like if they were part of the baseline product. In such a case, you'll want to expose you method as a PowerShell module, to ensure that it is made available to all users using PowerShell on the current machine. The most common scenario for creating custom modules is to take a PowerShell script (.ps1) containing the logic of the method you want to expose, and to convert it as a module. Consider the following script:

```
$script:Owner = "Nik"
function Get-Owner
{
    return $script:Owner
}

function Set-Owner($owner)
{
$script:Owner = $owner
}
```

It represents a very simple way of specifying who the current owner of a script is. It contains two methods, a "getter" and a "setter" and a generic script variable that stores the information pertaining to the owner's name. In order for this script to be converted into a PowerShell module, we'll need to save it with a .psm1 extension. Create a new folder at the root of your c:\ drive on your environment, and name it PSModules. Save this script in the newly created folder and name it MyOwnerModule.psm1. Now, open a new PowerShell session, and execute the following line of code to convert your script into a reusable module:

```
Import-module c:\PSModules\MyOwnerModule.psm1
```

That's it; your new custom module is now loaded into your PowerShell session. To confirm that it is loaded in memory, type the following command in your current PowerShell session:

```
Get-module
```

You should see it listed in the list of available modules. Please note that, at this point, your module only exists while your PowerShell session remains open. If you close your PowerShell window, and open a new one, you'll need to reimport it in order for it to be usable. If you want to make sure it stays available for all of your sessions, it would be a good idea to add the import command in your personal PowerShell profile. Now that your module is loaded, you can make direct calls to your method in the following fashion:

```
Get-Owner # Will print Nik
Set-Owner "Bob"
Get-Owner # Will print Bob
```

You should always consider creating modules when you want to reuse a set of methods and objects.

Leaping Ahead

As this book is being written, the Release to Manufacturers (RTM) version of Windows Server 2012 R2 has just been released. This new version of Microsoft's popular server operating system comes preloaded with PowerShell version 4.0. This section will give you a quick overview of what new features and tools have been introduced with this new version of the platform. It is important to note that Microsoft doesn't officially support installing SharePoint 2013 on top of PowerShell version 4.0. Even if it is possible to do so, we won't be covering the newest version throughout this book, as it is still unsure when Microsoft will officially start supporting SharePoint on the new operating system.

Desired State Configuration

This new feature is something administrators have been asking for since the early days of PowerShell. It allows a user to specify what the minimum conditions should be for the script to be able to execute properly. You can use Desired State Configuration code block, or DSC for short, in your scripts to specify what software, features, resources, or components should be present on specific machines, and what their status should be. PowerShell will then go and perform the required installation of the specified items before running your script.

Dynamic Method and Property Names

Imagine that you have a script in which you need to store information about what method or property of an object to call. In the current versions of PowerShell (version 3.0 and under), calling such an element using a value stored in a variable would require you to call in to some reflection assemblies. With PowerShell version 4, you can now make calls on object using variables values. The following example illustrates what I mean by dynamic naming:

```
$now = Get-Date
$dynamicProperty = "Month"

$now.$dynamicProperty
```

This example declares a new string variable that contains the name of the property you will want to call on the DateTime object, in this case Month, which will return the name of the current month. Instead of calling the Month property directly on the DateTime object, you now call the variable name that contains a string reference to the property name. This example is perfectly valid in PowerShell v4, and will return the name of the current month on screen.

Summary

In this chapter, you have learned the fundamentals of PowerShell. You should now be able to create and run your own PowerShell scripts and modules, and be able to customize your PowerShell experience using profiles. This chapter gave you an overview of the possibilities that PowerShell is offering you as a system administrator. Without getting into the low-level specifics of PowerShell, this chapter taught you the general concepts behind the use of PowerShell in real-life scenarios. You have now learned the fundamentals you require in order to start configuring and managing your SharePoint environment. The next chapter will focus on configuring a SharePoint 2013 environment from the groundup. From this point on, we will be assuming that you have a good understanding of all elements of PowerShell scripts. Refer to this chapter as needed throughout the rest of this book, as you may need to revise certain concepts explained in it for future examples.

CHAPTER 5

██ ██ ██

Installing & Deploying SharePoint with PowerShell

I am now ready to start digging into what PowerShell has to offer to us, SharePoint people. In this chapter I will go over the basic commands you can use in PowerShell to help you automate the build of your SharePoint environment. Through a set of different demos, you'll learn how you can write your own custom scripts, and reuse them to create new SharePoint machines on demand. I will be covering the installation automation of the following aspects of a new SharePoint farm:

- Installation and configuration of the Server Operating System's Roles and Features

- Installation and configuration of SQL Server

- Installation of the SharePoint prerequisites

- Installation of the SharePoint core components

- Configuration of your new SharePoint Farm

The SharePoint Farm environment that will have been created and configured at the end of this chapter will act as the foundation for all other chapters to come. The environment will be "self-contained," meaning that all required components will be installed on a single box. In real-life scenarios, you'll always want to offload the domai controller role to a separate server as well as have your SQL Server installation hosted elsewhere. SharePoint 2013 also gives us more flexibility than its predecessors, by allowing us to offload more service applications components than in the 2010 version of the product.

Components like the workflow engine, the machine translation, and search services would normally be installed on external application servers in order to keep the SharePoint Web front-end servers as lightweight as possible. It is important to note that the end-goal architecture will be achieving in this chapter is for learning purposes only, and should not be something you aim to replicate in a production environment. The following sections assume that your test environment has a fresh baseline copy of Windows Server 2012 Standard (x64) edition installed.

Requirements

In the following section, I will be covering both the hardware and the software requirements you will need in order to re-create the same development environment that was created in this chapter. Pay specific attention to the various drives that are required along with their respective installation media, as the script produced at the end of the chapter will not work otherwise.

Hardware Requirements

For you to be able to get through the rest of this book and experience all of the examples that follow in a reasonable fashion, you will need to create your new SharePoint farm on a machine that meets the following list of minimum requirements. These requirements are in line with Microsoft's recommendations:

- 8 Gb of RAM available

- 80 Gb of disk space

- 64-bit, 4 cores

- Windows Server 2012 as the operating system

- 3 DVD drives assigned to your machine (D:\, E:\, and F:\)

Software Requirements

The scripts and examples given in this chapter will require you to have a copy of the installation files for the following software:

- SQL Server 2012 Standard Edition with Service Pack 1 (x64)

- SharePoint Server 2013 (x64)

In addition, all of these scripts assume that you have the media shown in Table 5-1 available to automate the installation.

Table 5-1. *Required media and associated drives*

Drive	Media
D:\	SQL Server 2012 with SP1
E:\	Windows Server 2012
F:\	SharePoint Server 2013

Figure 5-1 shows the various drives that are required and their associated installation media in Windows Explorer.

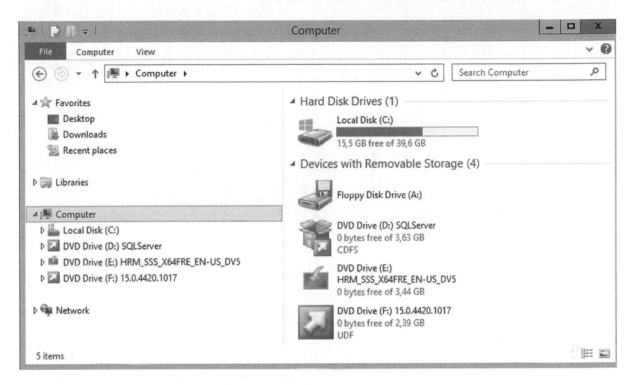

Figure 5-1. *Overview of the required instalaltion media*

Another requirement is to have the PowerShell execution policy set to be unrestricted. Please refer to Chapter 4 to learn how this can be achieved. Without this set properly, the scripts produced in this chapter will not execute properly, because PowerShell will block their execution.

Roles and Features

This section will help you automate the configuration of all Windows Server 2012 roles and features required by SQL Server 2012 and SharePoint 2013. I will go into the details of what roles and which PowerShell commands are required to have them enabled on your server.

■ **Caution**   Please note that the intent of this book is to help *you* understand the internals of how PowerShell works and how it can be used. Some of the scripts *that* you'll encounter in the following chapters may contain passwords that are exposed in plain text. This is not considered to be best practice, and you should always be careful how you expose sensitive information in your scripts.

.NET Framework 3.5

This component will require you to have the Windows Server 2012 installation media available. Some resources contained in the media are required to install the .NET Framework 3.5 bits. The following script assumes that the Windows Server 2012 installation files are loaded on drive E:\. The script will automatically enable the feature on the server. Figures 5-2 and 5-3 show the installation while in process and once completed.

```
Install-WindowsFeature –name NET-Framework-Core –Source E:\Sources\sxs
```

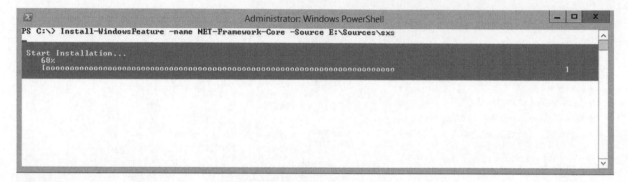

Figure 5-2. *Installing the .NET Framework*

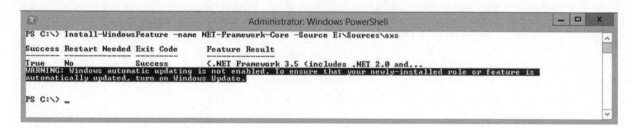

Figure 5-3. *Results of completing the .NET Framework installation*

Domain Controller

This role is probably the most important one of them all. Remember that your SharePoint machine will be self-contained; therefore, it needs to host its own domain. The good old days when you could simply call dcpromo in command prompt are long gone in Windows Server 2012. Trying to do so will result in getting an error similar to the one shown in Figure 5-4.

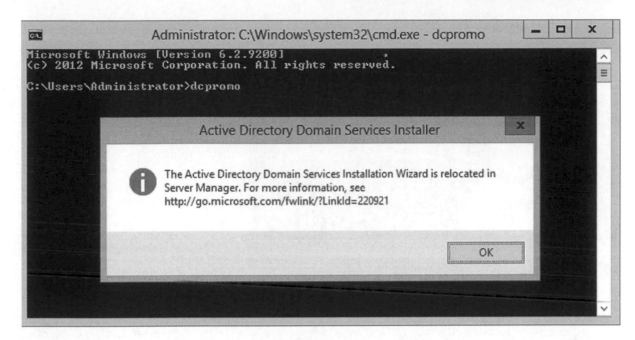

Figure 5-4. *DCPromo warning when running from command prompt*

PowerShell in Windows Server 2012 provides us with a set of various cmdlets that allow us to directly interact with the various Active Directory components. The following script excerpt will configure the domain controller role on the server environment (Figure 5-5 shows the script running):

```
$domainName = "contoso.com"
$safeModeAdminPassword = ConvertTo-SecureString "pass@word1" -asPlainText -force

Add-Windowsfeature AD-Domain-Services -IncludeManagementTools

Install-ADDSForest -DomainName $domainName -SafeModeAdministratorPassword $safeModeAdminPassword
-Confirm:$false
```

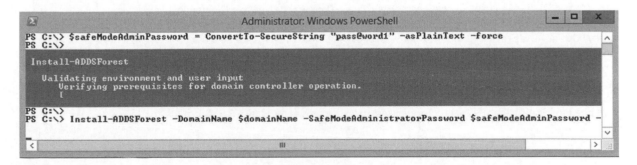

Figure 5-5. *Installing the Domain Controller role with PowerShell*

Running this script will declare a new domain, called contoso.com, and will automatically promote it. After running this script, the machine will automatically reboot after a few seconds to ensure that the new configuration is taken into effect. After the machine reboots, you should see your new domain name appended in front of your user name on the login screen (see Figure 5-6).

Figure 5-6. *Login screen with domain information*

Users and Groups

The next step will be to create a few test users and groups in your new Active Directory structure. I will try to mimic a real-world scenario with environment, in which I will have fictive users spread out across different business units in the Contoso organization. I will use PowerShell to create the following Active Directory groups to represent the following functional business units:

- Administration
- Finance
- Human Resources
- Directors
- Tech Support

The following lines of script will take care of automatically creating these groups.

```
New-ADGroup -DisplayName "Administration" -GroupScope DomainLocal -Name "Administration"
New-ADGroup -DisplayName "Finance" -GroupScope DomainLocal -Name "Finance"
New-ADGroup -DisplayName "Human Resources" -GroupScope DomainLocal -Name "Human Resources"
New-ADGroup -DisplayName "Directors" -GroupScope DomainLocal -Name "Directors"
New-ADGroup -DisplayName "Tech Support" -GroupScope DomainLocal -Name "Tech Support"
```

I will now create a user for each security group that I have just created using the following script. The default password for each of these users will be defaulted to *"pass@word1"*. This will prove useful in future example, when you will need to log into SharePoint as various users to test permissions. Figure 5-7 shows the created users.

```
$usersPassword = ConvertTo-SecureString "pass@word1!11" -asPlainText -force

New-ADUser -Name "JSmith" -GivenName "John" -Surname "Smith" -AccountPassword $usersPassword
-UserPrincipalName "jsmith@contoso.com" -DisplayName "John Smith"
Enable-ADAccount -Identity "JSmith"
Add-ADGroupMember -Identity "Administration" -Member "JSmith"
```

```
New-ADUser -Name "BMoores" -GivenName "Bob" -Surname "Moores" -AccountPassword $usersPassword
-UserPrincipalName "bmoores@contoso.com" -DisplayName "Bob Moores"
Enable-ADAccount -Identity "BMoores"
Add-ADGroupMember -Identity "Finance" -Member "BMoores"

New-ADUser -Name "PHarris" -GivenName "Peter" -Surname "Harris" -AccountPassword $usersPassword
-UserPrincipalName "pharris@contoso.com" -DisplayName "Peter Harris"
Enable-ADAccount -Identity "PHarris"
Add-ADGroupMember -Identity "Human Resources" -Member "PHarris"

New-ADUser -Name "KButtler" -GivenName "Kyle" -Surname "Buttlcr" -AccountPassword $usersPassword
-UserPrincipalName "kbuttler@contoso.com" -DisplayName "Kyle Buttler"
Enable-ADAccount -Identity "KButtler"
Add-ADGroupMember -Identity "Directors" -Member "KButtler"

New-ADUser -Name "MRanger" -GivenName "Mike" -Surname "Ranger" -AccountPassword $usersPassword
-UserPrincipalName "mranger@contoso.com" -DisplayName "Mike Ranger"
Enable-ADAccount -Identity "MRanger"
Add-ADGroupMember -Identity "Tech Support" -Member "MRanger"
```

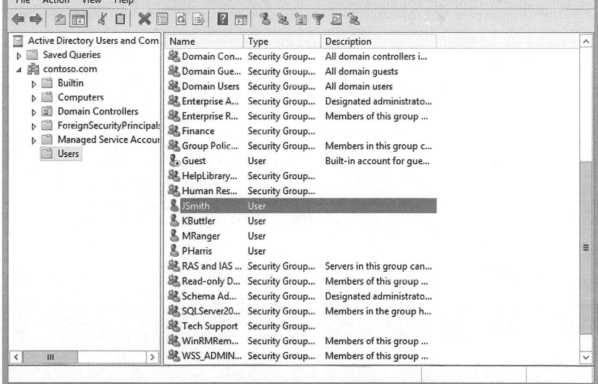

Figure 5-7. *List of users and groups*

Application Server Role

SharePoint requires your server to have the Application Server role enabled to leverage many .NET features such as the Windows Communication Foundation for web service calls. On top of activating this role, there are several specific features that also need to be turned on in order for SharePoint to install properly. The list in Table 5-2 identifies all features required.

Table 5-2. *All of the features required for your Application Server role*

Application-Server	AS-HTTP-Activation	AS-Named-Pipes
AS-Net-Framework	AS-TCP-Activation	AS-TCP-Port-Sharing
AS-WAS-Support	AS-Web-Support	Net-Framework-Features
Server-Media-Foundation	WAS	WAS-Config-APIs
WAS-NET-Environment	WAS-Process-Model	Web-App-Dev
Web-Asp-Net	Web-Basic-Auth	Web-Common-Http
Web-Default-Doc	Web-Digest-Auth	Web-Dir-Browsing
Web-Dyn-Compression	Web-Filtering	Web-Health
Web-Http-Errors	Web-Http-Logging	Web-Http-Tracing
Web-ISAPI-Ext	Web-ISAPI-Filter	Web-Lgcy-Scripting
Web-Log-Libraries	Web-Metabase	Web-Mgmt-Compat
Web-Mgmt-Console	Web-Mgmt-Tools	Web-Net-Ext
Web-Performance	Web-Request-Monitor	Web-Security
Web-Server	Web-Stat-Compression	Web-Static-Content
Web-WebServer	Web-Windows-Auth	Windows-Identity-Foundation
Xps-Viewer		

If you make the count, that's over 45 different features required. You could go and manually add each of them using the Server Manager console, but because this is a PowerShell book after all, just run a one-line command to have it all done automatically for you. The following line of script will take care of it all. Please give it a few minutes to complete.

```
Add-WindowsFeature Application-Server, AS-HTTP-Activation, AS-Named-Pipes, AS-Net-Framework,
AS-TCP-Activation, AS-TCP-Port-Sharing, AS-WAS-Support, AS-Web-Support, Net-Framework-Features,
Server-Media-Foundation, WAS, WAS-Config-APIs, WAS-NET-Environment, WAS-Process-Model, Web-App-Dev,
Web-Asp-Net, Web-Basic-Auth, Web-Common-Http, Web-Default-Doc, Web-Digest-Auth, Web-Dir-Browsing,
Web-Dyn-Compression, Web-Filtering, Web-Health, Web-Http-Errors, Web-Http-Logging, Web-Http-Tracing,
Web-ISAPI-Ext, Web-ISAPI-Filter, Web-Lgcy-Scripting, Web-Log-Libraries, Web-Metabase,
Web-Mgmt-Compat, Web-Mgmt-Console, Web-Mgmt-Tools, Web-Net-Ext, Web-Performance, Web-Request-Monitor,
Web-Security, Web-Server, Web-Stat-Compression, Web-Static-Content, Web-WebServer, Web-Windows-Auth,
Windows-Identity-Foundation, Xps-Viewer
```

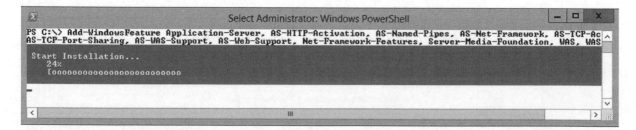

Figure 5-8. *Features being installed*

After you are done running this command, you will need to restart the server. Figure 5-9 shows the features being configured on restarting the server. You can simply run:

```
Restart-Computer
```

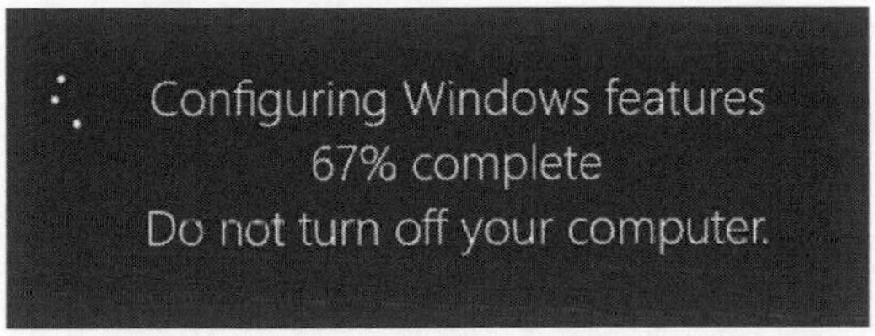

Figure 5-9. Applying the prerequisite features on restarting

Installing the Software Components

You are now ready to start installing the various components that make up a SharePoint farm. As mentioned earlier in this chapter, the environment that you are building in this chapter is self-contained. I will therefore cover how you can automate the installation of the SQL Server bits, the SharePoint 20103 prerequisites, and the SharePoint 2013 core components using PowerShell. In the next section, you will learn how to configure these components to make the most of your environment.

Installing SQL Server 2012

In order for you to be able to properly install the required components of SQL Server 2012, the following roles will need to be enabled on the server. The scripts that are detailed in the current section all assume that you have the SQL installation bits loaded on a drive mapped to D:\. You will be doing a minimal installation of a default SQL standalone instance, installing only the Database Engine Services core bits. The following script will perform an unattended installation of SQL Server:

```
$sqlSAPassword = "pass@word1"

$sqlProcess = new-object System.Diagnostics.Process
$sqlProcess.StartInfo.Filename = "D:\setup.exe"
$sqlProcess.StartInfo.Arguments = "/QS /ACTION=install /IACCEPTSQLSERVERLICENSETERMS=1
/FEATURES=SQL,Tools /INSTANCENAME=MSSQLSERVER /INSTANCEID=MSSQLSERVER
/SQLSYSADMINACCOUNTS=contoso\Administrator /SECURITYMODE=SQL /SAPWD=$sqlSAPassword
/INDICATEPROGRESS /AGTSVCSTARTUPTYPE=Automatic /TCPENABLED=1"
$sqlProcess.Start()
$sqlProcess.WaitForExit()
```

During the installation process, you will see several installation windows appear (see Figure 5-10). You do not have to interact with any of them. The parameters passed to the setup executable will automatically fill in the appropriate information required for you installation. The installation process will take about 10 minutes to complete, so now may be a good time for you to go grab a cup of coffee.

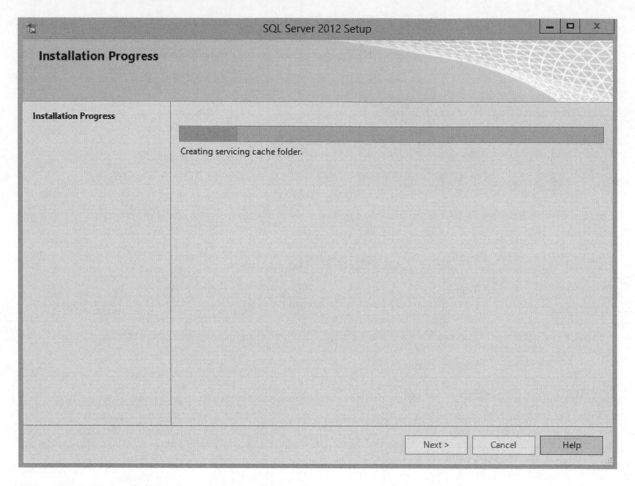

Figure 5-10. *Unattended SQL Server 2012 installation*

Installing SharePoint Prerequisites

Finally! You are now ready to install the SharePoint bits onto our server. The first step to installing SharePoint will be to download and install all of its prerequisites. You will be creating an automated PowerShell script that will automatically download each of them locally, and install them one at a time. The following list contains all the prerequisites that are required in order for the SharePoint Core installer to work:

- Microsoft SQL Server 2008 R2 SP1 Native Client
- Microsoft Sync Framework Runtime v1.0 SP1 (x64)
- Windows Server AppFabric
- Cumulative Update Package 1 for Microsoft AppFabric 1.1 for Windows Server (KB2671763)
- Windows Identity Foundation (KB974405)

- Microsoft Identity Extensions

- Microsoft Information Protection and Control Client

- Microsoft WCF Data Services 5.0

To download each of the required files, simply use the Invoke-WebRequest PowerShell cmdlet. The method takes two input parameters, one being the URL of the source file to download, and the second one being the local path of where to save the file. This method can be called in the following fashion:

```
$webClient = New-Object "System.Net.WebClient"
$webClient.DownloadFile("http://<source file URL>","c:\<local path>\<filename>")
```

The automated script that you will create will have a list of all of the prerequisites' files URLs stored in an array. It will loop through each of them and download them locally. Once all of the files have been downloaded locally, the script will call the SharePoint 2013 Products Preparation Tool, passing it the list of prerequisite files as an argument. The installer tool will then take care of installing and properly configuring each of them (see Figure 5-11).

```
$localPath = "C:\SP2013Prereqs\"

New-Item -ItemType Directory -Force -Path $localPath

# Array with all urls...a bit messy
$files = @("http://download.microsoft.com/download/9/1/3/9138773A-505D-43E2-AC08-9A77E1E0490B/1033/
x64/sqlncli.msi", "http://download.microsoft.com/download/E/0/0/E0060D8F-2354-4871-9596-
DC78538799CC/Synchronization.msi", "http://download.microsoft.com/download/A/6/7/A678AB47-496B-4907-
B3D4-0A2D280A13C0/WindowsServerAppFabricSetup_x64.exe",
"http://download.microsoft.com/download/7/B/5/7B51D8D1-20FD-4BF0-87C7-4714F5A1C313/AppFabric1.1-RTM-
KB2671763-x64-ENU.exe",
"http://download.microsoft.com/download/D/7/2/D72FD747-69B6-40B7-875B-C2B40A6B2BDD/Windows6.1-
KB974405-x64.msu", "http://download.microsoft.com/download/0/1/D/01D06854-CA0C-46F1-ADBA-
EBF86010DCC6/rtm/MicrosoftIdentityExtensions-64.msi",
"http://download.microsoft.com/download/9/1/D/91DA8796-BE1D-46AF-8489-663AB7811517/setup_msipc_x64.msi",
"http://download.microsoft.com/download/8/F/9/8F93DBBD-896B-4760-AC81-646F61363A6D/WcfDataServices.exe")

$fileName = ""
$pathParts

foreach($file in $files)
{
    $pathParts = $file.Split("/")
    $fileName = $pathParts[$pathParts.Length -1]
    $fullName = "$localPath$fileName"
    Invoke-WebRequest $file -OutFile $fullName
}

$prereqProcess = new-object System.Diagnostics.Process
$prereqProcess.StartInfo.Filename = "F:\prerequisiteinstaller.exe"
$prereqProcess.StartInfo.Arguments = "/SQLNCli:$localPath"+"sqlncli.msi /IDFX:$localPath" +
"Windows6.1-KB974405-x64.msu /IDFX11:$localPath" + "MicrosoftIdentityExtensions-64.msi
/Sync:$localPath" + "Synchronization.msi /AppFabric:$localPath" + "WindowsServerAppFabricSetup_x64.exe
```

```
/KB2671763:$localPath" + "AppFabric1.1-RTM-KB2671763-x64-ENU.exe /MSIPCClient:$localPath" +
"setup_msipc_x64.msi /WCFDataServices:$localPath" + "WcfDataServices.exe /unattended"
$prereqProcess.Start()
$prereqProcess.WaitForExit()
```

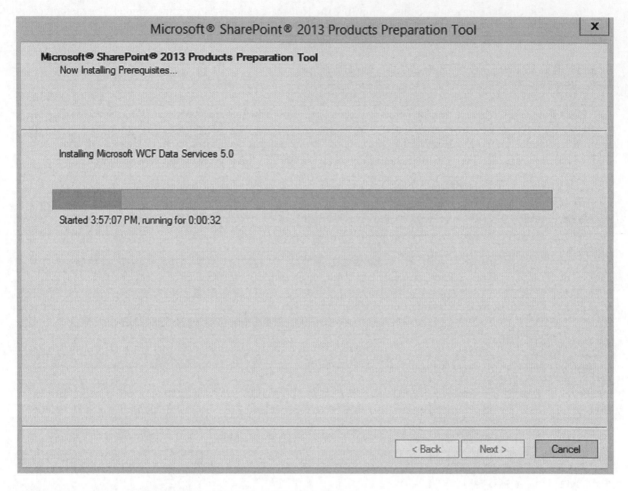

Figure 5-11. *Unattended Sharepoint 2013 prerequisites installation*

Allow this script about 5 to 10 minutes to finish its execution. Once completed, you will need to reboot the machine. After your machine has finished restarting, it will be properly configured and all ready to receive the SharePoint installation bits.

Installing SharePoint

Last but not least are the SharePoint core bits. The SharePoint installation media already contains a few different predefined configuration files to help us do an unattended installation of the product. Unfortunately, each of them requires you to manually specify your product key in order to be able to complete. The configuration files are nothing more than short XML files located under the /files/ folder at the root of the media.

In order to get your unattended installation working, you will need to copy the `setupfarmsilent` configuration file locally on drive `C:\`, modify it to include your product key, and then execute the installation process by referencing the newly modified configuration file.

```
$productKey = "XXXXX-XXXXX-XXXXX-XXXXX-XXXXX" # Replace by your own

$spLocalPath = "C:\SP2013\"
$spConfigFile = $spLocalPath + "config.xml"

New-Item -ItemType Directory -Force -Path $spLocalPath
Copy-Item F:\files\setupfarmsilent\config.xml $spLocalPath
$configContent =[io.file]::ReadAllText($spConfigFile)

Get-ChildItem $spConfigFile -Recurse |
    Where-Object {$_.GetType().ToString() -eq "System.IO.FileInfo"} |
    Set-ItemProperty -Name IsReadOnly -Value $false

$configContent = $configContent -Replace "<!--", ""
$configContent = $configContent -Replace "-->", ""
$configContent = $configContent -Replace "Enter Product Key Here", $productKey
$configContent = $configContent -Replace """none""", """basic"""

$configContent | Out-File $spConfigFile
```

This script takes care of copying the configuration file locally by creating a folder on your `C:\` drive, and creating a copy of the XML configuration file used by SharePoint to install all of its components. Open the newly copied file, and modify its content to include our own product key for SharePoint 2013. As the script indicates, please replace the generic product key provided with the one provided on your installation media or MSDN subscription. Next, initiate a new process that will execute the SharePoint 2013 installation wizard in silent mode (no graphical interfaces) by referencing the XML configuration file that you have just created locally with the previous script. Figure 5-12 shows the installation in process.

```
$spProcess = new-object System.Diagnostics.Process
$spProcess.StartInfo.Filename = "F:\setup.exe"
$spProcess.StartInfo.Arguments = "/config C:\SP2013\config.xml"
$spProcess.Start()
$spProcess.WaitForExit()
```

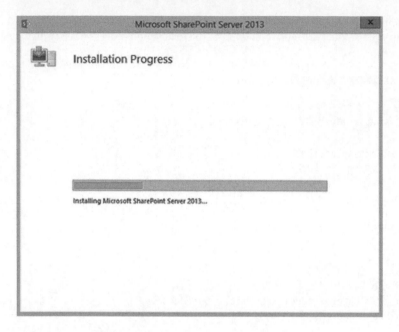

Figure 5-12. *SharePoint 2013 unattended installation*

Configuring Your SharePoint Farm

Now that all parts of our SharePoint environment have been installed, you need to configure the farm. Once again for this task we will be using PowerShell to create the various databases and service instances required by SharePoint to run properly. At the end of this section, your environment will be fully usable and will be ready for you to start playing with it.

Creating the Databases

Unless you've been living under a rock for the past few years, you've come to learn that since SharePoint 2010, the SharePoint Products Configuration Wizard, which is the default graphical tool to configure your SharePoint farm, adds a bunch of random numbers at the end of each database it creates. These numbers are referred to as a GUID, and are used by SharePoint to ensure your databases are uniquely named because the tool doesn't trust you to pick one yourself. If you are like me, I just hate it when software assumes that I don't know what I'm doing and makes decision on our behalf. Fear not my friends; with the help of some PowerShell goodness, there is a way to specify how you want these databases to be named.

In the SharePoint world, there are three main types of database that every farm should have: the Central Administration content database (referred to as the admin database), the configuration database (referred to as the config database), and the content database. The admin database is where the information about the central administration site collection is stored. There will always only be a single instance of this database per SharePoint farm. The second one, the config database, stores information about all other SharePoint databases in the farm. It also keeps track of all custom solutions, webparts, web applications, site templates, and all other farm setting. The content database, by contrast, can have multiple instances. It stores all information about a site collection in it. There could be more than one site collection stored in each content database.

Throughout the next few sections, I will describe how to automatically create each of these databases using PowerShell. With the core SharePoint bits now installed onto your machine, you now have access to use the `Microsoft.SharePoint.PowerShell` cmdlets, which will make your job easier.

The first database that you'll need to create is the config database. Because it is the main database keeping track of everything going on in our SharePoint farm, it makes sense to have created first. With the SharePoint cmdlets now available to you, you can call the New-SPConfigurationDatabase cmdlet to do the work. Calling this cmdlet will also automatically create an empty admin database that will act as a placeholder for the eventual Central Administration site collection that will be created in the next section.

```
$spConfigDBName = "SPConfig" # Config DB name, replace by your own;
$spAdminDBName = "SPAdmin" # Admin DB name, replace by your own;
$spPassphrase = "pass@word1" # Recommendation is to change this to something else;
$spFarmAdminPassword = "pass@word1" # replace by your admin account password;

# Convert the provided Passphrase to a secure string
$securePassphrase = ConvertTo-SecureString $spPassphrase -asPlainText -force

# Convert the provided Admin account's password to secure string and create a new PowerShell
Credentials object to represent the Administrator's account;
$secureAdminPassword = ConvertTo-SecureString $spFarmAdminPassword -asPlainText -force
$spFarmAdmin = new-object -typename System.Management.Automation.PSCredential -argumentlist
"contoso\administrator", $secureAdminPassword

# Load the SharePoint PowerShell cmdlets
Add-PSSnapin Microsoft.SharePoint.PowerShell

New-SPConfigurationDatabase -DatabaseServer $env:COMPUTERNAME -DatabaseName $spConfigDBName
-AdministrationContentDatabaseName $spAdminDBName -Passphrase $securePassphrase -FarmCredentials
$spFarmAdmin
```

The operation should take about four to five minutes to complete. Once completed, you should be able to see that your two databases have been properly created on your server by using the SQL Server Management Studio tool (see Figure 5-13).

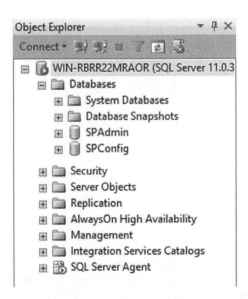

Figure 5-13. *SharePoint 2013 databases in SQL Server Management Studio 2012*

Configuring Central Administration

Now that your empty place holder for Central Administration has been created (config database), go ahead and populate it with information about its site collection. It is normally a good practice to have your Central Administration site deploy on a nonstandard port that is higher than 999. The following script lets you specify what port number you'd like to use. My personal preference is to always use port 7777 for development farms. Examples that will follow in the next few chapters will all assume that you have it deployed to this port, so unless you have a good reason to wanting to change it, I suggest that you leave it untouched. The execution of the PowerShell command should take about two minutes to execute.

```
$centralAdminPort = 7777
New-SPCentralAdministration -Port $centralAdminPort -WindowsAuthProvider "NTLM"
```

Once the process has completed, your Central Administration site will be all ready for you to use. Open a new browser window on your machine, and navigate to http://localhost:7777/. You should be able to view and navigate throughout the various administrative sections of the site (see Figure 5-14).

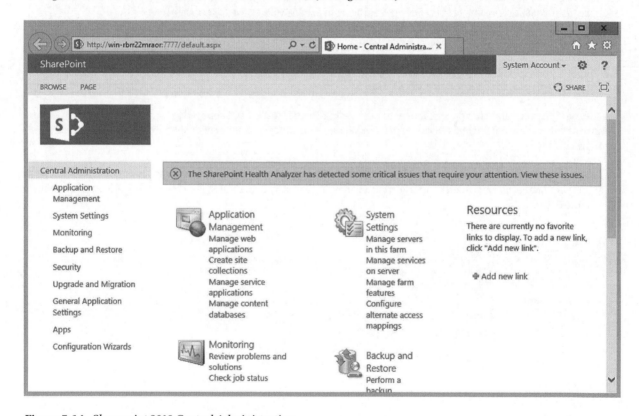

***Figure 5-14.** Sharepoint 2013 Central Administration*

Creating Your First Web Application

The title of this section is not 100 percent true; you already have a web application created in your farm, the Central Administration one. In order for you to start leveraging the collaborative side of SharePoint, you need to create another web application that will contain the site collections that you want to expose to the end users. My recommendation is to have your new web application created on port 80. It just makes it easier to access, and prevents you from having to remember what port it's on. Again, examples that are to follow in this book all assume that you have it configured on port 80. Feel free, however, to change it to whatever port you would like.

New web applications in PowerShell are created by calling the `New-SPWebApplication` cmdlet. This requires you to specify its name as well as the name of the Internet Information Services (IIS) application pool that will be associated with it. Each web application in SharePoint gets its own IIS application pool to manage its resources.

In this example, even if it is not required, you will also provide the cmdlet with the port number on which to create your web application. You will also provide the account to use to run the application pool, in this case the administrator account. In SharePoint 2013, the classic mode authentication has been deprecated, so you will need to define a new authentication provider so that your web application can use claims-based authentication. The script to have it created is the following:

```
$webAppPort = 80

$authProvider = New-SPAuthenticationProvider
$adminManagedAccount = Get-SPManagedAccount "contoso\Administrator"

New-SPWebApplication -Name "Demo Gateway" -ApplicationPool "DemoGatewayPool"
-ApplicationPoolAccount $adminManagedAccount -Port $webAppPort -AuthenticationProvider $authProvider

Install-SPFeature -AllExistingFeatures -Force # Active all required Farm Features
```

Creating Your Root Site Collection

You are almost there! All that is left is to create is a root site collection in the SharePoint Web Application that you have created in the previous section. SharePoint exposes several templates for creating new site collections out-of-the-box. For the purpose of simplicity, use the Blank Site template, which will create a new site with the minimum set of features activated by default.

```
$blankSiteTemplate = Get-SPWebTemplate STS#1
New-SPSite -Url "http://localhost/" -Name "Home" -Template $blankSiteTemplate -OwnerAlias
"contoso\administrator"
```

This script should only take a few seconds to execute. Once finished, open a new Internet Explorer window and navigate to `http://localhost/` to ensure that your new site collection was properly created.

Explorer Enhanced Security Configuration

Internet Explorer Enhanced Security Configuration (IE ESC) is a security mechanism put in place by Microsoft on its server operating systems to ensure that administrators do not browse the web on a server machine using their administrative accounts. As best practices would dictate, they should only browse it from a remote machine using a limited account to reduce risks of attacks on the server by an external website. Without going into too much detail about what IE ESC does exactly, you need to understand that it limits most functionalities available within Microsoft's web browser. For example, it will prevent the execution of scripts, which is essential for SharePoint to work correctly. Although you should normally never be browsing your SharePoint directly on the server, for demonstration purposes, I will be breaking this rule and disabling this security mechanism. If you don't disable this feature, you will get a page with an error at the top asking you to enable scripts and to reload the page (see Figure 5-15).

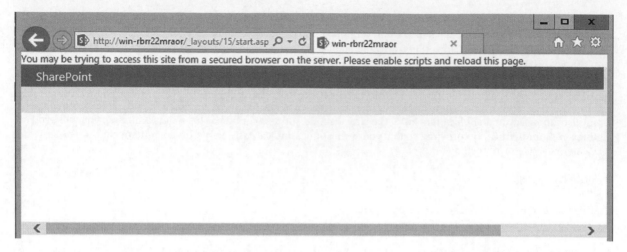

Figure 5-15. *Accessing your SharePoint 2013 site with Internet Explorer Enhanced Security Configuration enabled*

There are two levels of Enhanced Security Configuration you can set: one for administrator users and one for regular users. In this case, you will be disabling both levels using PowerShell. Internet Explorer Enhanced Security Configuration is disabled through the registry. The keys that control its state are listed in Table 5-3.

Table 5-3. *Ehanced Security Configuration levels and registery keys*

Level	Registry Key
Admin	HKLM:\SOFTWARE\Microsoft\Active Setup\Installed Components\{A509B1A7-37EF-4b3f-8CFC-4F3A74704073}
User	HKLM:\SOFTWARE\Microsoft\Active Setup\Installed Components\{A509B1A8-37EF-4b3f-8CFC-4F3A74704073}

You will need to set the IsInstalled property of both of these keys to '0.' The following lines of PowerShell will help automate this process:

```
$AdminKey = "HKLM:\SOFTWARE\Microsoft\Active Setup\Installed Components\{A509B1A7-37EF-4b3f-8CFC-4F3A74704073}"

$UserKey = "HKLM:\SOFTWARE\Microsoft\Active Setup\Installed Components\{A509B1A8-37EF-4b3f-8CFC-4F3A74704073}"

Set-ItemProperty -Path $AdminKey -Name "IsInstalled" -Value 0
Set-ItemProperty -Path $UserKey -Name "IsInstalled" -Value 0
```

Once executed, if you open your SharePoint site again, you should see that the error that you were previously getting is gone and that you are now able to use SharePoint to its full potential (see Figure 5-16). The most important thing to remember, however, is that in a real-world production environment, you do not want to disable these features, as they could easily expose it to real threats and cause irreparable damage to your environment.

Figure 5-16. *Accessing your SharePoint 2013 site with Internet Explorer Enhanced Security Configuration disabled*

Granting Users Access

Remember how you created five users and five security groups at the beginning of this chapter? Well, now is the time to set their permissions in our newly created SharePoint environment. You will be granting permissions to the Active Directory groups instead of granting permissions to the users directly. The permission list will look like Table 5-4.

Table 5-4. *Your Active Directory groups and permissions*

Group Name	Permission
Administration	Design
Finance	Contribute
Human Resources	Contribute
Directors	Read
Tech Support	Full Control

For a full description of what each role does and what privileges are granted with each one, I recommend that you read the following Microsoft article http://technet.microsoft.com/en-us/library/cc288074(v=office.14).aspx.

The following lines of PowerShell will automatically add the security groups you created earlier and will take care of granting the appropriate permission level to our site. In SharePoint, before being able to grant permission on a site to a user, you need to ensure that this user is registered against that site first. The SPWeb.EnsureUser() method ensures that a user is registered against a specific site and returns a reference to the user object.

```
$web = Get-SPWeb http://localhost
$user = $web.EnsureUser("Contoso\Administration")
Set-SPUser -Identity $user -web $web -AddPermissionLevel "Design"
```

```
$user = $web.EnsureUser("Contoso\Finance")
Set-SPUser -Identity $user -web $web -AddPermissionLevel "Contribute"

$user = $web.EnsureUser("Contoso\Human Resources")
Set-SPUser -Identity $user -web $web -AddPermissionLevel "Contribute"

$user = $web.EnsureUser("Contoso\Directors")
Set-SPUser -Identity $user -web $web -AddPermissionLevel "Read"

$user = $web.EnsureUser("Contoso\Tech Support")
Set-SPUser -Identity $user -web $web -AddPermissionLevel "Full Control"
```

Figure 5-17 shows the different SharePoint groups that have been created.

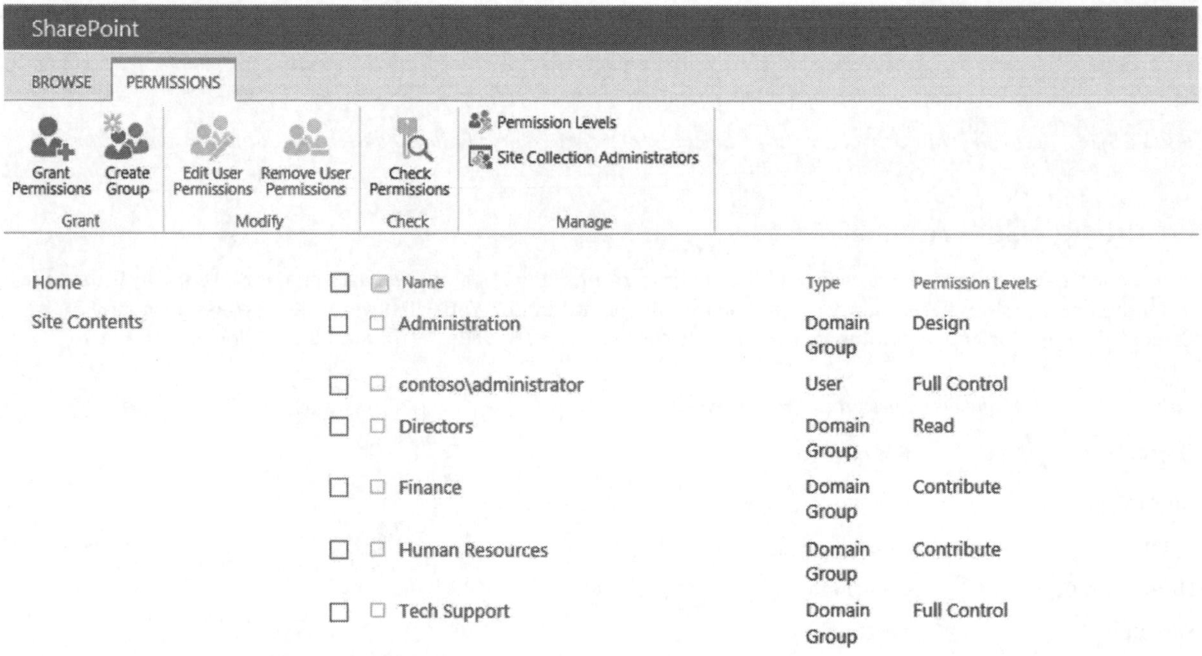

Figure 5-17. *List of users and groups and their associated permissions in SharePoint*

Putting It All Together

Throughout the previous sections of this chapter, you have learned how to configure different aspects of your SharePoint farm environment using PowerShell. Wouldn't it be awesome if you could now put it all together and simply start your script on a fresh installation of the operating system and let it run automatically, without requiring interaction at all? Simply putting all the lines of code together in a single PowerShell script file is not going to cut it. The installation requires the machine to reboot several times, so how do you ensure that PowerShell knows to restart its execution where it left off before the reboot? Also, because your machine will be joining a domain, how do you have the machine logon automatically after rebooting? You don't want to have to monitor the installation all the time and have to input your credentials to logon every time the machine starts.

Luckily, there is an old Windows trick that you can use that will ensure that you can create a fully unattended installation script. You can use PowerShell to write reboot instructions to the registry, and Windows will automatically read from these entries on rebooting.

Writing to the Registry

PowerShell provides a very simple way of creating and modifying properties of registry keys in Windows. The `Set-ItemProperty` cmdlet takes as parameters the registry path of the key to add/modify, the name of the property, and its value.

```
Set-ItemProperty -Path <KeyPath> -Name "<PropertyName>" -Value "<PropertyValue>"
```

As you've probably figured it out by now, the cmdlet to remove a key's property is `Remove-ItemProperty`, which only takes the key's path and its name.

```
RemoveItemProperty -Path <KeyPath> -Name "<KeyName>"
```

Automatic Login

The first registry key that you will need is the `WinLogon` key, which allows you to specify credentials for Windows to use to automatically logon when the machine boots. This key is found at the following location in the registry:

```
HKLM:\SOFTWARE\Microsoft\Windows NT\CurrentVersion\WinLogon
```

Remember that while this key is set, the computer will always attempt to login as the specified user. If you want to get the default login screen prompting you for your credentials, you will need to clear this key's properties first, or you can limit the number of times the automatic logon will happen by specifying the `AutoLogonCount` property. There are several properties, shown in Table 5-5, that you will need to set for the automatic logon to work properly.

Table 5-5. *Properties needed for automatic logon*

Property's Name	Description
DefaultUserName	User name to use to automatically logon
DefaultPassword	Password for the associated user account
AutoAdminLogon	0 - Disabled 1 - Enabled
AutoLogonCount	Number of times to automatically logon. Upon login on automatically, the counter will be decreased by 1.
DefaultDomainName	Domain name for the user account to use.

To achieve a fully unattended installation of SharePoint, encapsulate the code that sets the automatic logon key in a method for reusability purpose. Each time you will need the installation to reboot, you will make a call to this method to have the credentials set automatically on reboot. The method that you will use will look like the following:

```
Function AutoLogonAfterReboot
{
    $WinLogonKey = "HKLM:\SOFTWARE\Microsoft\Windows NT\CurrentVersion\WinLogon"

    set-itemproperty $WinLogonKey "DefaultUserName" "Administrator"
    set-itemproperty $WinLogonKey "DefaultPassword" "pass@word1"
    set-itemproperty $WinLogonKey "AutoAdminLogon" "1"
    set-itemproperty $WinLogonKey "AutoLogonCount" "1"
    set-itemproperty $WinLogonKey "DefaultDomainName" "Contoso"
}
```

Script Orchestrator

A piece of software or code that is used to determine what other piece of code to execute next is what we refer to as an orchestrator. In our case, an orchestrator will need to be developed to allow our installation to decide what to execute next on restarting. Our code will need to set a registry key containing instructions on what to execute next after rebooting. On rebooting, Windows will look at this registry key to determine if it needs to execute a command or not. The registry key to tell Windows what command to execute next on rebooting is the following:

```
HKLM:\SOFTWARE\Microsoft\Windows\CurrentVersion\Run
```

The orchestrator will break your installation down into several logical execution steps (configure domain controller, install SQL Server, install the SharePoint prerequisites, etc.). It will allow users to specify, through a parameter, what step of execution they would like to call next, and it will execute the appropriate piece of code based on this parameter.

Each execution step that requires the machine to reboot after completion will need to call your orchestrator to set the registry key, passing it the name of the next execution step. After the reboot is completed, PowerShell will automatically launch, call your installation script, and pass it the name of the next logical execution step to execute. The orchestrator's logical flow is summarized in Figure 5-18.

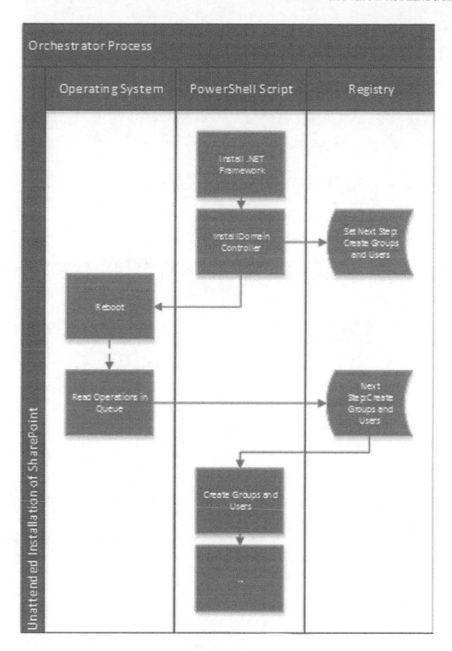

Figure 5-18. *Orchestrator flow of logic*

The orchestrator's code will need to have two main methods defined. One method will verify whether an execution step is the one that you should execute next, and one will store the value of the next command to execute in the registry.

```
# Receives the name of a step and determines if it's the next logical step to execute;
Function IsCurrentStep($nextStep)
{
    if ($global:startingStep -eq $nextStep -or $global:isStarted) {
        $global:started = $TRUE
    }
    return $global:started}

# Set the next command to execute upon rebooting in the registry key.
Function SetNextStep($script, $step)
{
    Set-ItemProperty $runKey $global:restartKey "$global:powershell $script -Step $step"
    Restart-Computer
    exit
}
```

The SetNextStep method will store the path to the PowerShell executable as the next command to execute, and will pass it the path for your script as well as the name of the next logical execution step to run as parameters (see Figure 5-19).

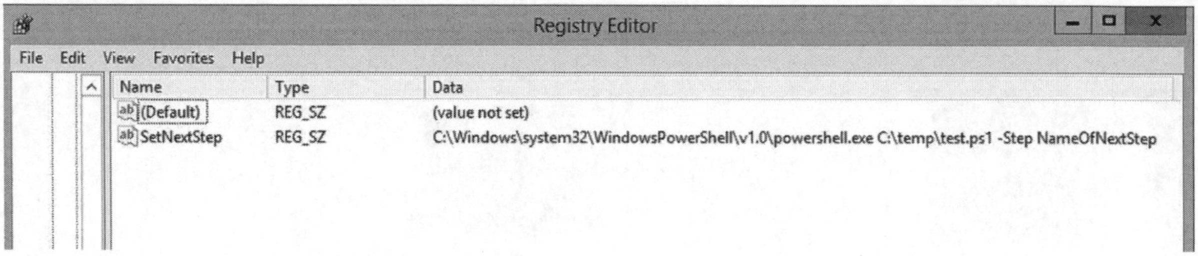

Figure 5-19. *Registry key used by the orchestrator*

With the orchestrator in place, all that is left to do is to wrap each execution step in our PowerShell script in if statements, and to call the IsNextStep method on them to decide whether or not to execute them.

```
if (IsCurrentStep "ASP.NET")
{
    ...
}

if (IsCurrentStep "DomainController")
{
    SetNextStep $script "GroupsAndUsers" # Computer will reboot after this line;
}

if (IsCurrentStep "GroupsAndUsers")
{
    ... # Execution will restart here after reboot;
    SetNextStep $script "NextStepName" # Computer will reboot after this line;
}
...
```

You should consult the electronic resources offered with this book to get your hands on the full script. The script will ask you to fill in certain details regarding your environment, such as what port to install the SharePoint Central Administration on, your administrator's account password, and so on. It will then start its execution and configure everything as expected. The script takes about an hour to execute. Once finished, it will automatically open a new Internet Explorer window and navigate to your new SharePoint 2013 homepage.

Summary

In this chapter, you have learned how you can automate the configuration of your SharePoint environment using PowerShell. You have had the chance, throughout the various demos, to familiarize yourself with the SharePoint 2013 PowerShell cmdlets, as well as how to use them to interact with the SharePoint 2013 object model. In the next chapter, I will build on this newly acquired knowledge and will dig into the various aspects of SharePoint that you can control using PowerShell. The environment built in the current chapter is the environment that will be used in all examples to come in this book.

CHAPTER 6

■ ■ ■

Managing SharePoint with PowerShell

I am now ready to take on the core of the subject of this book: how to interact with your SharePoint environment using PowerShell. In this chapter, I will make various analogies to compare how PowerShell relates to classic .NET interactions using the SharePoint object model. Throughout the following sections you will learn how you can write PowerShell scripts to manage and interact with different levels of SharePoint artifacts such as site collections, sites, lists, items, and so on. By the end of this chapter, you will have been exposed to the different components of SharePoint, and to their methods and properties that are made available through the object model. As mentioned earlier in this book, I am assuming that by now you have had some level of exposure to any version of SharePoint, and that you understand the different hierarchies of entities that exist within it.

Users who have previously done .NET development for SharePoint will recognize many concepts used in the examples that follow. Remember, PowerShell is built on top of the .NET Common Language Runtime (CLR), and therefore it can be used to interact with any .NET artifact just like you could do if you were using C# or Visual Basic. Just like any good piece of software, special care needs to be paid to objects' disposition in PowerShell. SharePoint object tends to take a lot of resources in memory, and it is important to free these resources once you are done working with the objects in question. I will dedicate an entire section of this chapter to discuss how to properly manage resources and memory.

By the end of this chapter, you will be able to write, test, and deploy PowerShell scripts that will allow you to perform large and repetitive operations on your SharePoint farms. You will be familiar with the various cmdlet made available to you through the `Microsoft.SharePoint.PowerShell` module that comes with SharePoint 2013, and you will be able to create your own reusable modules. You will learn how to modify configuration settings, create new objects, and interact with them using scripts. Several real-life scenarios will be given to help you understand how the various examples presented could apply to your work environment.

I will start by describing how to interact with high-level objects such as site collections and webs, and will slowly make my way down to lower-level objects such as list items and users. Farm administration and monitoring will be covered in Chapter 8.

Interacting with Objects

PowerShell in the context of SharePoint is all about interacting with the various artifacts made available to us by the server platform. SharePoint objects expose properties and methods just like any good old .NET object. For example, a list item exposes a property that indicates the date it was last modified. It also exposes a method that can induce a checkout operation on it. All of these properties and methods are available in PowerShell, and you can make direct calls to them, as long as you obtain a reference to the object that you wish to modify using a retriever method. I refer to methods as being retrievers when their sole purpose is to return a single or an array of objects. For example, the `Get-SPSite` method that returns a site collection object is a retriever method.

■ **Note**   Remember, you can always get a list of all available methods and properties for a specific object by passing it as a pipe operator to the Get-Member cmdlet.

PowerShell can also be used to execute long-lasting and repetitive operations against a farm. In many cases, PowerShell has been proven to be faster to execute administrative operations than its predecessor, the stsadm command line utility.

Throughout the following sections, I will give you a quick overview of the most important PowerShell cmdlets that you'll need to remember to help you do your daily work as a SharePoint administrator. This chapter should serve as a quick reference when you need to perform a specific operation against your SharePoint farm. Content in the next few pages will be presented as a cookbook, listing various operations with a short description that explains what they do and what you should be using them for. The list of cmdlets will be separated by the level of objects that they affect or with which they interact. All examples listed here will use the SharePoint environment that you built in Chapter 5.

Site Collections

Site collections in the SharePoint world represent the highest level of concrete objects with which your end users will interact. A site collection represents a set of websites that are logically linked together. Each site collection has its own set of permissions, solutions gallery, and other types of resources libraries dedicated to it. In the SharePoint object model, site collections are represented by the SPSite object.

Get-SPSite

The Get-SPSite cmdlet returns a list of site collections matching the specified criteria. You can use this cmdlet alongside with a URL for a specific site. There are also different parameters that could be used to retrieve different sets of site collections, but these are outside the scope of this chapter. Just know that you could, as an example, retrieve all site collections belonging to a specific content database.

```
$siteCol = Get-SPSite http://localhost
```

This PowerShell line will return the site collection associated with the http://localhost URL and will assign it to variable $siteCol (see Figure 6-1).

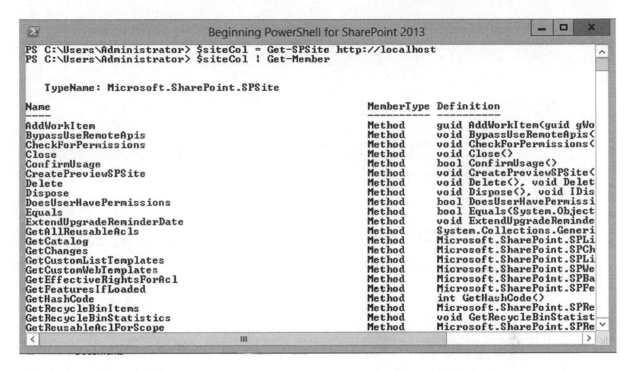

Figure 6-1. *Example of Get-SPSite in use*

Move-SPSite

Move-SPSite lets you move an existing site collection from one content database to another. It can be useful to regroup together various site collections for backup purposes. The following example assumes that the NewContentDB database already exists and that you are trying to move the specified site collection to it:

```
Move-SPSite http://localhost -DestinationDatabase NewContentDB
```

Copy-SPSite

The Copy-SPSite cmdlet makes a copy of an existing site collection. The copy can be done in the same content database or in a different one. You also can use this cmdlet to copy a site collection from one Web Application to another one, as shown in Figure 6-2.

```
Copy-SPSite http://localhost http://localhost/sites/destination
```

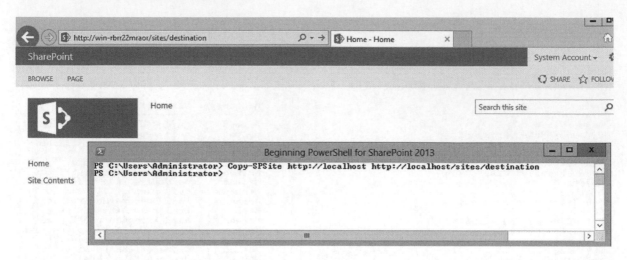

Figure 6-2. *New site created using the Copy-SPSite cmdlet*

New-SPSite

New-SPSite creates a new site collection under a SharePoint Web Application. You have the option of specifying under what content database to have it created. If no content databases are specified, SharePoint automatically determines where to store it. Take note that if you don't specify a template type when creating your new site collection, you will get a prompt asking you to select a template when you'll first try to access it through the SharePoint interface. If you wish to specify a default web template, you can do so by adding the -Template parameter to the cmdlet call and passing it the name of the template to use. You can find a full list of all template names that are available in SharePoint 2013 by using the Get-SPWebTemplate cmdlet. Figure 6-3 shows the creation of a new site collection using PowerShell.

```
New-SPSite http://localhost/sites/test -OwnerAlias "Contoso\Administrator"
```

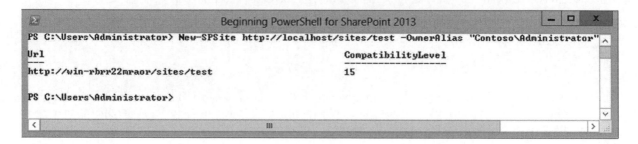

Figure 6-3. *Creating a new Site Collection using the New-SPSite cmdlet*

Set-SPSite

Set-SPSite applies the specified configuration parameters to a specific site collection. Note that you could also get a reference to your site and directly modify the properties you want. It is what I consider to be a "shortcut" cmdlet:

```
Set-SPSite http://localhost/sites/test -MaxSize 2000
```

This example sets a specific quota for the http://localhost/sites/test site collection. The same results could have been achieved by calling the following code:

```
$siteCol = Get-SPSite http://localhost/sites/test
$siteCol.Quota.StorageMaximumLevel = 2000
```

The PowerShell snippet in Figure 6-4 proves that the two methods are equivalent.

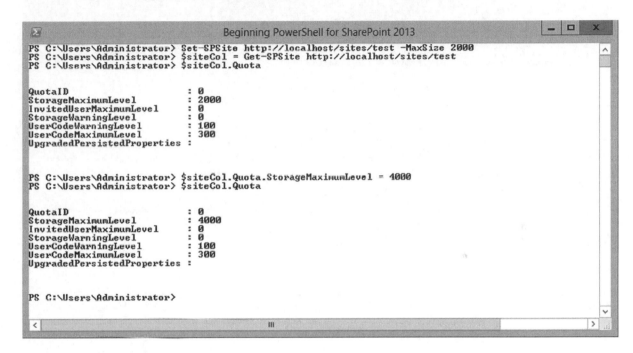

Figure 6-4. *Changing a Site Collection's quota using PowerShell*

Remove-SPSite

The Remove-SPSite cmdlet does exactly what you think it does. It deletes a specific site collection from a web application (see Figure 6-5). The only required parameter for this operation is the URL or GUID of the site collection to delete.

```
Remove-SPSite http://localhost/sites/test
```

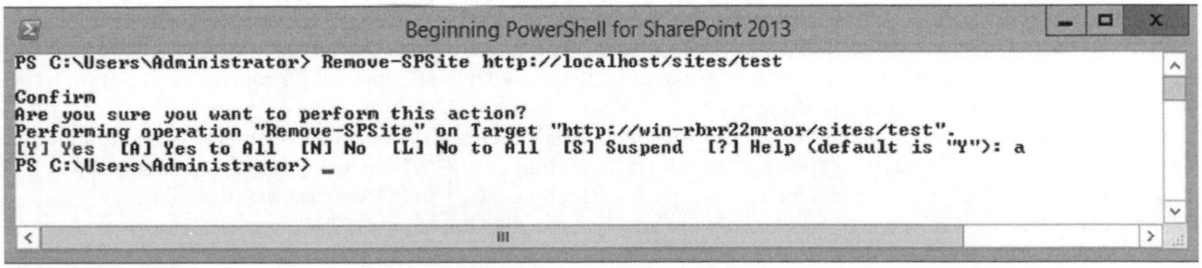

Figure 6-5. *Removing a Site Collection using the Remove-SPSite cmdlet*

Get-SPDeletedSite

Get-SPDeletedSite is a retriever method that returns a list of site collections that have been deleted based on specific research criteria. For example, you could get a list of all site collections that have been deleted under the "/sites" managed path (see Figure 6-6).

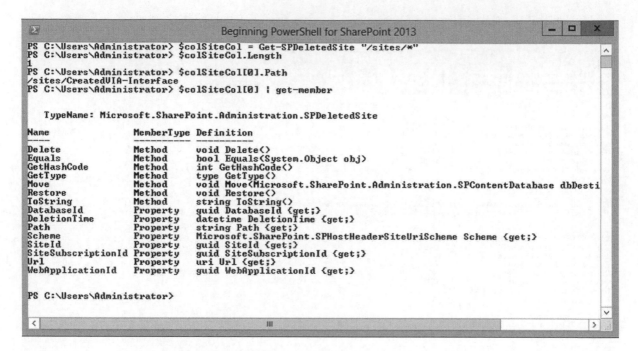

Figure 6-6. *Retrieving a deleted Site Collection using PowerShell*

■ **Note** This cmdlet only returns site collections that have been deleted via the SharePoint interface. The site collection we deleted using PowerShell in our previous example is long gone and cannot be retrieved.

```
$colSiteCol = Get-SPdeletedSite "/sites/*"
```

Remove-SPDeletedSite

As you've just seen, a special type of site collection object in SharePoint exists, called the Deleted Site Collection. This object is in limbo between life and death. Think of it as being a file in the recycle bin, which is given a second chance. From that state on, a site collection can either be permanently deleted or restored back. Of course, it can be moved over another content database but nothing more.

The Remove-SPDeletedSite cmdlet receives the identity of the deleted site collections you want to permanently delete and deletes it. You can either specify a specific site collection by its GUID, or specify a server-relative URL. Based on the Get-SPDeletedSite example in the preceding section, if we would like to remove the /sites/CreatedVIA-Interface site collection, we could execute the following line of PowerShell.

```
Remove-SPDeletedSite /sites/CreatedVIA-Interface
```

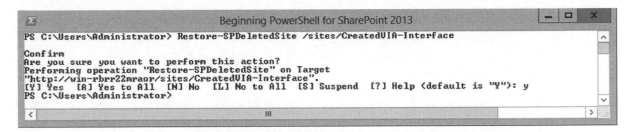

Figure 6-7. *Removing a deleted Site Collection from the recycle bin using PowerShell*

Restore-SPDeletedSite

As mentioned in the preceding section, a deleted site collection also can be restored. The `Restore-SPDeletedSite` cmdlet does the opposite of `Remove-SPDeletedSite` and actually brings a deleted site collection back from the dead into its former glory, assuming that it was deleted through the web interface and not through PowerShell (see Figure 6-8).

```
Restore-SPDeletedSite /sites/CreatedVIA-Interface
```

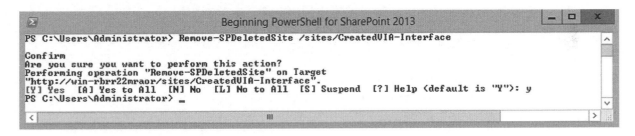

Figure 6-8. *Restoring a deleted Site Collection from the recycle bin using PowerShell*

Putting It Together: Creating a Site Collections Structure

Now that we have learned how easily we can interact with SharePoint site collections using PowerShell, we will build on the environment built in the previous chapter and will create a new site collection for every business unit identified in our fictive company, called Contoso. You will remember that when you created users in your domain, you also created five different security groups, each representing a different business unit. Those were:

- Administration

- Finance

- Human Resources

- Directors

- Tech Support

What you will want to do next is call the `New-SPSite` cmdlet and let it create these new business site collections. You could just call the cmdlet five times in a row with different parameters, but you've learned to do better. Put your newly acquired PowerShell skills to work and write something a bit more creative and reusable. What you are trying to achieve here can actually be achieved as a one liner using a pipe operation. Start by declaring an array containing the name of each business unit, and then pipe each of these names into your `New-SPSite` cmdlet. Then use the `$_` operand to insert the names into the new site collection's URL as follows (see Figure 6-9):

```
"Administration", "Finance", "Human Resources", "Directors", "Tech Support" |
%{New-SPSite http://localhost/sites/$_ -OwnerAlias contoso\administrator -Template "STS#0"}
```

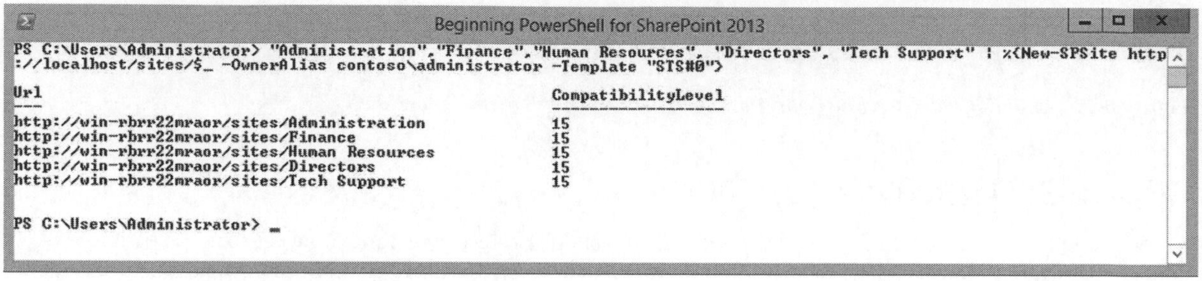

Figure 6-9. *Creating Site Collections in batch using PowerShell*

It doesn't get any simpler than this. You are now ready to dig deeper into the SharePoint object model and start looking at the various ways PowerShell can help you interact with webs.

Webs

Some of you may refer to webs as being SharePoint sites. I tend to prefer using "webs," just because it doesn't make it ambiguous as to whether we are talking about site collections (SPSite) or about an actual website. Microsoft identifies webs as being SPWeb objects in the SharePoint object model. A web in the context of SharePoint is what your users will be interacting with. It is something more tangible to end users than the concept of site collections. It is important to note that, in SharePoint 2013, every site collection needs at least one web in it. This web needs to exist directly at the root of its site collection and is being referred to as being the root web for the collection. By default, when using the `New-SPSite` cmdlet, PowerShell will automatically create a new root web inside the new site collection.

The following sections will give you an overview of the different cmdlets that are made available to you to interact with SharePoint webs. You will see several similarities in the naming and in the functionality to the ones made available for interacting with site collections.

Get-SPWeb

`Get-SPWeb` is the main retriever method to get a reference to a SPWeb object. It only requires you to specify the direct URL for the web you are trying to retrieve (see Figure 6-10).

```
Get-SPWeb "http://localhost/sites/Human Resources"
```

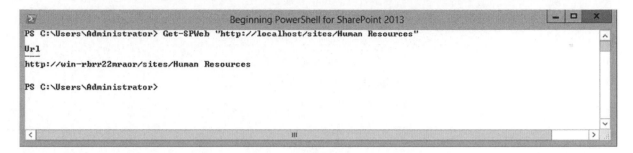

Figure 6-10. *Using the Get-SPWeb cmdlet to obtain a reference to a web*

New-SPWeb

The New-SPWeb cmdlet lets you create a new web under a specified site collection. Table 6-1 lists the different templates that can be used to create new SharePoint 2013 webs and their short names to use with PowerShell.

Table 6-1. *List of available SharePoint 2013 web templates*

Short Name	Title
ACCSRV#0	Access Services Site
ACCSRV#1	Assets Web Database
ACCSRV#3	Charitable Contributions Web Database
ACCSRV#4	Contacts Web Database
ACCSRV#5	Projects Web Database
ACCSRV#6	Issues Web Database
BDR#0	Document Center
BICenterSite#0	Business Intelligence Center
BLANKINTERNET#0	Publishing Site
BLANKINTERNET#1	Press Releases Site
BLANKINTERNET#2	Publishing Site with Workflow
BLANKINTERNETCONTAINER#0	Publishing Portal
BLOG#0	Blog
CENTRALADMIN#0	Central Admin Site
CMSPUBLISHING#0	Publishing Site
ENTERWIKI#0	Enterprise Wiki
GLOBAL#0	Global template
MPS#0	Basic Meeting Workspace
MPS#1	Blank Meeting Workspace
MPS#2	Decision Meeting Workspace

(*continued*)

Table 6-1. (*continued*)

Short Name	Title
MPS#3	Social Meeting Workspace
MPS#4	Multipage Meeting Workspace
OFFILE#0	(obsolete) Records Center
OFFILE#1	Records Center
OSRV#0	Shared Services Administration Site
PowerPointBroadcast#0	PowerPoint Broadcast Site
PPSMASite#0	PerformancePoint
PROFILES#0	Profiles
SGS#0	Group Work Site
SPS#0	SharePoint Portal Server Site
SPSCOMMU#0	Community area template
SPSMSITE#0	Personalization Site
SPSMSITEHOST#0	My Site Host
SPSNEWS#0	News Site
SPSNHOME#0	News Site
SPSPERS#0	SharePoint Portal Server Personal Space
SPSPORTAL#0	Collaboration Portal
SPSREPORTCENTER#0	Report Center
SPSSITES#0	Site Directory
SPSTOC#0	Contents area Template
SPSTOPIC#0	Topic area template
SRCHCEN#0	Enterprise Search Center
SRCHCENTERFAST#0	FAST Search Center
SRCHCENTERLITE#0	Basic Search Center
SRCHCENTERLITE#1	Basic Search Center
STS#0	Team Site
STS#1	Blank Site
STS#2	Document Workspace
TENANTADMIN#0	Tenant Admin Site
visprus#0	Visio Process Repository
WIKI#0	Wiki Site

The following example shows you how to create a new web using the Blank Site template. If you don't specify a template for it, you'll be prompted to select one the first time you access it through the SharePoint interface.

```
New-SPWeb http://localhost/NewWeb -Template "STS#1"
```

Remove-SPWeb

Remove-SPWeb lets you delete an existing web by specifying its URL. Note that deleting a web using PowerShell deletes it permanently, unless you specify the -Recycle parameter:

```
Remove-SPWeb http://localhost/NewWeb
```

If a web is deleted through the SharePoint interface, it becomes a SPDeletedSite object! Yes, you've heard me; just like in the case of a deleted site collection, a deleted web becomes the same object. Why is that? Because when you delete a site collection, all you're doing is actually deleting the webs contained in it. When you restore at least one web in the site collection, you're automatically restoring the site collection itself. There is such a thing as a SPDeletedSiteCollection object, but it does not expose any methods to remove or to restore itself.

The sad part, however, is that you cannot use the Get-SPDeletedSite cmdlet to retrieve webs that have been deleted in a site collection that still exists. To get a reference to such a web, you'll need to get a reference to the site collection's recycle bin, and then obtain a reference to the deleted web by iterating through the list of deleted objects. The example in Figure 6-11 shows you how you could retrieve a list of deleted webs from the recycle bin, and restore them back using PowerShell.

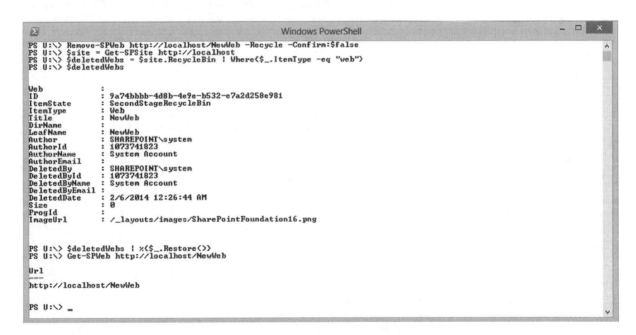

Figure 6-11. *Restoring all deleted webs from the recycle bin using PowerShell*

Set-SPWeb

Just like the Set-SPSite cmdlet, the Set-SPWeb is a shortcut command that allows you to configure a specified web. It allows you to specify a new URL, a new name, or a new description, or lets you apply a new template for the web. Again, just as is the case with the site collection level method, you could easily accomplish the same operation by getting a reference to the object using its retriever method, and by assigning values to its properties directly. The following example shows you how you could change the URL of a web using this PowerShell cmdlet (see Figure 6-12).

```
Set-SPWeb http://localhost/NewWeb -RelativeUrl ModifiedWeb
```

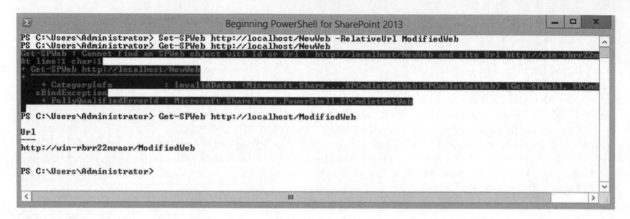

Figure 6-12. *Change a web's URL using PowerShell*

Export-SPWeb

Export-SPWeb lets you export a web along with all of its lists and libraries and their contents. The operation creates the backup file locally on disk, and generates an associated backup log. If you do not wish to have an export log generated on disk, you can simply us the -NoLogFile parameter. It is also important to note that this cmdlet will not preserve permissions for lists with broken inheritance and for item-level permissions.

```
Export-SPWeb http://localhost/ModifiedWeb -Path "C:\ExportedWeb.cmp"
```

Import-SPWeb

Peanut butter is to jam what Import-SPWeb is to Export-SPWeb: they just go along together. Cheesy analogy, I know, but what can you do with a backup of something if you don't have a means to restore it? This cmdlet lets you import a web along with all of its lists, libraries, and items. Just as in the case of the export method, it creates an operation log on disk. You can restore the backup on top of the existing site, or you could make a copy of it by creating a new site and restoring it at this new location, as shown in the following example (see Figure 6-13).

```
New-SPWeb http://localhost/MyImportedWeb
```

```
Import-SPWeb http://localhost/MyImportedWeb -Path "C:\ExportedWeb.cmp"
```

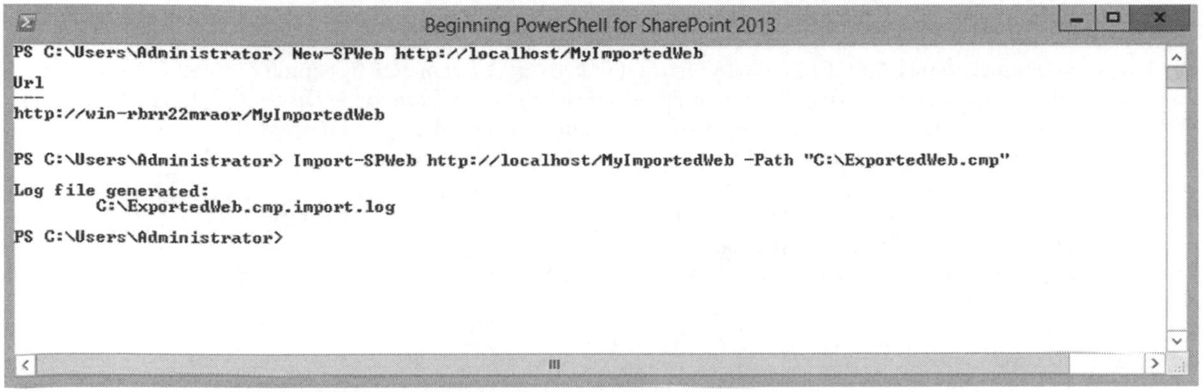

Figure 6-13. *Importing a web using the Im port-SPWeb PowerShell cmdlet*

■ **Note** There are no `Copy-SPWeb` cmdlets available by default in SharePoint 2013. However, you could easily build on top of the existing set of available cmdlets and create your. A combination of Export/Import on a specific web would have the same anticipated result as a `Copy-SPWeb` method.

Putting It Together: Creating Supporting Webs

You have now learned how easy it is to interact with SharePoint webs using PowerShell. You will now put your new learnings to good use, and continue to build on the example you've started in the previous section of this chapter. Now that you've created a site collection for each business unit within your organization, you will create workspaces for each team within the business unit. You will declare a multidimensional array with two dimensions: one representing the unit and one that will contains its associated teams. The logic will then loop in each row and create the new webs using the Team Site template (STS#0, as seen earlier in Table 6-1). To make things more exciting, each business unit will see their webs use a different theme to make sure that they can be easily differentiated. We will begin by declaring the array as follow:

```
$teamArray = @{}
$teamArray["Finance"] = @("Payroll", "Financial Systems", "Procurement")
$teamArray["Human Resources"] = @("Training", "Staff Services", "Recruiting")
$teamArray["Administration"] = @("Executive Assistants", "Planification")
$teamArray["Directors"] = @("CIO", "CEO", "COO")
$teamArray["Tech Support"] = @("Help Desk", "Applications", "Infrastructure")
```

Your next step is to define what the theme will be for each of these team sites. In SharePoint 2013, themes are now referred to as "Composed Looks." However, the ApplyTheme method is what you need to use to apply custom theming. A composed look is made of three important parts: a color palette, a font scheme, and a background image. You will declare a second multidimensional array to keep track of what composed look will get applied to what web. The array contains the name of the SharePoint theme that you want to apply. The array will be declared as follows:

```
$themeArray = @{}
$themeArray["Finance"] = "Sea Monster"
$themeArray["Human Resources"] = "Sketch"
$themeArray["Administration"] = "Characters"
$themeArray["Directors"] = "Wood"
$themeArray["Tech Support"] = "Nature"
```

In order to get a reference to the appropriate color palette, font scheme, and background image, you need to get a reference to the composed look based on its name, as specified in the previous array. In order to achieve this, you need to get a reference to the site collection's design catalog. This can be achieved by getting a reference to the site collection and calling the .GetCatalog(<name>) method. Once you have obtained the reference to the catalog, all that's left to do is to query it based on the composed look's name. You could get a reference to the Sea Monster theme for the Finance unit by using the following piece of PowerShell code (see Figure 6-14):

```
$site = Get-SPSite http://localhost/sites/Finance
$designCatalog = $site.GetCatalog("Design")
$seaMonsterTheme = $designCatalog.Items | Where {$_.Name -eq "Sea Monster"}

# Color Palette
$seaMonsterTheme["ThemeUrl"].Split(',')[1]

# Font Scheme
$seaMonsterTheme["FontSchemeUrl"].Split(',')[1]

# Image
$seaMonsterTheme["ImageUrl"].Split(',')[1]
```

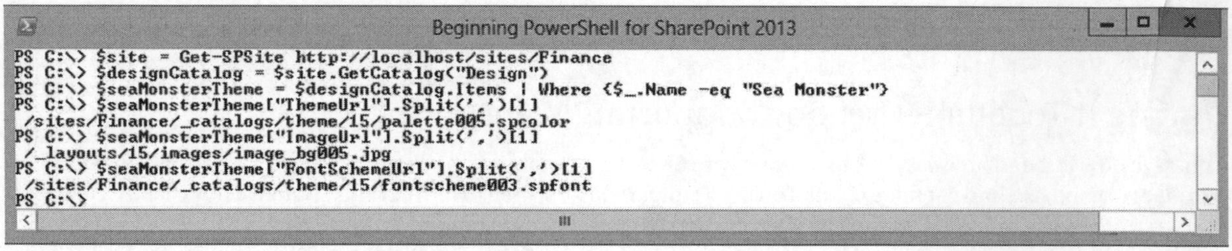

Figure 6-14. Creating webs in batch and applying custom themes using PowerShell

Now that both of our arrays have been properly declared and initialized, you can loop through each of the entries and make calls to the New-SPWeb cmdlet for each one. You will need to loop through each of the team array's keys and use its key value to determine what the associated team is for a given business array:

```
foreach($businessUnit in $teamArray.Keys) # this returns a list of business units
{
    oreach($team in $teamArray[$businessUnit]
    {
        # At this point we have access to the teams' names, and we can dynamically
        # build the urls for the composed looks using that information     }
}
```

If you now try to put it all back together, your script will look like the following. You can use a unique set of foreach loops to access both the team and theme arrays. The script should take about five minutes to execute, at the end of which all of your webs will have been properly created:

```
#Declaring all teams in business units
$teamArray = @{}
$teamArray["Finance"] = @("Payroll", "Financial Systems", "Procurement")
```

```
$teamArray["Human Resources"] = @("Training", "Staff Services", "Recruiting")
$teamArray["Administration"] = @("Executive Assistants", "Planification")
$teamArray["Directors"] = @("CIO", "CEO", "COO")
$teamArray["Tech Support"] = @("Help Desk", "Applications", "Infrastructure")

#Declaring the various components of composed look for each team
$themeArray = @{}
$themeArray["Finance"] = "Sea Monster"
$themeArray["Human Resources"] = "Sketch"
$themeArray["Administration"] = "Characters"
$themeArray["Directors"] = "Wood"
$themeArray["Tech Support"] = "Nature"

foreach($businessUnit in $teamArray.Keys)
{
    $site = Get-SPSite "http://localhost/sites/$businessUnit"
    $catalog = $site.GetCatalog("Design")
    $theme = $catalog.Items | Where {$_.Name -eq $themeArray[$businessUnit]}

    foreach($team in $teamArray[$businessUnit])
    {
        #Remove-SPWeb "http://localhost/sites/$businessUnit/$team" -Confirm:$false
        $web = New-SPWeb "http://localhost/sites/$businessUnit/$team" -Template STS#0
                -Name $team

        $color = $theme["ThemeUrl"].Split(',')[1].Trim()
        $font = $theme["FontSchemeUrl"].Split(',')[1].Trim()
        $image = $theme["ImageUrl"].Split(',')[1].Trim()
        write-host $color
        $web.ApplyTheme($color, $font, $image, $true)
        write-host $team -backgroundcolor green

        $web.Dispose()
    }
    $site.Dispose()
}
```

To ensure that everything worked as expected, navigate to http://localhost/sites/Finance/Payroll/. Your team site should have been created with the Sea Monster composed look, which is made of an orange suite bar at the top (where you see the mention "SharePoint"), and of green tiles and icons.

I am now ready to dig deeper in the SharePoint object model and start playing with lists and libraries.

Lists

A SharePoint list is probably the type of object that is the most widely used. Almost any out-of-the-box "apps" (remember that in 2014 everything is an app) uses lists in the backend. Document libraries, as an example, are just a SharePoint list with a special SharePoint Content Type associated with it. Just as with the other types of artifacts we already touched on in this chapter (site collections and webs), SharePoint lists can have unique permissions or inherit permissions from their parent web. Since SharePoint 2010, lists also have a new feature called *throttling*, which prevents large lists from bringing a server down to its knees because of large lists. Users have a maximum number of items they can have in a list before SharePoint stops trying to render its content on screen.

A list in the SharePoint object model is represented by the SPList object. It represents a set of items that have different properties associated with them. I tend to think as a list in the SharePoint context as being a data table with columns and rows, like a table you would find in an Excel spreadsheet, for example. The rows would be the list's items, and the columns would be represented by the properties associated with the items. These properties are also referred to as fields. Each field has a data type associated with them, and it represents the type of data that this one can accept as input value.

Lists can also have a predefined set of filters, sorting options, and display fields. These are referred to as views. Think of a SharePoint view just like you would think of a view in the database world. It is a way to present data from a specific source in a format and in a fashion that makes sense to the end user. For example, assume that you are a regional manager in charge of managing a store for the city of Ottawa. Your organization keeps track of every transaction made across all the different stores in the region into a single SharePoint list. It may not make sense for you to view the transactions for the city of Toronto, for example. What you want to do is to create yourself a view on the list so that the data display only ever shows records for the store you are managing. You could also decide to hide certain fields that you may judge are not necessary to display. Creating such a view does not affect the data source; it simply changes its presentation layer.

Throughout the following sections, you will learn how you can use PowerShell to interact with the structure and the configuration properties of SharePoint lists. I will not be discussing list items at this point. This will be addressed in a later section. In comparison to site collections and webs, there aren't any cmdlets that deal directly with lists. Instead, you need to obtain your own instance of a list and manipulate it through its methods and properties.

Getting a List Instance

SharePoint lists are contained at the web level. Every SPWeb object has a property called Lists that represents an array of all the lists contained in that specific web. In order to get a reference to a specific list, you'll need to get it from that list array using either its name or its GUID. Another option would be to use the GetList method that expects the list's relative URL as a parameter. The following example shows you how to get a reference to the Style Library located at the root of our site collection on http://localhost:

```
$web = Get-SPWeb http://localhost
$list = $web.Lists["Style Library"]
$fields = $list.Fields.InternalName
$fields | Where {$_ -like '*workflow*'}
```

This gets a list of all the internal names of the fields contained in the Style Library list. Think of internal names as being unique IDs. Each field has two names, an internal one and a display one. There is nothing preventing a list from having two fields with the same display names, but you cannot have two fields with the same internal name being part of the same list. Once you've retrieved a list of all internal names, you can query it using the pipeline operator, to retrieve only the field names that contain the word workflow (see Figure 6-15).

```
PS C:\> $web = Get-SPWeb http://localhost
PS C:\> $list = $web.Lists["Style Library"]
PS C:\> $fields = $list.Fields.InternalName
PS C:\> $fields | Where {$_ -like '*workflow*'}
WorkflowVersion
WorkflowInstanceID
PS C:\> _
```

Figure 6-15. *Obtaining a list of all fields' names in a SharePoint list using PowerShell*

Creating a New List

To create a new list instance, you will need to first obtain a reference to the web in which you want to add the list. After the reference is obtained, the new list can be created by calling the .Add() method on the Lists properties of the web object. In most cases, you will be calling the Add() method using three parameters: a title, a description, and the list template associated with your list. To get a full list of all available list templates, as shown in Figure 6-16, you can simply run the following PowerShell command:

```
$web = Get-SPWeb http://localhost
$web.ListTemplates.Name
```

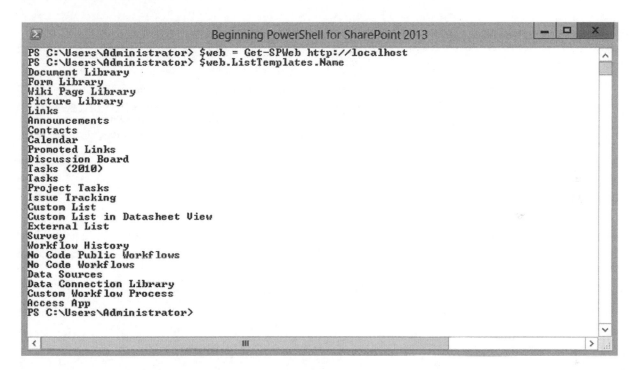

Figure 6-16. *Listing all available list templates using PowerShell*

Once you have determined what list template you wish to use for your new list, you can call the following commands to have your list created (see Figure 6-17). Note that the Add() method returns a GUID associated with your newly created list, not a SPList object. You will need to get an instance of your new list using either the list's name or obtained GUID to interact with it further.

```
$web = Get-SPWeb http://localhost
$ID = $web.Lists.Add("My List", "My Description", $web.ListTemplates["Custom List"])
```

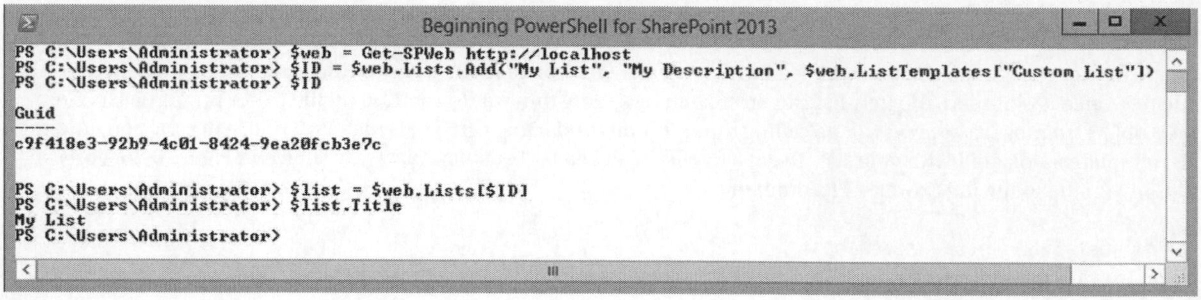

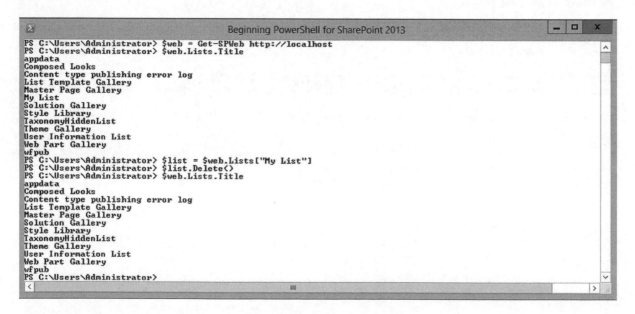

Figure 6-17. Creating a new SharePoint list using PowerShell

Removing a List Instance

In order for you to be able to delete a list instance, you will need to get an instance of it first. After an instance has been obtained, you can simply call the Delete() method on it. Just like site collections and webs, deleting a list instance using PowerShell will permanently remove the list, and it won't be recoverable through the recycle bin. The following code example shows you how to delete the "My List" instance that was created in the previous section:

```
$web = Get-SPWeb http://localhost
$list = $web.Lists["My List"]
$list.Delete()
```

In Figure 6-18, I list the titles of all of the lists that exist at the specified web level. You can clearly see that after calling the Delete() method on your list's instance, it doesn't show up in the list anymore, which means it has been properly deleted.

Figure 6-18. Listing all existing lists from a web using PowerShell

Restoring a List Instance

A SharePoint list that gets deleted makes it into the recycle bin before being deleted from the server for good. You then have the option of restoring it by getting a reference to the current site's recycle bin object, and by iterating through its items. Once you have obtained a reference to the appropriate item in the recycle bin, simply call the Restore() method on it (see Figure 6-19). To have the list deleted permanently, you should call the Delete() method instead.

```
$spsite = Get-SPSite http://localhost
$bin = $spsite.RecycleBin
$myList = $bin | Where{$_.ItemType - eq "List"}
$myList.Restore()
```

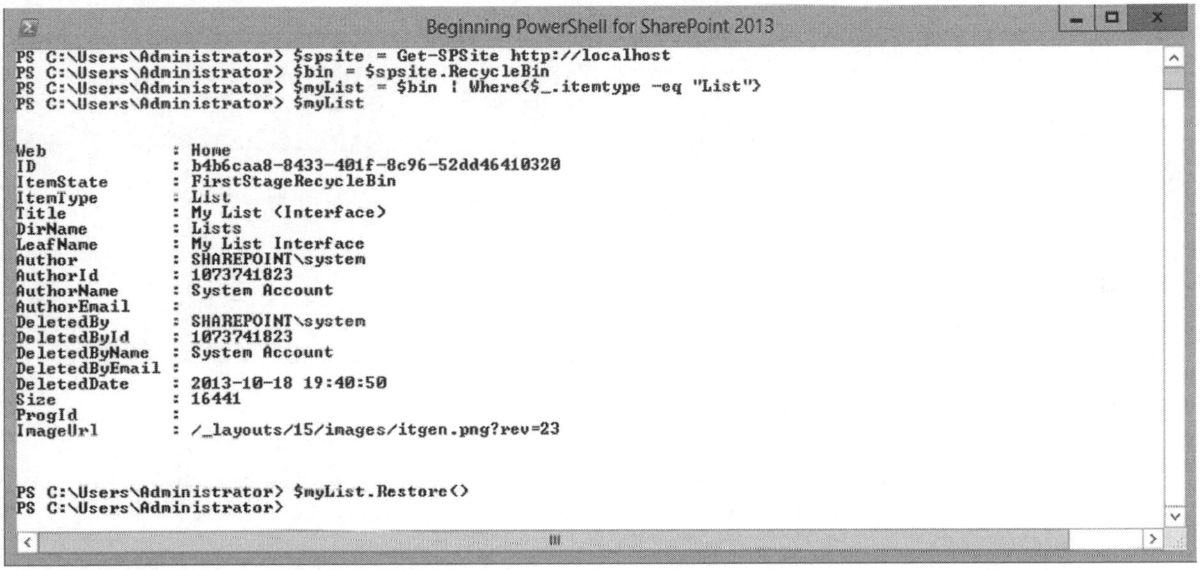

Figure 6-19. Restoring a deleted list from the recycle bin using PowerShell

Copying a List Instance

Sadly, there are no direct ways to copy a SharePoint list using PowerShell. Despite this fact, you could still copy an existing list along with all of its data using a combination of two operations. To be able to copy a SharePoint list instance using PowerShell, you will need to first save your list as a List Template and then create a new copy of the list using that template. Saving a list as a template is as simple as calling the SaveAsTemplate() method on a SharePoint list instance. This method requires you to specify a name for the resulting .stp (template) file, a title for your template, a description, and lets you specify if you'd like to save the list's content and data as part of the template:

```
$web = Get-SPWeb http://localhost
$list = $web.Lists["My List"]
$list.SaveAsTemplate("MyTemplate", "My Template", "This is my custom list", $true)
```

Custom list templates in SharePoint are stored at the site collection level. To get a list of available custom list templates, you'll need to call the GetCustomListTemplates() method on the site collection object (see Figure 6-20):

```
$site = Get-SPSite http://localhost
$customTemplates = $site.GetCustomListTemplates($site.RootWeb)
```

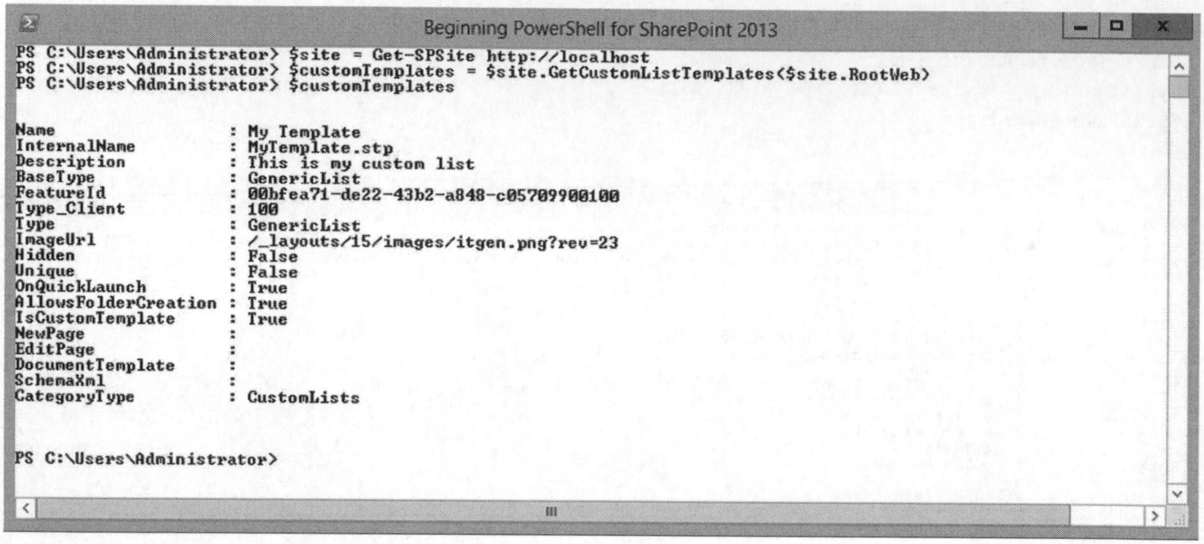

Figure 6-20. *Listing custom SharePoint list templates using PowerShell*

With this information in hand, you are now ready to create a new list using your custom list template. This will result in a new copy of the original SharePoint list to be created. You will need to begin by obtaining a reference to your custom list. This can be achieved by calling the following line of PowerShell:

```
$myListTemplate = $customTemplates | Where {$_.Name -eq "My Template"}
```

To create the copy of your list, you will need to call the Add() method on a specific web list collection, like you did in the "Creating a New List" section. This time, however, you will call an overload of the method, meaning that you will call the method using a different set of parameters as input. In order to create a list based on a custom list template, you need to call the method using six parameters as shown here:

```
$web.Lists.Add("My Copy", # Title
        "Description", # List Description
        "Lists/MyCopy", # Relative URL $myListTemplate.FeatureId, # Feature Id of custom template
        100, # List Type - 100 is for none
        "101") # Document Template Type - 101 is for none
```

Remember that there is an opportunity to create your own cmdlet to automate these two operations into a single one. You could easily create a new Copy-SPList cmdlet taking the source list, and its destination title as input parameters.

Putting It Together: Creating Common Lists

I will now continue to build upon this demo environment, and put your latest acquired knowledge to use. In real-life scenarios, business units will most likely share some very similar processes. For example, every business unit in an organization will be subject to a set of policies, procedures, and guidelines. It would be considered best practice to keep all documents related to these in a SharePoint document library under each business unit workspace. Another important feature that each business unit may also want to have is a task list to allow various tasks assigned to their employees to be tracked.

You will create a new PowerShell script that will iterate through all the various sites created earlier, and that will create a new document library at its root named "Business Documents" as well as a new task list named "Unit Tasks." The following script will allow you to do just that, but this time you'll add a little twist to it. In the previous demo ("Putting it Together: Creating Support Webs"), you had obtained references to each site collection by generating their URLs dynamically. This time around, you will delve into some of the material covered in the next chapters to obtain a reference to the SharePoint web application that you've created on port 80. Remember, a web application can be thought of as a container for site collections. All site collections that are hosted on port 80 logically belong to the same web application. By obtaining a reference to this object, you will be able to iterate through all of its contained site collections, and then in turn iterate through the set of webs they each contain:

```
$webApp = Get-SPWebApplication http://localhost

foreach($site in $webApp.Sites)
{
    foreach($web in $site.AllWebs)
    {
        $web.Lists.Add("Business Documents", "",
            $web.ListTemplates["Document Library"]);
        $web.Lists.Add("Unit Tasks", "", $web.ListTemplates["Tasks"]);
    }
}
```

As you can see from this example, in order to get a reference to a SharePoint web application, you can call the Get-SPWebApplication PowerShell cmdlet.

List Items

The next logical progression of object in the SharePoint object model hierarchy is a list item. A list item in the SharePoint world represents a logical unit that contains pertinent information. For example, a Word document stored in a SharePoint library would be considered to be a list item, as would a new project task stored in a task list. Descriptive data associated with them is referred to as metadata. Think of metadata as being a field in the list. Each field captures different information about each list item. You will learn more about fields in the next section. List items are also the lowest level of objects in the hierarchy that can have unique permissions applied to. SharePoint permissions is also a topic that will be covered later in the chapter.

This section focuses on explaining the basics of list items and how we can interact with them using PowerShell. As with SharePoint lists, the SharePoint modules provided for PowerShell don't include cmdlets that let you interact directly with list items. You will need to obtain them manually by drilling down into the object model.

Getting List Items

To obtain a reference to a list item, you need to obtain a reference to the list that contains it. Once the reference has been obtained, you can get access to a collection of all list items contained in the list by calling the Items property on it. Other than accessing an item directly by its position in the list (e.g., $list.Items[2] where 2 is the position in the list) there is no way to obtain a reference to a single list item in SharePoint. The best you can do to get a reference to a specific item is to query a collection of items back based on certain criteria, and hope that there is only one item contained in it.

To get a collection of items back, you could either write a CAML query and use it to get a specific set of items back from a list, or you could simply use PowerShell to iterate through the collection of returned items and find the item based on a specific property's value. Both options are explained in the following example. Figure 6-21 shows the SharePoint list used for the example.

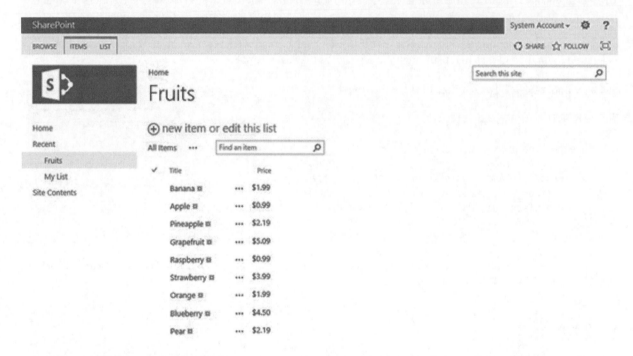

Figure 6-21. *SharePoint list containing information about various fruits and their associated unit price*

```
# Assuming a SharePoint List that contains a list of fruits and their unit price.

$web = Get-SPWeb http://localhost
$fruitsList = $web.Lists["Fruits"]

# Scenario A - Get a reference to the apple item

# Option 1 - Write a CAML Query
$query = "<Where><Eq><FieldRef Name='Title' /><Value Type='Text'>Apple</Value></Eq></Where>";
$spQuery = New-Object Microsoft.SharePoint.SPQuery
$spQuery.Query = $query
```

```
$items = $fruitsList.GetItems($spQuery)
$items[0].Title

# Option 2 - Use PowerShell to query by property
$items = $fruitsList.Items | Where {$_.Title -eq "Apple"}
$items.Title
```

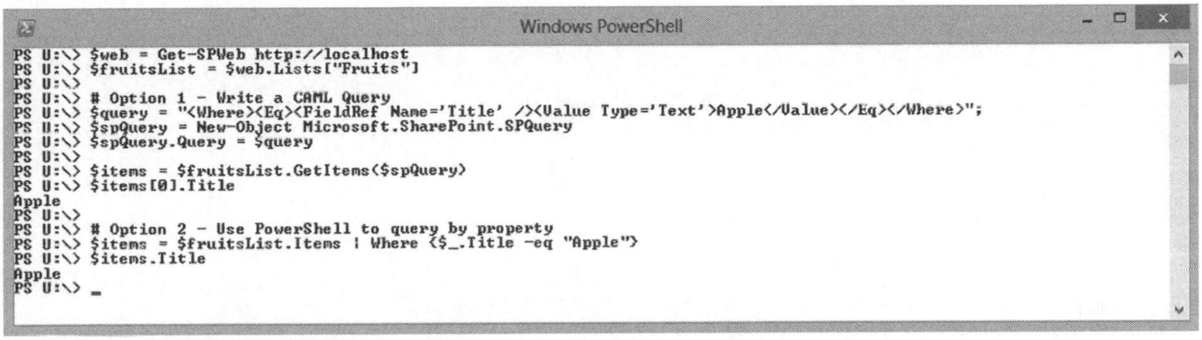

```
Windows PowerShell

PS U:\> $web = Get-SPWeb http://localhost
PS U:\> $fruitsList = $web.Lists["Fruits"]
PS U:\>
PS U:\> # Option 1 - Write a CAML Query
PS U:\> $query = "<Where><Eq><FieldRef Name='Title' /><Value Type='Text'>Apple</Value></Eq></Where>";
PS U:\> $spQuery = New-Object Microsoft.SharePoint.SPQuery
PS U:\> $spQuery.Query = $query
PS U:\>
PS U:\> $items = $fruitsList.GetItems($spQuery)
PS U:\> $items[0].Title
Apple
PS U:\>
PS U:\> # Option 2 - Use PowerShell to query by property
PS U:\> $items = $fruitsList.Items | Where {$_.Title -eq "Apple"}
PS U:\> $items.Title
Apple
PS U:\> _
```

Figure 6-22. *Comparing two option to get specific items from a SharePoint list using PowerShell*

Here is a second example using the same list, to obtain a list of all items that have a unit price of 4$ or more:

```
# Scenario B - Get items that are 4$ and over

# Option 1 - Write a CAML Query
$query = "<Where><Gt><FieldRef Name='Price' /><Value Type='Currency'>4</Value></Gt></Where>"
$spQuery = New-Object Microsoft.SharePoint.SPQuery
$spQuery.Query = $query

$expItems = $fruitsList.GetItems($spQuery)

# Option 2 - Use PowerShell to query by property
$expItems = $fruitsList.Items | Where{$_["Price"] -gt 4}
```

```
PS U:\> # Option 1 - Write a CAML Query
PS U:\> $query = "<Where><Gt><FieldRef Name='Price' /><Value Type='Currency'>4</Value></Gt></Where>"
PS U:\> $spQuery = New-Object Microsoft.SharePoint.SPQuery
PS U:\> $spQuery.Query = $query
PS U:\>
PS U:\> $expItems = $fruitsList.GetItems($spQuery)
PS U:\> $expItems | select Title

Title
-----
Grapefruit
Blueberry


PS U:\>
PS U:\>
PS U:\> # Option 2 - Use PowerShell to query by property
PS U:\> $expItems = $fruitsList.Items | Where($_["Price"] -gt 4)
PS U:\> $expItems | select Title

Title
-----
Grapefruit
Blueberry


PS U:\> _
```

Figure 6-23. *Getting a list of items based on a specific property using PowerShell*

Removing a List Item

The operation to delete a list items is fairly simple. All you need to do is obtain the ID of the object that you wish to delete, and then call the Delete() method on the list's item collection, passing the item's position in the list as a parameter. As with webs and lists, a deleted list item makes it into the site's recycle bin and can be restored or deleted from there. As always, remember that only list items that have been deleted through the SharePoint interface are given a second chance in the recycle bin. Those deleted through PowerShell are deleted permanently.

You need to pay special attention when deleting an item from a SharePoint list. The index you're passing to the Delete() method is actually referencing the position of the item to delete in the list. Simply getting the ID position of the object may not end up deleting the proper object. IDs assigned to items in a list are automatically incremented. Once an item has been deleted, its ID stays reserved, and no other items in that list can have the same id. This could prove to be very confusing, and often results in catastrophic results when forgotten.

For example, assume that you have a list of five different items, say user names. When the list first gets created, all items are given a unique number starting from 1 to 5; this is their ID property. In addition, items in a list are also assigned a relative position in the list, based on the order in which they were added. In the beginning, our five users are all assigned a position number that matches their ID. The next user to be added to the list will automatically be granted an ID of 6, with a position value of 6. Now, let's assume that user #2 is deleted; what happens to the position values? User #3 will now be shifted down one position in the list, and so will the other three users. Only user #1 will keep its original position. With this in mind, if you were to call the Delete() method passing a position value of 4 as a parameter, user #5 is the user that would actually be deleted.

To make sure that you delete the appropriate item in your list, you need to loop through the list of items and get their exact positions. Then you can call the Delete() method on the collection to have the proper item deleted. To illustrate this, see the SharePoint list in Figure 6-24. I've used the following PowerShell code to list each item in the list along with their current position:

```
$web = Get-SPWeb http://localhost
$fruitsList = $web.Lists["Fruits"]
$position = 0
```

```
foreach($fruit in $fruitsList.Items)
{
    Write-Host "Position $position :" $fruit.Title "- ID: " $fruit.Id: $position++
}
```

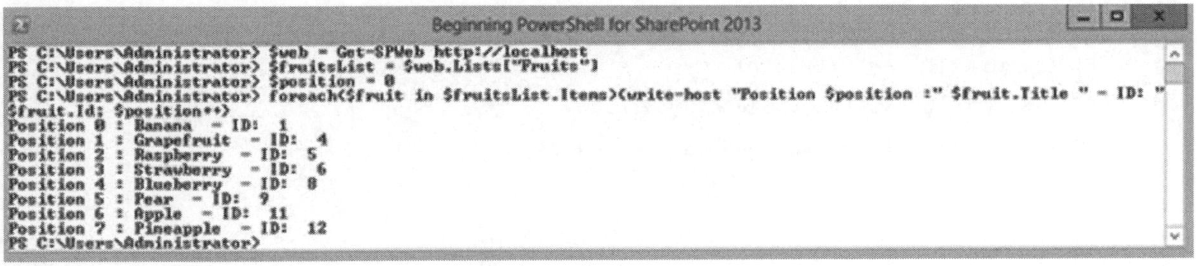

***Figure 6-24.** Listing items position and IDs from a SharePoint list using PowerShell*

The following lines of code will loop through the entire collection of items and compare each item's ID with the ID of the apple item. If a match is found, then the item at the current position (the apple item) will be removed from the collection (see Figure 6-25):

```
$web = Get-SPWeb http://localhost
$fruitsList = $web.Lists["Fruits"]
$appleItem = $fruitsList.Items | Where {$_.Title -eq "Apple"}
$appleId = $appleItem.ID

$position = 0;
foreach($fruit in $fruitsList.Items)
{
    if($fruit.ID -eq $appleId)
    {
        $fruitsList.Items.Delete($position)
    }
    $position++ # Increases the current position
}
```

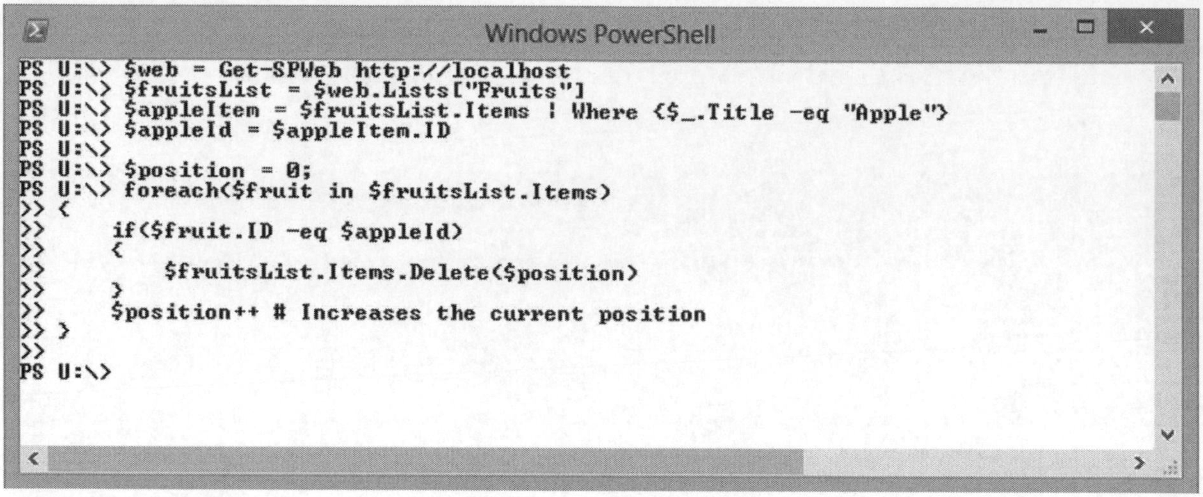

Figure 6-25. *Deleting a list item using PowerShell*

Creating a List Item

There are two methods available in the object model that will allow you to create a new list item in a list. The first one is the AddItem() method from the SharePoint list object, and the second is the Add() method available on the collection of items associated with a list. Both methods have the exact same behavior. You can simply use the one you prefer. You should always remember to use the Update() method on an item once you've created it; otherwise, it will not get registered with its parent list and, therefore, won't be accessible through the SharePoint interface. Figure 6-26 shows the results of using the two methods included in the following code:

```
$web = Get-SPWeb http://localhost
$fruitsList = $web.Lists["Fruits"]

$newItem1 = $fruitsList.AddItem()
$newItem1["Title"] = "Kiwi";
$newItem1["Price"] = 6.99;
$newItem1.Update()

$newItem2 = $fruitsList.Items.Add()
$newItem2["Title"] = "Grape"
$newItem2["Price"] = 5.99
$newItem2.Update()
```

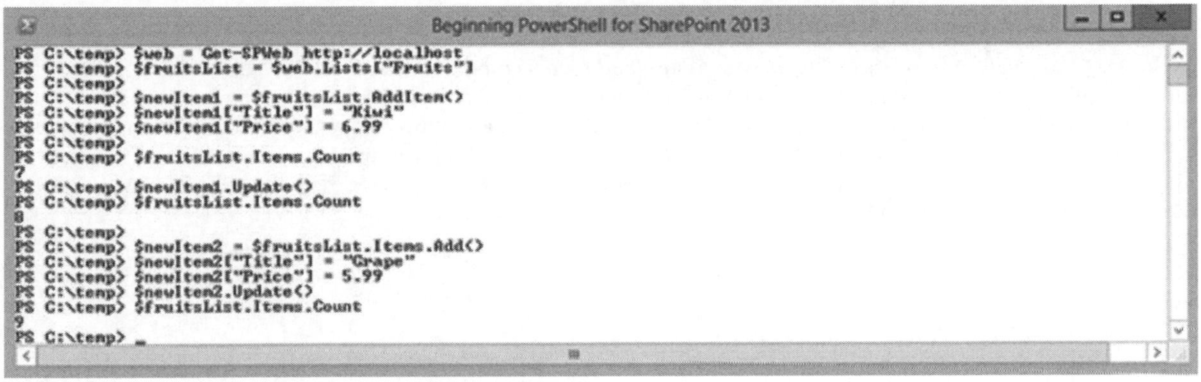

Figure 6-26. *Creating a new list item using PowerShell*

Updating a List Item

Just like any good artifacts supporting CRUD (create, read, update, and delete) operations, list items in SharePoint allow you to update an existing item's properties. What you'll need to do is to first get a reference to the item you wish to update, and then modify the value of the property you wish to change by accessing it directly in the fields' collection. In the current example, a common scenario may be to update the unit price of a specific fruit on a regular basis. The following lines of PowerShell script provide more details on how you could achieve this update, which is then shown in Figure 6-27. Note that once you've modified a list item's property, you do need to call the Update() method on it for the changes to be reflected.

```
$web = Get-SPWeb http://localhost
$fruitsList = $web.Lists["Fruits"]

$bananaItem = $fruitsList.Items | Where {$_.Title -eq "Banana"}
$bananaItem["Price"] = 0.99
$bananaItem.Update()
```

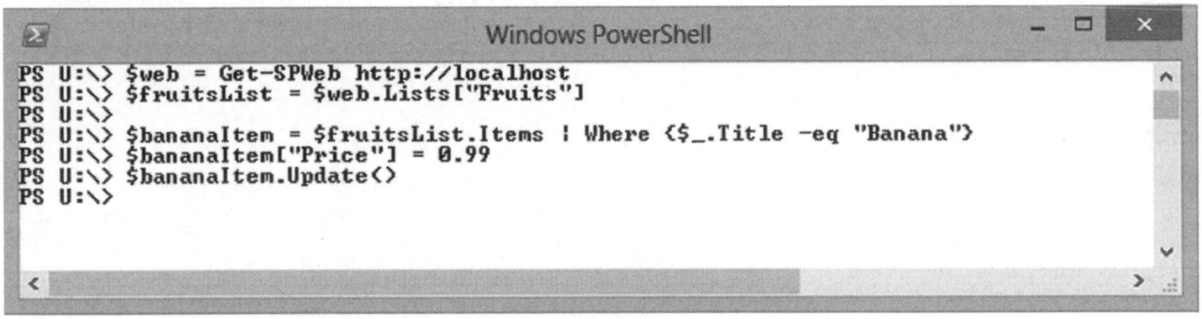

Figure 6-27. *Updating an existing list item using PowerShell*

Putting It Together: Creating Default Tasks Items

In this section, you'll continue building on your SharePoint organizational workspaces. The goal of this exercise is to loop through all the various business unit sites that you have and add a default task in each team's "Unit Tasks" list. The default task will simply be called "Get familiar with your unit's SharePoint workspace," and it will have a deadline scheduled a week from today. The key thing to take from this exercise is that you will have to use objects that are of the SharePoint scope, and use objects that are built in the core .NET Framework. In this case, you will be using the .NET DateTime object to get next week's date.

```
$webApp = Get-SPWebApplication http://localhost

foreach($site in $webApp.Sites)
{
    foreach($web in $site.AllWebs)
    {
        $list = $web.Lists["Unit Tasks"]

        $newTask = $list.AddItem();
        $newTask["Title"] = "Get familiar with your unit's SharePoint workspace"

        $today = [System.DateTime]::Now
        $nextWeek = $today.AddDays(7)

        $newTask["DueDate"] = $nextWeek
        $newTask.Update()
    }
}
```

List Fields

I've already briefly touched on the subject of List Fields in this chapter. I've explained that a field contains a specific type of information about a list item contained in a list. List fields can have many types, such as text, number, currency, choice, data, and so on. Each field is given two name properties, an internal name and an external name. These two names can be the same, but the internal name has to be unique within the list. This internal name is used by SharePoint to reference a field. Think of it as being the unique identifier for a specific field in a list. In the present section, we will learn how to interact with fields in a SharePoint list using PowerShell.

Getting an Instance of a Field

You've already seen how to get a reference to a specific field's value in the previous section's examples. When you called a list item property by using a field's internal name as an index, you're actually getting a reference to a specific field's value for a given item. For example, calling $item["FieldName"] will return the value of field "FieldName" associated with the list item $item. To get a reference to the actual field, all you need to do it use the internal name of the field as an index on the list object's Fields property. This property represents an array containing all of the fields associated with a SharePoint list. The following lines of PowerShell script will create a new SharePoint list, and will iterate through all of its fields and display their internal names:

```
$web = Get-SPWeb http://localhost
$listID = $web.Lists.Add("DemoList", "", $web.ListTemplates["Custom List"])
$list = $web.Lists[$listID]
```

```
foreach($field in $list.Fields)
{
    write-host $field.InternalName" - Hidden:" $field.Hidden" - ReadOnly:" field.ReadOnlyField
}
```

You will see that some fields listed by the script in Figure 6-28 will look familiar (e.g., title, author, and attachments). Others, however, aren't recognizable. These are most likely hidden fields that are required by SharePoint. In addition to having a data type defining the type of value that they can accept, fields can have two other properties that can be set to determine their behaviors: the ReadOnlyField and the Hidden properties. One of these two properties set to true on a field will normally indicate that this field is reserved by SharePoint.

Figure 6-28. *Listing information related to a list's fields using PowerShell*

Creating a New Field

Fields are created by calling the Add() method on the array of fields associated with a SharePoint list instance. When calling this method, you will need to specify a title for the field, the type of data this field should be accepting, as well as specifying if the field is required or not.

```
$web = Get-SPWeb http://localhost
$demoList = $web.Lists["DemoList"]
$fieldID = $demoList.Fields.Add("HairColor", [Microsoft.SharePoint.SPFieldType]::Choice, $true)
$myNewChoiceField = $demoList.Fields["HairColor"]

$myNewChoiceField.Choices.Add("Brown")
$myNewChoiceField.Choices.Add("Blond")
$myNewChoiceField.Choices.Add("Red")
$myNewChoiceField.Choices.Add("Black")
```

```
$myNewChoiceField.Choices.Add("Grey")
$myNewChoiceField.Choices.Add("None")

# Need to call the Update() method in order for the choices to appear on interface
$myNewChoiceField.Update()
```

As you can see in Figure 6-29, the new field has been created in SharePoint with all the values that you provided in PowerShell.

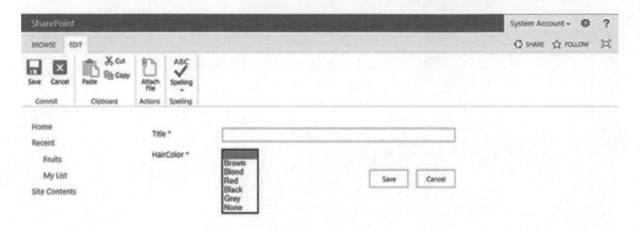

Figure 6-29. *New item form showing a list field created by PowerShell*

Removing a Field

To remove a field, simply get a reference to the field in question and call the `Delete()` method on it. The operation of deleting a field is permanent and cannot be recovered. Once a field has been deleted, all of the data that was contained in it is removed as well.

```
$web = Get-SPWeb http://localhost
$demoList = $web.Lists["DemoList"]
$field = $demoList.Fields["HairColor"]
$field.Delete()
```

Permissions

Up to this point, you've learned about how you can interact with various types of artifacts in your SharePoint environment using PowerShell. I have now arrived at what I consider to be the most important topic: permissions. With the exception of fields, specific permissions can be applied on all the types of artifacts that I've covered in this chapter. By default, permissions are applied at a site collections root web and inherited down to every web, every list, and every list item contained within it, which means they all use the same set of permissions. For example, if a list inherits its permissions for its parent web, changes to the permissions on that parent web will automatically be reflected in the list's permissions, as well. You do have the option, if you want, to break the permission inheritance on any object that inherits permissions from a parent.

For example, if I have a web that contains a document library storing information about salaries for my employees, I would probably want to prevent users that should not have access to information about others' salary from seeing the information in the library. One way of achieving this could be to break the inheritance at the document library level and only grant access to those authorized. This way, users that are not authorized to see the information contained in the library would not even see the library at all.

Another option may be to break the inheritance at the document level. For example, if each user is entitled to see their own salary information, I could break the inheritance on each document in the library and simply grant access to each employee to their own files. This will result in each employee seeing the library, but only being able to view one document in it. Documents for which they are not granted permissions would be hidden and made inaccessible to them.

In the context of SharePoint, permissions are made up of two different pieces of information: a role definition that specifies what privileges a permission entry is granting, and a role assignment that specifies who is assigned to the role definition entry. In this section, you will learn how easy it is to interact with SharePoint permissions using PowerShell. For the sake of simplicity, I will keep my explanations of permissions at the list level. To interact with permissions at a web, or at a list item level, the same methods and operations apply.

List Permissions on an Object

The following request is something that always comes back: given a specific artifact in SharePoint, I want to know who has access to it. Using PowerShell, it becomes extremely easy to get such information about an object. To illustrate how to obtain information about permissions for a list, I will start by creating a new SharePoint list using PowerShell:

```
$web = http://localhost
$newListId = $web.Lists.Add("Secure", "", $web.ListTemplates["Custom List"])
$secureList = $web.Lists[$newListId]
```

By default, using the Add() method with the signature I used here will create the new list and inherit permissions from its parent web. If you want to list the permissions that are applied to it by default, you can simply get access to the RoleAssignments properties of your new list. Doing this will return a list of all users that have some level of access to your list, along with information about what their role definition is (see Figure 6-30):

```
$newListId = $web.Lists.Add("Secure", "", $web.ListTemplates["Custom List"])
$secureList = $web.Lists[$newListId]
$secureList.RoleAssignments
```

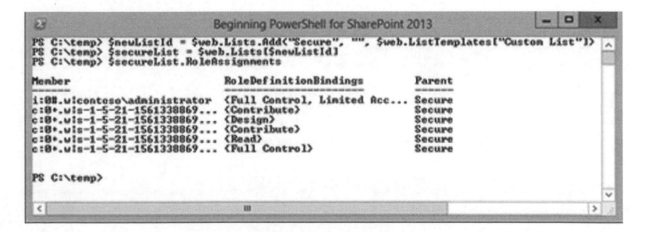

Figure 6-30. *Listing all role assignments on a specific list using PowerShell*

Breaking Permission Inheritance

The concept of breaking inheritance describes the scenario in which we want to stop permissions on an object from being inherited from its parent container. When breaking inheritance on a container, we are given the choice to copy the parent permissions down to the object's permissions, or to start fresh. Once the permission inheritance has been broken on an object, modifying the permissions for its parent will not have any impact on it, and vice versa. Permissions inheritance from the parent container can be restored at any time by calling the ResetRoleInheritance() method on the object. The following example shows you how to break inheritance for your list and start fresh with no role assignments (see Figure 6-31):

```
$web = Get-SPWeb http://localhost
$secureList = $web.Lists["Secure"]
$secureList.BreakRoleInheritance($false)
```

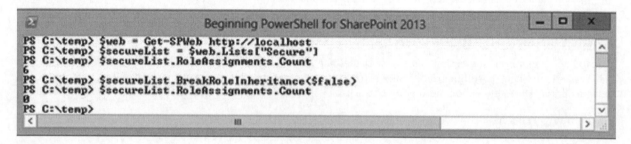

Figure 6-31. *Breaking permission inheritance on a SharePoint list using PowerShell*

Granting New Permissions

In order for you to be able to grant new permissions on a SharePoint artifact, you'll need to start by determining what role definition you want to map the user to and obtain a reference to it. A role definition instance can be obtained at the web level, as shown with the following example code and in Figure 6-32:

```
$web = Get-SPWeb http://localhost
$fullControlRoleDefinition = $web.RoleDefinitions["Full Control"]
```

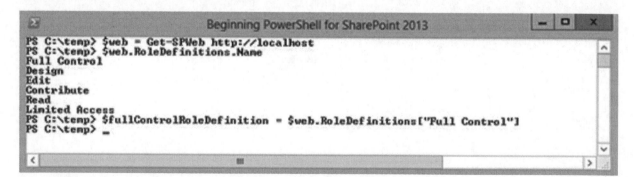

Figure 6-32. *Declaring a new role definition using PowerShell*

Once a reference has been obtained, you will need to declare a new RoleAssignment variable as follows:

```
$roleAssignment = New-Object Microsoft.SharePoint.SPRoleAssignment("DOMAIN\\UserName",
"username@domain.com",
"Display_Name","Notes about the assignment");
```

Now comes the tricky part: linking the role definition you've obtained previously with the newly created SPRoleAssignment object. In order to achieve this, you need to declare a new object of type SPRoleDefinitionBindingCollecton, and associate both entities through it:

```
$bindings = $roleAssignment.RoleDefinitionBindings
$bindings.Add($fullControlRoleDefinition)
```

Once the linkage has been created, you are now ready to add your new role assignment definition to your list:

```
$secureList.RoleAssignments.Add($roleAssignment)
```

This will automatically grant Full Control permission on your secure list to the administrator account, as shown in Figure 6-33.

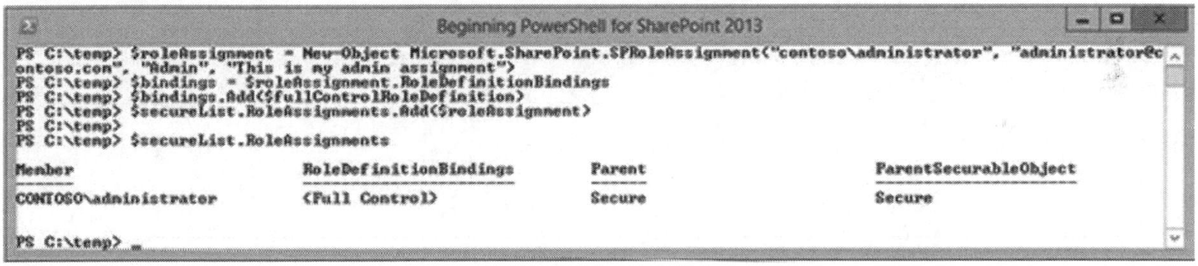

Figure 6-33. *Creating a new role assignment on a SharePoint list using PowerShell*

Removing Permissions

To remove permission for a user on a specific artifact, simply get a reference to the associated role assignment item, and remove it from the list of assignments on the artifact. For example, if you want to remove the permission that you just granted to the administrator account on your secure list, you could call the following lines of PowerShell script:

```
$web = Get-SPWeb http://localhost
$secureList = $web.Lists["Secure"]
$secureList.RoleAssignments.Remove($web.EnsureUser("CONTOSO\Administrator"))
```

Updating Permissions

The most straightforward way to update a permission would be to remove the existing one and add a completely new one. Normally, you would update only the role definition portion of an assignment; otherwise, you'd be changing the user associated with a permission entry, which really comes back to creating a new entry all together. There are no ways of updating an existing role assignment without first removing the existing one and adding a new one instead.

Objects Disposal

SharePoint is a beast when it comes down to memory consumption. For the sake of performance, when dealing with large objects such as site collections and webs, the .NET Framework keeps entire SharePoint objects in memory. The responsibility of properly disposing of SharePoint objects in memory once they are done with them comes back to the user that deals with them. Many large objects in the SharePoint world implement the IDisposable interface behind the scene, meaning that they all expose a Dispose() method to force the removal of objects from memory.

Most of the examples provided throughout this chapter did not properly dispose of objects. Almost all of them have declared a web object without implicitly calling the dispose method on it. In these scenarios, the impact of not properly disposing of items was minimal, but imagine a scenario in which there are thousands of site collections, each having a few hundred sites under them. If you iterate through all these site collections and webs using PowerShell without properly disposing of them, you risk bringing the server to its knees.

To illustrate the effects of memory disposition using PowerShell to interact with SharePoint artifacts, I have created a demo that will loop 10,000 times through all the site collection in a web application and get an instance of all of its webs. The web application used for this demo has about a dozen site collections, with 1,000 webs in each. The first scenario will showcase what happens to the server if you don't properly dispose of objects in memory, and the second one will show what happens when memory management is properly performed. I have monitored the memory usage for both scenarios.

Scenario #1 - Bad Memory Management

The following PowerShell code example shows a scenario in which memory is not being freed up and objects not disposed of properly:

```
$webApp = Get-SPWebApplication http://localhost
for($i = 0; $i -le 10000; $i++)
{
    foreach($site in $webApp.Sites)
    {
        foreach($web in $site.AllWebs)
        {
            Write-host $web.Title
        }
    }
}
```

In Figure 6-34, you can see that the memory usage of our PowerShell script keeps increasing as time goes by without ever releasing it in a significant way. This is because all of the webs and site collection objects used by our script are kept in memory.

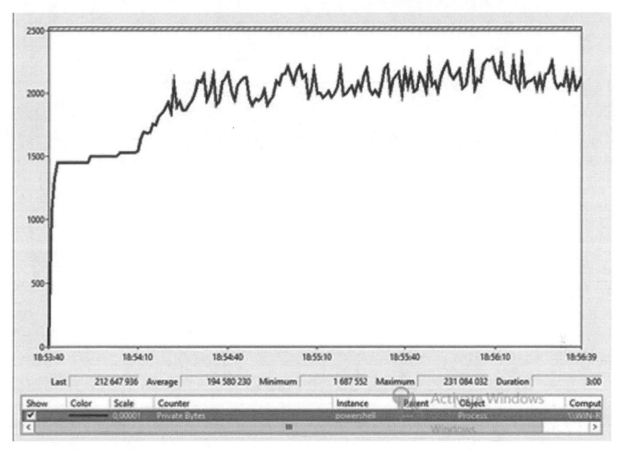

Figure 6-34. *Performance monitor window for code running without properly disposing of SharePoint objects in memory*

Scenario #2 - Good Memory Management

The following lines of PowerShell code ensure that you dispose of objects in memory after you are done using them:

```
$webApp = Get-SPWebApplication http://localhost
for($i = 0; $i -le 10000; $i++)
{
    foreach($site in $webApp.Sites)
    {
        foreach($web in $site.AllWebs)
        {
            Write-host $web.Title
            $web.Dispose()
        }
        $site.Dispose()
    }
}
```

You can clearly see in Figure 6-35 that the memory usage has greatly improved over your previous scenario. Yes, there are spikes of memory usage, but as objects are being disposed from memory, the overall memory usage goes back to normal right away.

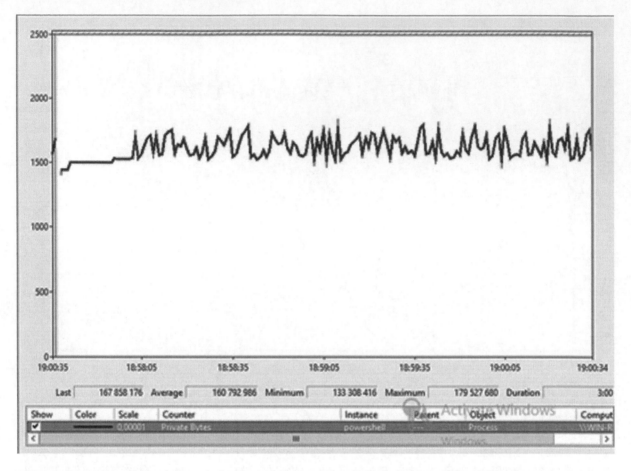

Figure 6-35. *Performance monitor window for code running that properly disposes of SharePoint objects in memory*

Summary

In this chapter, you've learned how you can interact with SharePoint objects using PowerShell. To a certain extent, the objects that you've been dealing with in this chapter are what I consider to be front-end artifacts: normally tangible objects with which end users can interact, such as list items and webs. In the traditional scenario, automating operations on these types of objects has always been done by developers. However, this reality has changed drastically in the past few years. Administrators are now given the ability to write scripts of their own using PowerShell, without ever having to "open code." I consider PowerShell to be a gray zone for sure when it comes to governance and responsibility. Even if your organization decides that PowerShell scripts are to be handled by the development team, the fact that these are actually written in plain text and use an administrative scripting language will allow your administrators to at least take a peek at the code and understand what is being executed.

In the next two chapters, I will show you how to use PowerShell to monitor and manage the administrative side of SharePoint, something that the end users don't see. This chapter has given you an overview of how you can interact with objects that you'll see in the SharePoint interface, and Chapter 7 will give you an overview of how to use PowerShell to interact with objects that are normally managed through the Central Administration interface.

CHAPTER 7

■ ■ ■

Managing Apps and Solutions Using PowerShell

Those of you that are SharePoint administrators are probably starting to feel dirty doing all these examples and going through all of these scripts that are normally the job of developers and end users. Now's the time go take a shower and to start back fresh. What you will learn in this chapter is what SharePoint administrators would normally do in their daily jobs. This chapter builds on the concepts learned in the previous chapters and will allow you to understand how certain configuration changes made to a SharePoint farm can affect artifacts that business users use daily.

In this chapter, you will learn how to deploy and manage custom code solutions developed by developers in your organization or by external companies. You will also be introduced to a new development model in SharePoint 2013 known as the app model and will learn how, as an administrator, you can leverage PowerShell to manage these custom solutions. At the end of this chapter, you will have a complete understanding of the differences between what a farm solution and a SharePoint app are and will have all the tools to help you manage them in your day-to-day work.

Solutions

In this section, we will learn how, as a SharePoint administrator, you can use PowerShell to manage solutions in your SharePoint environment. SharePoint solutions are contained a Windows SharePoint (.wsp) file, and contain pieces of functional logic that will get installed in your environment. Solutions can contain different SharePoint features, list definitions and instances, documents, and so on.

Types of Solutions

In SharePoint 2013, there are three types of solutions that are officially supported by Microsoft: farm solutions: sandboxed solutions, and SharePoint apps. Table 7-1 details the differences between each type of solution.

Table 7-1. *Types of solutions in SharePoint 2013*

Solution Type	Description
Farm Solutions	When installed, these can interact with the entire farm. Their contents can be used across various site collections.
Sandboxed Solutions	These are limited to the site collection in which they have been uploaded to. That's right, sandboxed solutions can be uploaded, meaning anyone that has the site collection administration role in a site collection can build their own sandbox solutions and deploy them themselves. However, their contents can't affect other site collections. When Office 365 originally launched back in July 2011, sandbox solutions were the only way of deploying reusable customization to your cloud environment. I will cover the topic of Office 365 in Chapter 9.
	In SharePoint 2013, sandbox solutions are said to be deprecated. What this means is that they will continue to work the way they did in SharePoint 2010, but that most likely, the next version of SharePoint won't be supporting them, or at least not in the way it is currently supported. Microsoft released an official statement saying that sandbox solutions containing user code components are in fact deprecated, but that the ones containing only declarative content (design packages, list definition, templates, files, etc.) will still be supported in the future. Proof of this is the new design manager feature of SharePoint 2013 that allows you to create packaged themes, called *design packages*. When you export a design package you built, it always generates a sandbox solution file for you to reuse.
SharePoint Apps	This is a new type of solution that was introduced in SharePoint 2013. These can be executed outside of the SharePoint environment and are allowed to interact with its artifacts using calls to the various SharePoint 2013 web services and REST APIs. I will be covering these in more details later on in this chapter.

My word of advice when it comes to building new solutions in SharePoint is the following: If the solution that you are trying to build serves solely an administrative function, use farm solutions. If all you need to do is to package a set of SharePoint artifacts that you would like to make reusable, then see if sandbox solutions are appropriate depending on what's the scope of accessibility you want. For example, if you need your artifacts to be accessible across an entire SharePoint farm with over 50 site collections, a sandboxed solution may not be the best fit because it would require you to activate its features on every site collection manually. Remember that sandboxed solutions cannot include code in them. If your solution needs to be accessed throughout the farm, in every site collection, then go with farm solutions. For anything else, you should consider building an app.

Because of the uncertain future of sandbox solutions, the focus of this section will remain on farm solutions. We will learn how you can use PowerShell to deploy, install, uninstall, remove, and upgrade farm solutions in your SharePoint environment. One thing to note is that the process of adding or removing a farm solution in SharePoint automatically recycles the application pools associated with your SharePoint environment in the Internet Information Service manager, causing interruption for the end users. This is not the case when deploying sandbox solutions.

Adding a New Farm Solution

Before you can actually install a SharePoint farm solution in your environment, you need to add it to the solutions store by calling the Add-SPSolution PowerShell cmdlet and by passing it the full path to the solution file you're trying to add (see Figure 7-1). Doing so will automatically add an entry to the list of available farm solutions under Central Administration ➤ System Settings ➤ Manage farm solutions (see Figure 7-2).

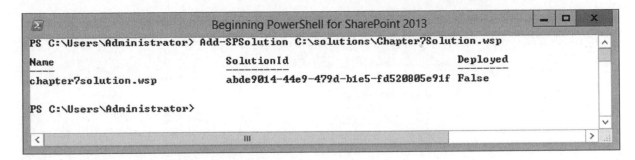

Figure 7-1. Adding a new SharePoint Farm solution

Figure 7-2. New Farm solution viewed from the Central Administration interface

Installing a Farm Solution

At this point, the solution has been added to your farm. In reality, all that you've done so far is upload the .wsp file as a blob in your SQL database. You can find information about the solutions that have been added to SharePoint in the configuration database in the Objects table.

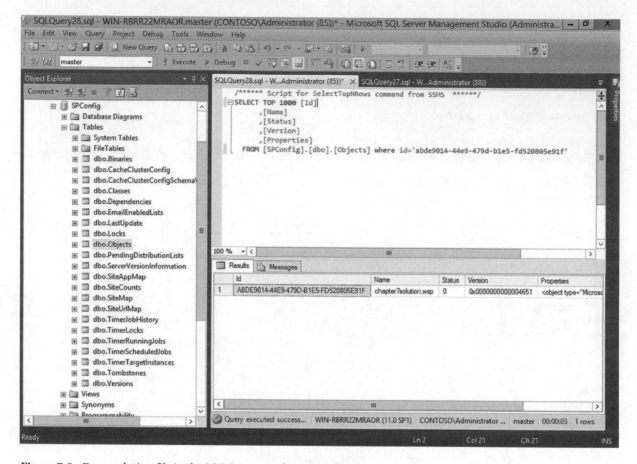

Figure 7-3. *Farm solution file in the SQL Server configuration database*

In order to be able to use the content of your solution, you need to have it installed on your farm. The PowerShell cmdlet to use to install a specific farm solution in our SharePoint environment is `Install-SPSolution`. Most solutions that you will encounter as an administrator will require you to deploy assemblies in the .NET Global Assembly Cache (GAC). Assemblies deployed in the GAC are made available to the entire farm by default. If you would like to prevent solutions from having to be deployed to it, you'll need to ask your developers to package their solution using the `WebApplication` assembly target instead of the default `GlobalAssemblyCache` value in Visual Studio (see Figure 7-4).

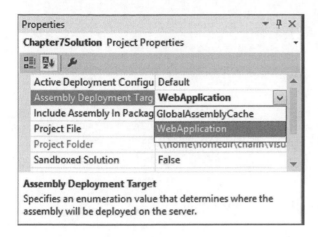

Figure 7-4. *Changing the Assembly Deployment Target Type of a SharePoint solution in Visual Studio*

If the Assembly Deployment Target is set to WebApplication (as shown in Figure 7-4), then you will need to provide the URL of the destination web application to which you wish to deploy your solution (see Figure 7-5). Please note, however, that deployments to web applications' bin folder (local folder containing assemblies for a web application) that are not using the Global Assembly Cache are considered deprecated since the 2010 version of SharePoint. Microsoft's recommendation is that you deploy it globally, using the GACDeploy parameter. If you do, however, need for some reason to deploy your solution in the bin folder, you will need to add the FullTrustBinDeploment parameter to your method call.

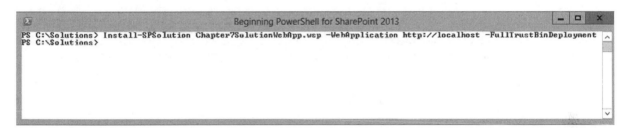

Figure 7-5. *Deploying a farm solution to the web application's full trust bin directory*

When you install a solution, the changes take effect immediately. You have, however, the option of specifying a schedule for the deployments to occur using the -Time parameter. For example, the following line of PowerShell code will create a deployment schedule for our custom solution at 6PM on the 27th of October 2013. A timer job will be scheduled to execute at that time, and will take care of installing the solution.

```
Install-SPSolution Chapter7Solution.wsp -GACDeploy -Time "2013-10-27 18:00:00"
```

To verify that a scheduled job has correctly been created for your solution to deploy, you can open the SharePoint Central Administration interface and go to Monitoring ➤ Check job status. In the top left menu, click on Scheduled job to view a complete list of all scheduled instances of timer jobs. You should see an instance of your scheduled job in there if everything worked as expected (see Figure 7-6).

Microsoft SharePoint Foundation Solution Deployment for "chapter7solution.wsp"	WIN-RBRR22MRAOR	10/27/2013 6:00 PM

Figure 7-6. *Deployment scheduled job entry for a custom farm solution*

Once the job executes, you'll be able to validate the status of your solution's deployment by going back to the Solution Management page. You should now see a mention that your solution was globally deployed (see Figure 7-7).

Figure 7-7. *Deployed farm solution viewed in Central Administration*

Uninstalling a Farm Solution

Uninstalling a farm solution is the process of unbinding its logical components from the farm. It doesn't remove the solution file from the database; it simply deactivates it. To uninstall a solution from the farm, you'll need to use the Uninstall-SPSolution PowerShell cmdlet and pass it the name of the solution to uninstall. You can use the -Confirm parameter to prevent PowerShell from prompting you to confirm before doing the uninstallation process of your farm solution.

```
Uninstall-SPSolution Chapter7Solution.wsp -Confirm:$false
```

Removing a Farm Solution

Removing a farm solution from your SharePoint environment deletes the solution from the Config database. The PowerShell cmdlet that allows you to remove a solution from your SharePoint farm is the Remove-SPSolution cmdlet. If you no longer need a farm solution in your environment, the recommendation is to uninstall and then remove it from your farm using the PowerShell cmdlets. Once again, you can use the -Confirm parameter to prevent PowerShell from prompting you to confirm your changes before committing them to your environment.

```
Remove-SPSolution Chapter7Solution.wsp -Confirm:$false
```

Updating a Farm Solution

You can update an existing farm solution only if the set of files and features contained in the new version of the solution is the same as the one contained in the old one. Otherwise, you will need to uninstall/remove the existing solution and reinstall the new version.

```
Update-SPSolution Chapter7Solution.wsp -LiteralPath "C:\Solutions\Chapter7Solutionv2.wsp"
-GACDeploy
```

If the new version of the solution has the same GUID as the previous one, then the latter gets removed completely from the Config database.

Apps

In SharePoint 2013, a new development model, the *app model*, was introduced. In the new SharePoint lingo, everything except for webs are apps: custom lists, picture libraries, contacts, everything is an app in SharePoint 2013. The idea behind this new model was to allow developers to build components and have them run outside of SharePoint. This new paradigm was introduced to help minimize problems introduced in SharePoint environments by poorly designed custom farm solutions that did not properly make use of the resources and caused several performance issues. At the same time, this new model also helped Microsoft build their new Office Store component that allows users to "shop" online for preexisting SharePoint solutions meeting their needs. Apps are packaged as .app files and, just like solutions, they can be deployed and installed on the SharePoint farm. In this section you will learn how to use PowerShell to interact with these new apps inside SharePoint. All the content covered in this section is new for SharePoint 2013 and does not apply to SharePoint 2010 and earlier.

Configuring your Environment to Support Apps

Before I begin playing with SharePoint apps, I need to get the environment configured. In order to be able to install apps within your farm, you'll need to create an instance of two essential components: the App Management Service and Microsoft SharePoint Foundation Subscription Settings Service applications.

App Management Service Application

The App Management Service application is responsible for storing information about app licenses and permissions. It acts as the police between the server that serves the app and the end users to determine if they are authorized or not to use the app in question. It is accessed every time an app is requested in your SharePoint environment. It is this component that allows you to purchase apps straight from the SharePoint store.

To create a new instance of this component using PowerShell, I recommend that you start by creating a new application pool in IIS that will be dedicated to serving requests to the service application. To create a new IIS application pool, you can use the following lines of PowerShell. This will create a new IIS application pool named "AppMgmtServiceAppPool" that will use the identity of our administrator's account to run (see Figure 7-8).

```
$adminAcc = Get-SPManagedAccount "contoso\administrator"
$appMgmtPool = New-SPServiceApplicationPool -Name AppMgmtServiceAppPool -Account $adminAcc
```

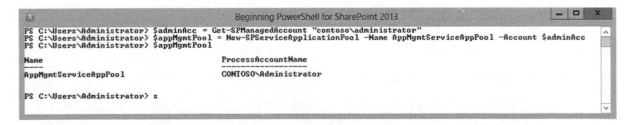

Figure 7-8. Creating a new IIS application pool using PowerShell

Once your new application pool has been created, you can create a new instance of our App Management Service application by calling the following cmdlet. This will create a new instance of the service application named "AppManagementServiceApp" and will also create an associated database named "AppManagementDB".

```
$appMgmtSvc = New-SPAppManagementServiceApplication –ApplicationPool $appMgmtPool –Name
AppManagementServiceApp –DatabaseName AppManagementDB
```

To verify that the creation was successful, open Central Administration and browse to the list of service applications on the server (under the Application Management section). You should see an entry for the instance that you just created, as shown in Figure 7-9.

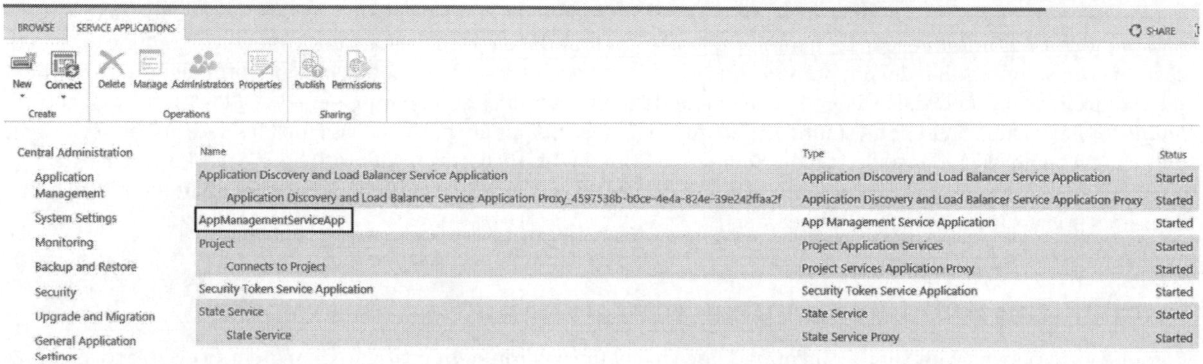

Figure 7-9. *New App Management Service Application in Central Administration*

You're almost done! The next step is to create the associated proxy for the instance of the service application we just created. This will allow your Web application to communicate with the instance itself.

```
$appMgmtProxy = New-SPAppManagementServiceApplicationProxy -ServiceApplication $appMgmtSvc
-Name AppManagementProxy
```

Once executed, you should see a new entry under the previously created AppManagementServiceApp instance, as shown in Figure 7-10.

Figure 7-10. *New App Management Service Application Proxy in Central Administration*

You now have the service application instance and its associated proxy created, but that is not enough for the App Management Service to be enabled on the farm. You need to turn the App Management Service on. To do so, you could navigate to Central Administration and then choose Manage services on server under the System Settings header and then activate the service manually, but you're a wannabe PowerShell expert, aren't you? To begin, you need to get a reference to the instance of the App Management Service. This service's instance can be obtained by using the Get-SPServiceInstance cmdlet. This cmdlet doesn't take any parameters by default. Calling it directly will simply return a list of all available services on the current server. To get your reference to our specific service (see Figure 7-11), you'll need to query the returned dataset containing all the services by specifying the type name of the service instance you're trying to get.

```
$service = Get-SPServiceInstance | Where{$_.TypeName -eq "App Management Service"}
```

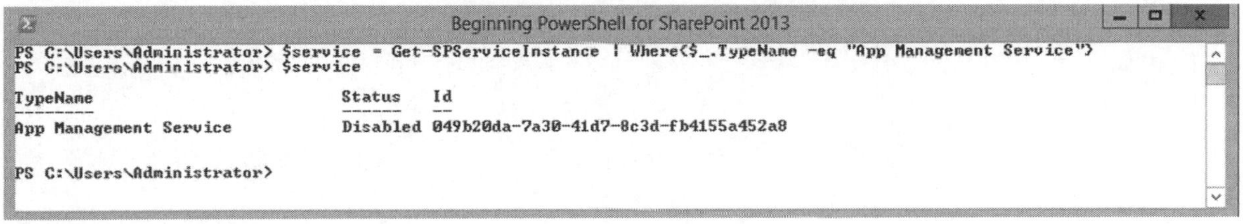

Figure 7-11. *Obtaining a reference to the App Management Service on a SharePoint 2013 server using PowerShell*

You can clearly see from the figure that the status of the service instance is set to Disabled, meaning that it is not activated on the server. To start the service instance, you have two choices: you can either manually set the Status property of our service instance to Online, or you can use the Start-SPServiceInstance PowerShell cmdlet and pass it the reference to your service instance. Both would work in this situation.

Option A:

```
$service.Status = [Microsoft.SharePoint.Administration.SPObjectStatus]::Online
$service.Update()
```

Option B:

```
Start-SPServiceInstance $service
```

To confirm that the App Management Service has been properly started, navigate to the Services on Server page in Central Administration and verify that the service is set to Started (see Figure 7-12).

Figure 7-12. *The App Management Service entry marked as started through the Central Administration interface*

You now have the App Management component of your SharePoint farm up and running. Sadly, this is not enough to allow your users to use the app model and install apps in the environment. There is still another service application that needs to be installed before that. At this point, if users try to go an install an app from the SharePoint Store, they'll get a notice like the one in Figure 7-13 that apps are turned off in their environment, and that they should contact their administrator.

Figure 7-13. *Notification that the apps are turned off in the SharePoint Store*

Microsoft SharePoint Foundation Subscription Settings Service Application

The second SharePoint service application that is required to enable the use of apps in your environment is called the Microsoft SharePoint Foundation Subscription Settings Service application. This service application is used to manage subdomains for your apps. Basically, every app that you install in your farm, with the exception of the default apps such as lists and documents library, will each have its own subdomain. By default, apps' URLs will take the following structure:

```
http://[app prefix]-[app id].[domain name]
```

where the app prefix is a value you specify in your farm's configuration (I'll get to this soon), and the app id is a random unique identifier for your app. One very interesting fact with this service application is that, compared to other service applications in the farm, this one is not available to create through the Central Administration interface. You must use PowerShell if you wish to create an instance of it, how's that! Figure 7-14 shows you the available service applications from the interface. The Subscription Settings Service is not one of them.

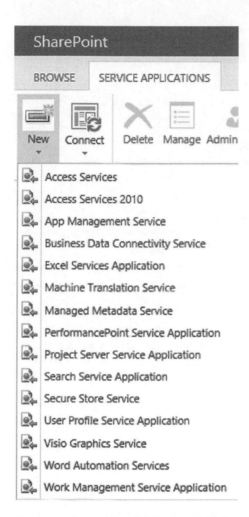

Figure 7-14. *List of available service applications in the Central Administration interface*

Just like for the App Management Service application, PowerShell provides us with a pre-built cmdlet for creating an instance of the Subscription Settings Service application. The cmdlet in question is New-SPSubscriptionSetting sServiceApplication. (Is it just me or do these keep getting longer and longer?) This cmdlet, just like the one for the App Management Service, take three parameters: a name, a database name, and an application pool to use.

```
$adminAcc = Get-SPManagedAccount "contoso\administrator"
$subSettingsPool = New-SPServiceApplicationPool -Name SubSettingsServiceAppPool -Account $adminAcc

$subSettingsService = New-SPSubscriptionSettingsServiceApplication -Name SubSettingsService
-DatabaseName SubSettingsDB -ApplicationPool $subSettingsPool
```

As with the previous application service, you need to create an associated proxy instance. Just when you thought cmdlets' names couldn't get any longer, along comes New-SPSubscriptionSettingsServiceApplicationProxy! If you can place this on a Scrabble board, victory is yours for sure. This cmdlet takes a reference to your service application and a name as parameters.

```
$subSettingsProxy = New-SPSubscriptionSettingsServiceApplicationProxy -ServiceApplication
$subSettingsService
```

Again, to verify that both your service application and its associated proxy got created properly, open Central Administration and navigate to the Service Applications page. You should see the two entries shown in Figure 7-15.

Security Token Service Application		Security Token Service Application		Started
State Service		State Service		Started
State Service		State Service Proxy		Started
SubSettingsService		Microsoft SharePoint Foundation Subscription Settings Service Application		Started
Microsoft SharePoint Foundation Subscription Settings Service Application Proxy		Microsoft SharePoint Foundation Subscription Settings Service Application Proxy		Started

Figure 7-15. *Microsoft SharePoint Foundation Subscription Settings Service pplication and its proxy viewed in Central Administration*

As explained in the previous section, it is not enough to just create the service application and proxy instances. You also need to enable the associated service on the server. The name of the associated service is Microsoft SharePoint Foundation Subscription Settings Service. You will use the piping method learned in Chapter 4 to obtain a reference to the instance of the service, and to turn it on.

```
$subSettingsSvc = Get-SPServiceInstance | Where{$_.TypeName -eq "Microsoft SharePoint Foundation
Subscription Settings Service"}

Start-SPServiceInstance $subSettingsSvc
```

Final Configuration Steps

You are now down to the last step of configuring SharePoint apps for your environment. As mentioned earlier in this section, apps in the context of SharePoint 2013 are accessed using a very specific URL. The first part of that URL is the app prefix, which can be any identifier you want to specify. By default, I tend to simply use the word "Apps" as a prefix. It helps me quickly identify if what I'm looking at is an app or a SharePoint page by simply looking at the URL in the browser.

Before proceeding to configuring the app prefix using PowerShell, let's have a look at how one would normally do it using the web interface. Notice that when you open Central Administration in SharePoint 2013, the interface looks very similar to what you were accustomed to in the 2010 version of the product. However, one big difference jumps at us right from the start: the introduction of a totally new section called Apps, and that is represented by two white octagons on a blue background. This is a brand new management section that Microsoft introduced in 2013 to allow administrators to easily manage settings related to the configuration and the licensing of apps. To configure the app's prefix through the interface, navigate to the Apps section by clicking on the header, and then choose Configure App URLs. This will bring a page up that will allow you to specify the app domain to use, as well as the app prefix.

I will now do it the PowerShell way. I'll start by configuring the app domain using the Set-SPAppDomain cmdlet. This cmdlet takes a single parameter, the appdomain parameter that lets you mention the DNS of the domain your SharePoint farm is on. In our case, I will use the following line of PowerShell to get it configured properly within my environment:

```
Set-SPAppDomain -AppDomain "app.contoso.com"
```

The next step is to configure the app prefix. The cmdlet's name for this is less intuitive; it is the Set-SPAppSiteSubscriptionName cmdlet that takes a single parameter called Name that represents the app prefix that you wish to use across your farm. The following line of PowerShell will configure our farm to use the prefix "apps" for all of its SharePoint apps' URLs.

```
Set-SPAppSiteSubscriptionName -Name "apps" -Confirm:$false
```

o verify that everything has been configured properly, you can navigate to the Configure App URLs page in Central Administration. You should now see both the app domain and app prefix values specified in the text boxes, as shown in Figure 7-16.

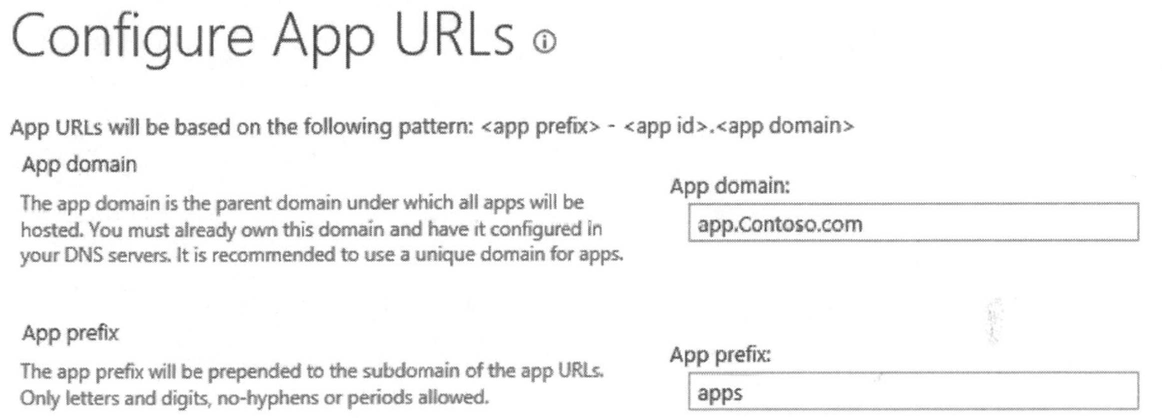

Configure App URLs ⓘ

App URLs will be based on the following pattern: <app prefix> - <app id>.<app domain>

App domain

The app domain is the parent domain under which all apps will be hosted. You must already own this domain and have it configured in your DNS servers. It is recommended to use a unique domain for apps.

App domain:

app.Contoso.com

App prefix

The app prefix will be prepended to the subdomain of the app URLs. Only letters and digits, no-hyphens or periods allowed.

App prefix:

apps

Figure 7-16. *App domain and prefix viewed through the Central Administration interface*

At this point, you are now ready to deploy and install apps within your SharePoint 2013 environment. If you navigate back to the SharePoint Store page, you should see that the yellow notification banner is now gone, indicating that apps are configured properly. In the next section, you will learn how to use PowerShell to interact with app instances and have them automatically deployed within your environment.

Only one problem remains; the app URLs are not being resolved by our DNS service. In order to allow your DNS service to resolve them, you need to create a new subdomain on your main contoso.com domain. Before PowerShell version 3, interacting with DNS entry using PowerShell required you to do all sorts of gymnastics using obscure Windows Management namespaces. Starting with version 3, you now have a full set of extremely useful PowerShell cmdlets that allow you to interact directly with DNS entries. You need to create a new alias for the apps prefix in your DNS server. The following line of PowerShell will take care of it for you:

```
Add-DnsServerResourceRecordCName -Name "*.app" -HostNameAlias "contoso.com" -ZoneName "contoso.com"
```

To verify that the entry was properly created, run the DNS manager console, by typing dnsmgmt.msc in the run console of windows (Windows key + R). When the console opens, expands the node representing your server, expand the Forward Lookup Zone folder, and click on the contoso.com node. You should see the entry shown in Figure 7-17.

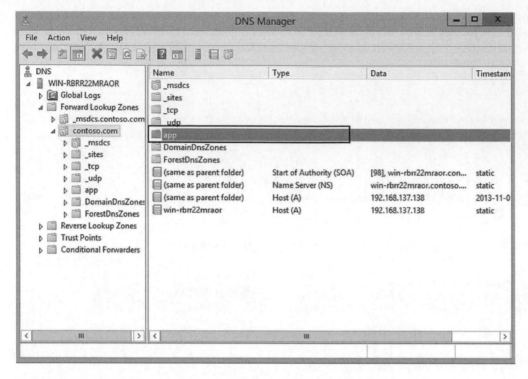

Figure 7-17. *New entry in the DNS manager console for app management*

Importing an App Package

Before being able to deploy and install a SharePoint app in your environment, you'll need to import an instance of it in your farm. The PowerShell cmdlet that lets you import an instance of an app is Import-SPAppPackage. To use this command, you'll need to pass it the local path to your .app package, and also specify the URL of the site collection in which it is to be imported. You also need to specify the source of the app package to import. To use this command, you need to pass it the local path to your .app package and specify the URL of the site collection into which it will be imported. (The user who is calling the cmdlet must be a member of the site owners' group for this site collection.) You also need to specify the source of the app package to import. Table 7-2 enumerates the possible values that can be passed for an app package's source. Note there is a sixth value—InvalidSource—that indicates an error and can be seen only as a return value.

Table 7-2. *Valid Value Options for an App Package Source*

Value	Description
Marketplace	Indicates that the app is taken from the Office Marketplace
CorporateCatalog	Indicates that the app is taken from the Corporate Catalog. This means that the application has been made available to all employees by the farm administrator
DeveloperSite	Indicates that the app is taken from a developer's site. Normally developers will push their development apps onto a special type of site called a Developers' site
ObjectModel	Indicates that the app has been compiled onto a local package and that it is that local app package that we are trying to import
RemoteObjectModel	Indicates that the app that you're trying to import was uploaded using the Client Object Model

The following example will import a custom local SharePoint app, as shown in Figure 7-18, into our root site collection:

```
$app = Import-SPAppPackage -Path C:\Apps\Chapter7App.app -Site http://localhost/
-Source ([Microsoft.SharePoint.Administration.SPAppSource]::ObjectModel)
```

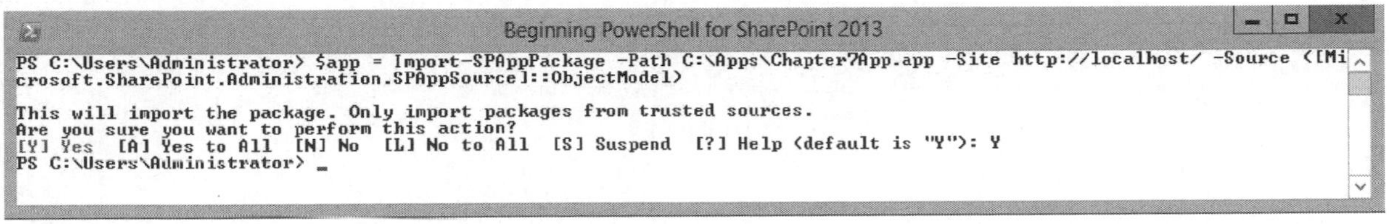

Figure 7-18. *Importing a SharePoint 2013 app package using PowerShell*

As mentioned earlier, Microsoft made a big push with the 2013 release of SharePoint to help developers make their apps available to the largest amount of users by enabling the Office Store. I expect that most organizations will mainly start their SharePoint 2013 app journey by browsing the Office Store and by installing from that source.

The Microsoft Office SharePoint Store can be accessed at http://office.microsoft.com/en-us/store/apps-for-sharepoint-FX102804987.aspx. When accessed, that URL allows you to search for various apps that have been made available by freelance developers and by larger development companies. Some apps are free, and some require that you purchase a license before being able to download them. Because of the order of operations, installing apps from the SharePoint Store will be discussed in the "Installing an App Package" section later in this chapter.

Exporting App Packages

It is important here to note the difference between an app package and an app instance. The term *package* represents the actual .app file that is produced once SharePoint code is compiled. An instance, by contrast, represents an installed entity of a specific app. An instance is associated with a particular web onto which it has been deployed. Assuming that for some reason you have lost the original .app package of a custom app in your organization, if there is still an instance of that app existing in your SharePoint environment, PowerShell provides you with a mechanism to extract the .app package that is associated with your instance. The Export-SPAppPackage cmdlet expects two parameters: an app instance, and a path that specified where to store the extracted app package.

The following example describes how you can get an app package from the SharePoint store. The app used in this example is the Yammer app provided by Microsoft. First you have to install it manually in your farm, and then retrieve its related information using the Get-SPAppInstance cmdlet. I won't be covering the details of how you can install an app from the SharePoint Store using the web interface. This is a very straightforward process that I'm sure you'll be able to figure out easily. Calling the cmdlet will give you an app instance object. To retrieve its associated package, you need to look at its App property (see Figure 7-19). One important point to note is that an administrator account is not allowed to install apps on a SharePoint web. In order for you to be able to install an app using the environment that you built in Chapter 5, you will need to log on with one of the custom user accounts we created (e.g., Contoso\JSmith).

```
$app = Get-SPAppInstance -Web http://localhost | Where {$_.Title -like "Yammer*"}
```

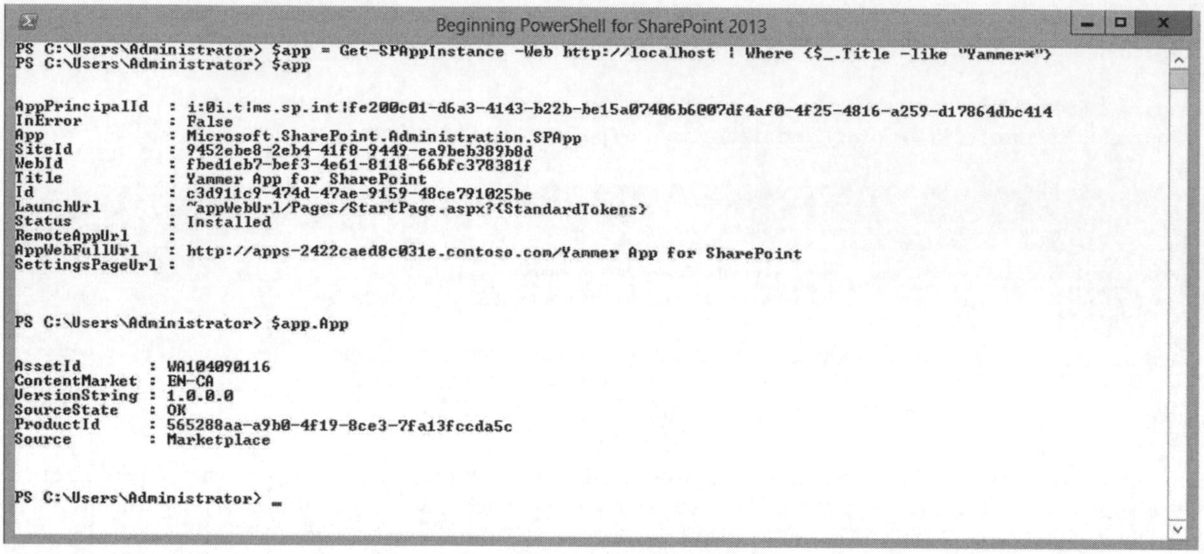

Figure 7-19. *Obtaining a reference to a SharePoint App instance and to its associated app package using PowerShell*

With this information in hands, you can now call the Export method, specifying the app package object, as well as a local path to extract the app package to:

```
Export-SPAppPackage -App $app.App -Path "C:\temp\Yammer.app"
```

Navigate to the specified path, and verify that the local .app package has been created as expected. You are now ready to move forward and install an app package within our SharePoint environment.

Installing an App Package

In the two preceding sections of this chapter, you've learned how to import a local app package within your environment and how to produce a local package from an already installed app instance. Now let's have a look at how you can take those local app packages and install them within your SharePoint environment for everyone in the organization to use and consume. The cmdlet that you need to use to install an app package is Install-SPApp. You need to pass it the URL of the web onto which you wish to install it, as well as a reference to the imported app package.

One thing to watch out for here is that for security reasons the administrator account is never allowed to install apps in a SharePoint farm. Therefore, you will need to launch PowerShell as a separate user before running the scripts below. This user will need to be granted special permissions against the content databases associated with the web where you're trying to install the app package. In order to grant these permissions, you can run the Add-SPShellAdmin cmdlet and specify the user name and the GUID of the content database in question. The following code example will grant permissions to execute PowerShell commands to user John Smith against the content database that hosts the root site collection of your SharePoint 2013 environment:

```
$contentDB = Get-SPContentDatabase -WebApplication http://localhost
Add-SPShellAdmin -UserName Contoso\JSmith -Database $db
```

This code example assumes that there is only one database returned for the web application; otherwise, the variable db will represent an array of content databases and you will need to specify the one to which you wish to grant permissions.

The following example will import and install the Yammer app that you extracted locally in the previous section (see Figure 7-20). Note that because this app package was taken from the online store, it requires you to specify two additional parameters when importing it: the AssetId, and the ContentMarket, both of which you obtained in the preceding section of this chapter.

```
$yammerApp = Import-SPAppPackage -Path "C:\temp\Yammer.app" -Site http://localhost
-Source ([Microsoft.SharePoint.Administration.SPAppSource]::Marketplace)
-AssetId WA104090116 -ContentMarket EN-CA

Install-SPApp -Web http://localhost -Identity $yammerApp
```

Figure 7-20. Installing a SharePoint app package on a web using PowerShell

Once executed, an installation process for the specified app will be initiated. As you can see in Figure 7-20, the app instance status is set to installing. Give it a few seconds and navigate to the All Site Contents page of your root web (http://localhost). If everything went as expected, you should see your Yammer app installed in the list of available SharePoint apps, as shown in Figure 7-21.

Site Contents

Lists, Libraries, and other Apps

add an app

My List (Interface)
0 items
Modified 3 weeks ago

My List Copy
0 items
Modified 3 weeks ago

My List
3 items
Modified 3 weeks ago

Style Library
0 items
Modified 6 weeks ago

Yammer App for
SharePoint
new!

Figure 7-21. *Yammer SharePoint 2013 app installed on a web*

Uninstalling a SharePoint App

To uninstall an app instance, the cmdlet to use is Uninstall-SPAppInstance, and as a parameter, it simply takes a reference to the app instance to uninstall. You need to understand that what you are actually doing here is simply removing a specific instance of an app on a particular web. You are not removing the app entirely from our farm. Just like it was the case for installing an app, the default administrator account is prohibited from uninstalling apps. You will have to run PowerShell using another administrator account. The following example will show you how to uninstall the instance of the Yammer app we've just installed at the root of our main site collection (see Figure 7-22):

```
$yammerApp = Get-SPAppInstance -Web http://localhost | Where{$_.Title -like "Yammer*"}
Uninstall-SPAppInstance -Identity $yammerApp
```

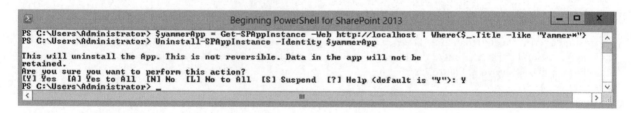

```
PS C:\Users\Administrator> $yammerApp = Get-SPAppInstance -Web http://localhost | Where{$_.Title -like "Yammer*"}
PS C:\Users\Administrator> Uninstall-SPAppInstance -Identity $yammerApp

This will uninstall the App. This is not reversible. Data in the app will not be
retained.
Are you sure you want to perform this action?
[Y] Yes  [A] Yes to All  [N] No  [L] No to All  [S] Suspend  [?] Help (default is "Y"): Y
PS C:\Users\Administrator> _
```

Figure 7-22. *Uninstalling a Sharepoint 2013 app from a web using PowerShell*

One very important piece information you'll probably want to obtain as an administrator is a list of webs on which a specific app is installed on. You could easily create a short PowerShell script using everything that you've learned so far and get the result printed out on screen. Our script would need to begin by obtaining a reference to the Web Application instance in which you want to check for instances of your apps. You would then loop through each site collections and each webs to determine if the specified app is installed or not. The following lines of PowerShell would allow you to create such a useful script:

```
# Prompt the user to enter the name of the app to check for instances of
$appTitle = Read-Host "What is the name of your app?"

# Get a reference to the Web Application on port 80
$webApp = Get-SPWebApplication http://localhost

# Loop through all site collections in the Web Aplication
foreach($site in $webApp.Sites)
{
    # Loop through each Web in the current site collection
    foreach($web in $site.AllWebs)
    {
        # Query the current site for an instance of our app
        $appInstance = Get-SPAppInstance -Web $web.Url |
            Where {$_.Title -like "*$appTitle*"}

        # If the appInstance variable is not null, then an instance was found
        if($appInstance -ne $null)
        {
            Write-Host $web.Url -BackgroundColor "green"
        }

        $web.Dispose()
    }
    $site.Dispose()
}
```

This example assumes that a custom SharePoint 2013 app named "Timer Clock" has been installed on two webs across your farm. Executing the script will loop through each web in our Web Application, and print out the URLs of the webs where the app has been installed, as shown in Figure 7-23.

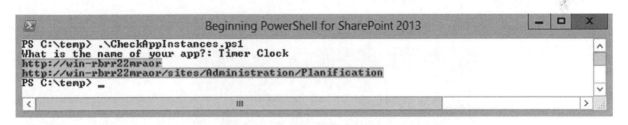

Figure 7-23. *Checking for an instance of a SharePoint 2013 app on all webs using PowerShell*

The App Catalog

SharePoint 2013 introduced a brand new site collection template called the App Catalog. An app catalog is a site that makes custom built apps available to your organization. It lets administrators control apps for Office and for SharePoint, and it also allows users to request apps from the Office Store. App requests can then be approved or rejected by the administrator. An app catalog is an essential piece to any SharePoint 2013 farm in which apps are enabled to end users.

Creating an App Catalog

By default, the new App Catalog template is not made available via the New Site Collection page. If you wish to create an app catalog through the web interface, you will need to go in Central Administration and navigate to the *Apps* ➤ *Manage App* Catalog page using the option shown in Figure 7-24. This page will let you create a new app catalog and specify the primary and secondary administrators, as if you were just creating a normal site collection.

Figure 7-24. *The Manage App Catalog link in Central Administration*

Using PowerShell, things are almost as easy. We simply call the New-SPSite cmdlet as if we were creating a new site collection, and we specify the custom "APPCATALOG#0" template name. The following line of PowerShell shows you how to create a new app catalog for our environment (shown in Figure 7-25). The app catalog will be created at http://localhost/sites/appcatalog:

```
$catalogSite = New-SPSite -Url http://localhost/sites/appcatalog -OwnerAlias "contoso\administrator"
-Name "App Catalog" -Template "APPCATALOG#0"
```

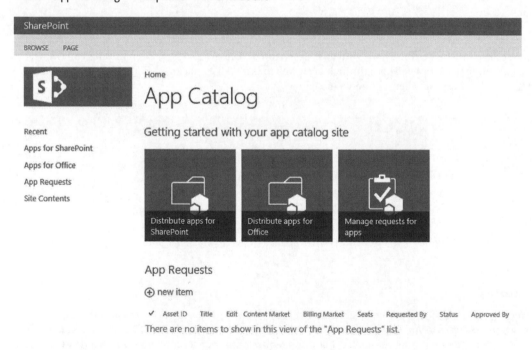

Figure 7-25. *Main page of an App Catalog site collection in SharePoint 2013*

At this point, your app catalog site collection has been properly created, but it is not yet associated with your current Web application. Even if you were to add new applications in it at this point, they would not be discoverable by users on other sites. What you need to do now is associate it with your current web application. Each web application in a SharePoint environment can have an instance of an app catalog associated with them. You cannot have more than one catalog per web application, however. To associate your catalog, you need to execute the following line of PowerShell:

```
Update-SPAppCatalogConfiguration -Site http://localhost/sites/appcatalog
```

To verify that the app catalog has been properly associated with your web application, you can navigate back to the Manage App Catalog page in central administration, and ensure that the site collection is configured properly.

Figure 7-26. *Manage App Catalog screen in Central Administration*

Adding an App to the Catalog

Once your app catalog is up and running, one of the first things you'll probably want to do is add authorized apps for your end users to start consuming. Although it is very easy for you to upload custom app packages through the catalog's web interface, there might be scenarios in which you will want to use PowerShell to achieve this instead. In fact, in many organizations the process of adding apps to the corporate catalog is controlled by the administration team, which uses PowerShell scripts to add, remove, and modify app packages from the catalog. Unfortunately for us, there are no "shortcut" cmdlets that will let us do this in an easy way. You need to treat the app catalog site as if it was just any other site, and upload our local .app package in the appropriate document library.

Each app catalog site has three main document libraries that are made available to SharePoint administrators: Apps for SharePoint, Apps for Office, and App Requests. The first one is the one that I am interested in. It contains a list of all apps that have been made available by the administrators to users in the organization. The following lines of PowerShell will allow you to get a reference to it and to upload a custom .app file in it. Assume this app file (Chapter7RestrictedApp.app) was provided to us by developers within our organization:

```
$web = Get-SPWeb http://localhost/sites/appcatalog

#Gets a reference to the AppCatalog library
$appCatalog = $web.GetFolder("AppCatalog")
$appFiles = $appCatalog.Files

$myAppPackage = Get-ChildItem C:\Apps\Chapter7RestrictedApp.App
$appFiles.Add("AppCatalog/Chapter7RestrictedApp.App", $myAppPackage.OpenRead(), $false);
```

Executing these lines of PowerShell will automatically make the uploaded app package available to everyone in the organization. To confirm that the upload process worked as expected, simply navigate to the Apps for SharePoint library of your app catalog. You should now see an entry in there for your new app package, as shown in Figure 7-27.

Figure 7-27. A SharePoint 2013 app uploaded in the app catalog

With this package deployed, users who try to add a new app to their sites will now see the newly added app as an available choice (see Figure 7-28).

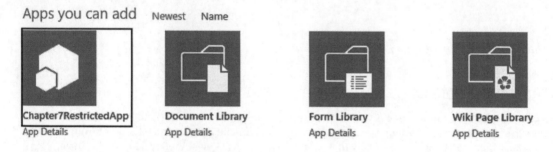

Figure 7-28. Available apps on a SharePoint 2013 web

Managing App Permissions

As a SharePoint administrator, you may decide to prevent users from installing apps on certain sites in your environment. PowerShell provides you with various cmdlets that will give you better control on how you want apps to be automatically deployed throughout your organization. However, with PowerShell there are no ways for us to specify granular permissions for end users on specific apps. To clarify what I mean by this, you need to start by defining how permissions work within the context of SharePoint 2013 apps.

In SharePoint 2013, every app package contains an XML declaration file known as the manifest. An app manifest file contains information about its associated resources such as its app's title, product Id, and version. It also contains very important information about the set of permissions it needs in order to be installed. When installing an app, the installation process looks at the permissions of the user who's trying to install the app to determine whether or not the minimum set of permissions required is attained. A user trying to install an app needs to be able to meet every single permission requirement for the app in order for him to be granted rights to install it. Once the app is installed, every user trying to use the app will also need to meet the minimum permission requirement. Because the minimal installation permissions are set in the app package directly, there are no ways with PowerShell to block specific users from installing apps. If you need to prevent a certain group of users from being able to install and use a specific app using PowerShell, you will need to lower their permissions, making sure they don't meet the minimum required set of permissions to use the app.

To illustrate this, let's take a look at the Chapter7RestrictedApp app. When developed by developers in Visual Studio, the app had the permissions shown in Figure 7-29 applied to it.

Scope	Permission	Properties
Web	Manage	
Site Collection	FullControl	

Figure 7-29. *SharePoint 2013 custom app permissions viewed in Visual Studio*

This basically means that in order for a user to be able to install and use this app, they'll need to be granted permissions to manage the web on which the app is to be installed, and be an administrator of its site collection. Now, let's assume a new user named Bob Houle has Full Control role on the web on which he wants to install your app, but he is not a site collection administrator, which is a requirement for the app to install. The user does not have any access whatsoever on the app catalog site on which your custom app has been deployed. When the user goes to the Add an App page and looks at the apps that are available to him, he won't see the Chapter7RestrictedApp listed (see Figure 7-30).

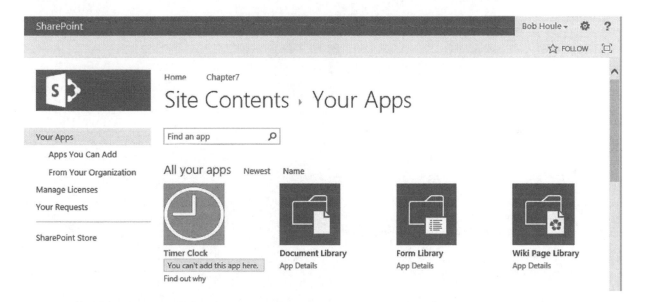

Figure 7-30. *Custom app not listed on available apps page*

In order for him to even be made aware that this app is available to his organization, he needs to be granted at least Read access to the app catalog site. We can use what we've learned in Chapter 6 and grant the user read access to the site using PowerShell. Once the access has been granted, the user will see the app appear on the From Your Organization page but won't be given the option to install it. Clicking on the app details will give the message shown in Figure 7-31 to the user.

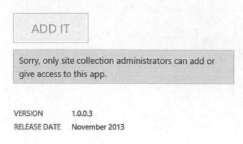

Details

There is no description available.

ADD IT

Sorry, only site collection administrators can add or give access to this app.

VERSION   1.0.0.3
RELEASE DATE   November 2013

Figure 7-31. *Denied permission to install a custom app*

In order for you to allow the user to install your custom app, you'll need to make him a site collection administrator. Doing so will automatically allow the user to install and trust the application for the current site (see Figure 7-32).

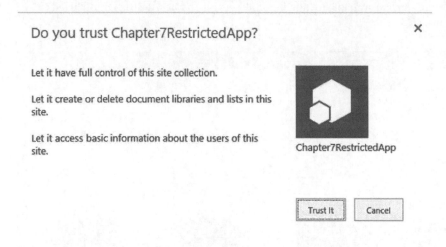

Figure 7-32. *Trust a custom SharePoint 2013 app dialog*

Updating an Existing App

The new app model allows for several different versions of a same app to run across various webs. For example, the Finance division in our organization could have deployed version 1.0.0.4 of our Chapter7RestrictedApp, while the Human Resources division can have the 1.0.0.5 version deployed. As a SharePoint administrator, this is something you need to be aware of and is something you should pay close attention to. From an app catalog perspective, a different version of an app is simply another version of an app package you need to upload to your Apps for SharePoint library.

Notice in Figure 7-33 that there are different versions of the app version in the version history. Remember, an app package uploaded to the app catalog is just a file like any other document you upload to SharePoint. You can take a look at its history to determine the list of changes that occurred on it. You can clearly see from the figure that the app is now up to version 1.0.0.4. As discussed earlier, in your example the finance division has version 1.0.0.3 deployed, even if the latest version is 1.0.0.4. If a user of the Finance division navigates to the list of apps on the site, and looks at the About page for your app by clicking on the "…" link and choosing About, they see a notification saying that there's a newer version of their app available and asking them if they would like to upgrade (see Figure 7-34).

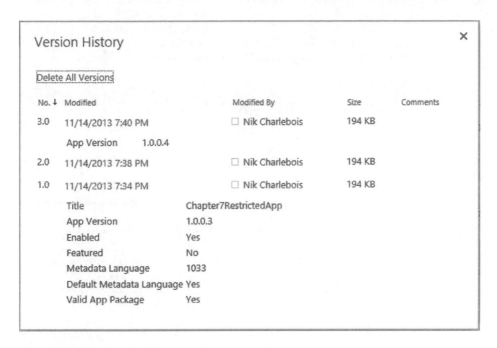

Figure 7-33. *App version history in the app catalog*

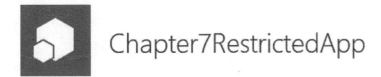

Figure 7-34. *New app version notification screen*

You may argue that running several versions of the same app is somehow good for your organization because it offers backward compatibility, but personally I smell nothing but trouble coming out of this. As a SharePoint administrator, you'll probably want to be able to tell, when deploying a new version of an app, what sites are using the previous version of your app. This would allow you to figure out who the client for the site is, and try to see if there's a way for them to upgrade to the latest version. Out-of-the-box, this is not something that is easily feasible, but with PowerShell, the sky is the limit! Every app package object in SharePoint exposes a property called VersionString that contains the version of the current app package that is installed on a specific web. Given our example, the Figure 7-35 shows the result of obtaining our app instance on both the Finance and Human Resource sites.

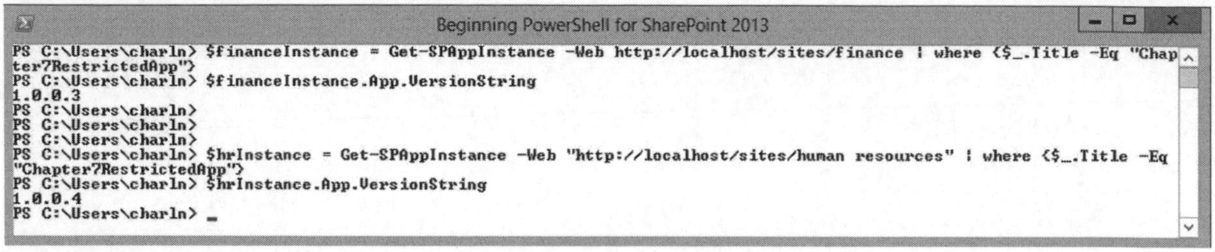

```
PS C:\Users\charln> $financeInstance = Get-SPAppInstance -Web http://localhost/sites/finance | where {$_.Title -Eq "Chap
ter7RestrictedApp"}
PS C:\Users\charln> $financeInstance.App.VersionString
1.0.0.3
PS C:\Users\charln>
PS C:\Users\charln>
PS C:\Users\charln>
PS C:\Users\charln> $hrInstance = Get-SPAppInstance -Web "http://localhost/sites/human resources" | where {$_.Title -Eq
"Chapter7RestrictedApp"}
PS C:\Users\charln> $hrInstance.App.VersionString
1.0.0.4
PS C:\Users\charln> _
```

Figure 7-35. *Displaying two versions of the same app on different sites using PowerShell*

All right, so you now know that the finance site needs some upgrading of their Chapter7RestrictedApp app. The question now is how do you make sure that you upgrade to the latest version of our app using PowerShell? Fear not my friends; Update-SPAppInstance is coming to your rescue. This cmdlet takes two parameters: App, a reference to the newest version of the app package; and Identity, a reference to the app instance to upgrade. Normally, you would get a reference to the newest app package using the .app file on disk. Assume the newest package of your app is located on disk at C:\temp\Chapter7RestrictedApp-1.0.0.4.app. You should get a reference to this package using Get-SPAppInstance:

```
$financeAppInstance = Get-SPAppInstance -Web http://localhost/sites/Finance |
Where {$_.Title -eq "Chapter7RestrictedApp"}

$newestPackage = Import-SPAppPackage -Path C:\Temp\Chapter7RestrictedApp-1.0.0.4.app
-Site http://localhost/sites/Finance
-Source ([Microsoft.SharePoint.Administration.SPAppSource]::CorporateCatalog)

Update-SPAppInstance -Identity $financeAppInstance -App $newestPackage
```

To recap, in order to update an app to its latest version, you need to begin by importing the newest version of the app package onto the web where the outdated app is located. Then once the package has been imported, you can simply get a reference to the outdated app instance, and then call the Update-SPAppInstance cmdlet passing both values as parameters.

Summary

In this chapter, you've learned how, as a SharePoint administrator, to control custom solutions and apps produced by your developers using PowerShell. I've also gone through the process of creating new service application instances using scripts. In the next chapter, I will continue to build on this topic and will explain how to use PowerShell to automate the creation of other service applications in SharePoint 2013. You will also learn how to use PowerShell to validate the health of your SharePoint farm as well as manage and execute maintenance jobs known as Timer jobs.

CHAPTER 8

■ ■ ■

Administering and Monitoring SharePoint with PowerShell

This chapter is where most of you will get the biggest bang for your buck. It is full of IT Pro goodness and will really get into the guts of SharePoint administration. As mentioned earlier in this book, there used to be a time when SharePoint administrative tasks all had to be done using a command line tool called STSAdm. This legacy tool came from the time when the SharePoint product as we came to know it today was called SharePoint Team Sites (therefore the STS prefix in the tool's name). This tool was good, but it was extremely slow to execute heavy operations against the server, and it was difficult for administrators to really know what its methods were really doing in the background.

The story has changed dramatically with the appearance of PowerShell. Now administrators can easily automate long-lasting operations against their SharePoint farms, and have full control over what steps are being executed as part of it. In this chapter, I will be covering various aspects of SharePoint administration using PowerShell. I will be covering several real-life examples, and will provide multiple code samples that could be reused in your respective organizations to help assist you in your day-to-day jobs. Topics covered will include the automation of backups and restores, the monitoring of timer jobs, and the management of services, as well as monitoring the overall SharePoint 2013 farm's well-being using the Health Analyzer.

Most of the things I will cover in the present chapter are things that can be achieved manually by using the SharePoint Central Administration web interface. However, if you add PowerShell to the mix, you can create new reusable and repeatable scripts that can improve performance, and save you from a lot of headaches. By the end of this chapter, you will have learned the basics of everything a SharePoint farm administrator has to do in order to be successful in his role.

Features

In this section, you will learn how to use PowerShell to interact with SharePoint 2013 features. More specifically, you will learn how to enable and disable features on site collections and webs. A feature, in the context of SharePoint, represents a self-contained set of elements that can be made available at various levels of a SharePoint environment. A SharePoint solution (.wsp package) can contain one ore many features, each associated to a different deployment scope (farm, web application, site collection or web).

When creating custom SharePoint solutions, developers are given the option to choose against which scope they wish to associate their features. For example, assume that you have a custom farm solution that contains a webpart that you wish to deploy to your environment. The web part will be associated with a feature and this feature is scoped at the site collection level. The simple fact of deploying your farm solution will not automatically make that web part available to end users to use in all site collections. In order for the web part to become available, the feature will need to be activated for every site collection on which you wish to use the web part. The process of activating a feature against a specific scope is called "Feature Stapling."

Getting a Reference to an Existing Feature

The Get-SPFeature PowerShell cmdlet lets you get a reference to the list of all features deployed in your local SharePoint environment, no matter the scope. Each feature is given a unique identifier, a name, and an associated scope. Figure 8-1 shows how to get a list of all existing features in your SharePoint environment using PowerShell. It also shows how you can get a reference to a specific feature using only its name, in your case, the ExcelServer farm feature:

```
$excelServer = Get-SPFeature | Where{$_.DisplayName -eq "ExcelServer"}
$Get-SPFeature
```

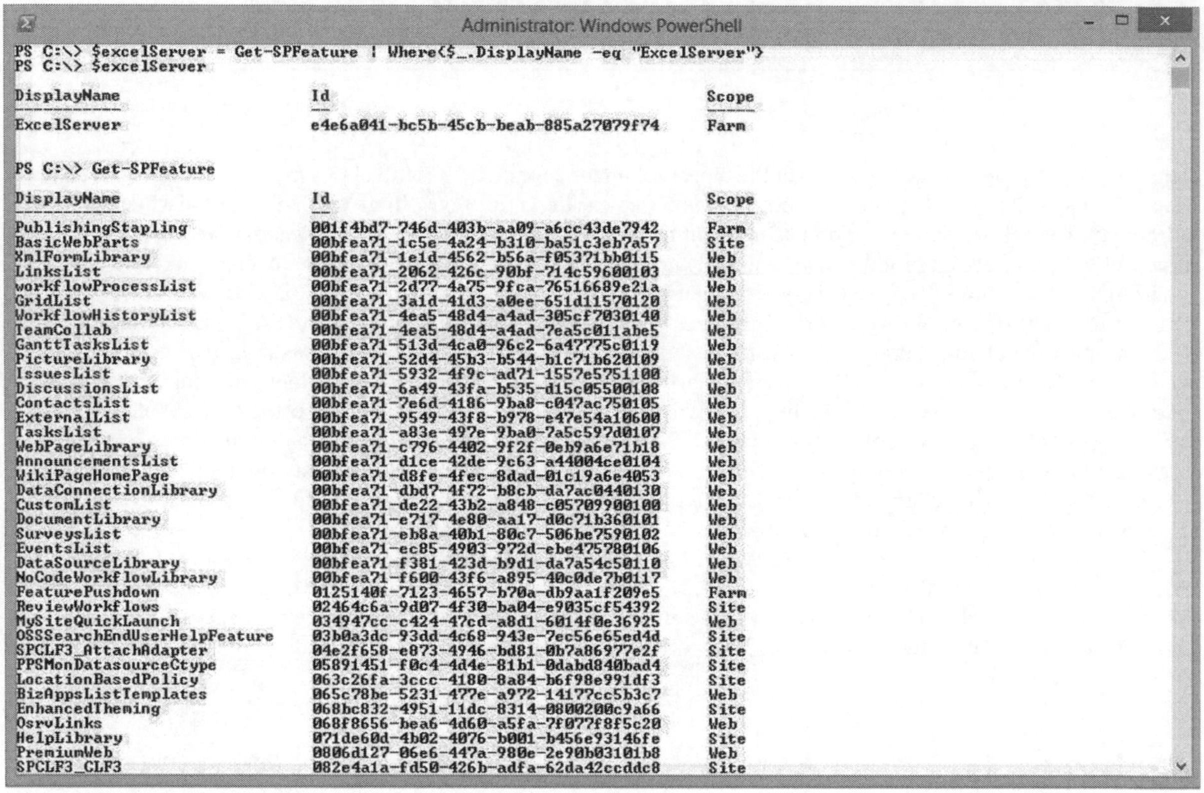

```
PS C:\> $excelServer = Get-SPFeature | Where{$_.DisplayName -eq "ExcelServer"}
PS C:\> $excelServer

DisplayName                    Id                                       Scope
-----------                    --                                       -----
ExcelServer                    e4e6a041-bc5b-45cb-beab-885a27079f74     Farm


PS C:\> Get-SPFeature

DisplayName                    Id                                       Scope
-----------                    --                                       -----
PublishingStapling             001f4bd7-746d-403b-aa09-a6cc43de7942     Farm
BasicWebParts                  00bfea71-1c5e-4a24-b310-ba51c3eb7a57     Site
XmlFormLibrary                 00bfea71-1e1d-4562-b56a-f05371bb0115     Web
LinksList                      00bfea71-2062-426c-90bf-714c59600103     Web
workflowProcessList            00bfea71-2d77-4a75-9fca-76516689e21a     Web
GridList                       00bfea71-3a1d-41d3-a0ee-651d11570120     Web
WorkflowHistoryList            00bfea71-4ea5-48d4-a4ad-305cf7030140     Web
TeamCollab                     00bfea71-4ea5-48d4-a4ad-7ea5c011abe5     Web
GanttTasksList                 00bfea71-513d-4ca0-96c2-6a47775c0119     Web
PictureLibrary                 00bfea71-52d4-45b3-b544-b1c71b620109     Web
IssuesList                     00bfea71-5932-4f9c-ad71-1557e5751100     Web
DiscussionsList                00bfea71-6a49-43fa-b535-d15c05500108     Web
ContactsList                   00bfea71-7e6d-4186-9ba8-c047ac750105     Web
ExternalList                   00bfea71-9549-43f8-b978-e47e54a10600     Web
TasksList                      00bfea71-a83e-497e-9ba0-7a5c597d0107     Web
WebPageLibrary                 00bfea71-c796-4402-9f2f-0eb9a6e71b18     Web
AnnouncementsList              00bfea71-d1ce-42de-9c63-a44004ce0104     Web
WikiPageHomePage               00bfea71-d8fe-4fec-8dad-01c19a6e4053     Web
DataConnectionLibrary          00bfea71-dbd7-4f72-b8cb-da7ac0440130     Web
CustomList                     00bfea71-de22-43b2-a848-c05709900100     Web
DocumentLibrary                00bfea71-e717-4e80-aa17-d0c71b360101     Web
SurveysList                    00bfea71-eb8a-40b1-80c7-506be7590102     Web
EventsList                     00bfea71-ec85-4903-972d-ebe475780106     Web
DataSourceLibrary              00bfea71-f381-423d-b9d1-da7a54c50110     Web
NoCodeWorkflowLibrary          00bfea71-f600-43f6-a895-40c0de7b0117     Web
FeaturePushdown                0125140f-7123-4657-b70a-db9aa1f209e5     Farm
ReviewWorkflows                02464c6a-9d07-4f30-ba04-e9035cf54392     Site
MySiteQuickLaunch              034947cc-c424-47cd-a8d1-6014f0e36925     Web
OSSSearchEndUserHelpFeature    03b0a3dc-93dd-4c68-943e-7ec56e65ed4d     Site
SPCLF3_AttachAdapter           04e2f658-e873-4946-bd81-0b7a86977e2f     Site
PPSMonDatasourceCtype          05891451-f0c4-4d4e-81b1-0dabd840bad4     Site
LocationBasedPolicy            063c26fa-3ccc-4180-8a84-b6f98e991df3     Site
BizAppsListTemplates           065c78be-5231-477e-a972-14177cc5b3c7     Web
EnhancedTheming                068bc832-4951-11dc-8314-0800200c9a66     Site
OsrvLinks                      068f8656-bea6-4d60-a5fa-7f077f8f5c20     Web
HelpLibrary                    071de60d-4b02-4076-b001-b456e93146fe     Site
PremiumWeb                     0806d127-06e6-447a-980e-2e90b03101b8     Web
SPCLF3_CLF3                    082e4a1a-fd50-426b-adfa-62da42ccddc8     Site
```

Figure 8-1. *Getting a reference to SharePoint features using PowerShell*

Activating a Feature

To activate a SharePoint feature using PowerShell, you need to use the Enable-SPFeature cmdlet and pass it a reference to the feature that you wish to activate. Note that you cannot decide against what scope you wish to activate a specific feature. Each feature is already preassociated with a specific scope, and this cannot be changed using PowerShell. Figure 8-2 shows how to activate the web-scoped GroupWork feature against your root web.

```
$groupWork = Get-SPFeature | Where{$_.DisplayName -eq "GroupWork"}
Enable-SPFeature -URL http://localhost -Identity $groupWork
```

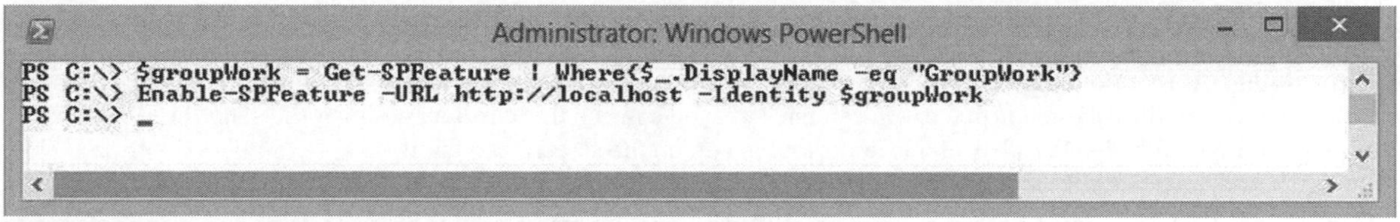

Figure 8-2. *Enabling a SharePoint feature using PowerShell*

Disabling a Feature

If you wish to use PowerShell to disable a SharePoint feature that has previously been activated, you will need to use the `Disable-SPFeature` cmdlet. This method requires you to pass a reference to the feature that you wish to disable. Figure 8-3 shows you how to use PowerShell to disable the GroupWork feature we activated in the previous section.

```
$groupWork = Get-SPFeature | Where{$_.DisplayName -eq "GroupWork"}
Disable-SPFeature -URL http://localhost -Identity $groupWork -Confirm:$false
```

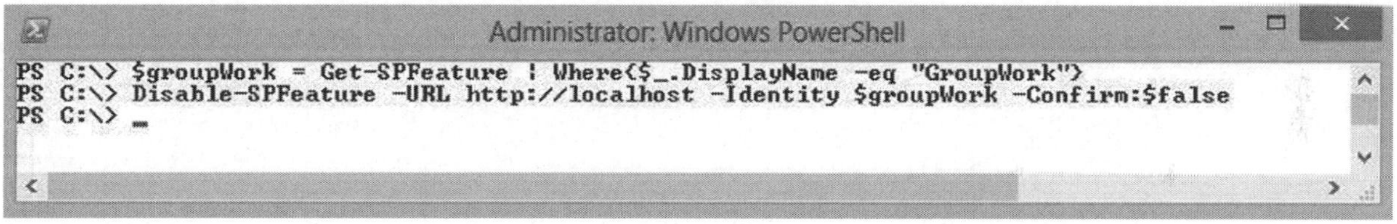

Figure 8-3. *Disabling a SharePoint feature using PowerShell*

Backups

In the SharePoint world, there are several types of backups available. When backing up entities, SharePoint creates .bak files. These files are essential when trying to restore a SharePoint instance to a previous state. It is important to note that you can also use the built-in SharePoint backup mechanism to assist in transferring site collections or web applications from one SharePoint farm over to another, as long as the destination server has the exact same product version as the source server.

You can back up any SharePoint entities from any level of the hierarchy (farm, web application, and site collection). By default, PowerShell provides us with four main cmdlets to interact with SharePoint 2013 backups: one for backing up the configuration database, one for backing up the enterprise search index, another one for backing up the entire farm or specific content databases, and, finally, one for backing up site collections. In this section, you will learn how to use PowerShell to automate backups of different architectural components of a SharePoint farm (content databases, web applications, site collections, etc.) using PowerShell. Content related to backing up the enterprise search content of SharePoint 2013 is outside the scope of the present book.

Automating a Farm Backup

There are two types of farm backups you can do in the SharePoint world: a full backup and a differential one. A full backup creates a backup of all content along with all of its history, whereas a differential backup simply saves what changed since the last full backup was completed.

A farm backup represents the operation of creating a full-trust, offline copy of an existing SharePoint 2013 farm, and storing it elsewhere on a shared location. Farm backups can be automated with PowerShell using the Backup-SPFarm cmdlet. As mentioned previously, you can choose what level of SharePoint artifacts you wish to back up. In order to determine the different artifacts you can back up, you can call this cmdlet passing it the -ShowTree switch. This will automatically display all available items for backup on the screen (see Figure 8-4).

Figure 8-4. *Listing all available SharePoint 2013 artifacts available for backup using PowerShell*

Once you've determine the type of backup (full or differential), and the artifacts you wish to back up, you can proceed with the backup process. The following code will initiate a full farm backup. The backup files will be stored in a local share you've created at c:\Backups\. To perform a differential backup, you simply replace Full with Differential.

```
Backup-SPFarm -Directory \\localhost\Backups\ -BackupMethod Full
```

Executing this code can take several minute depending on the size of your farm. When executing this code, PowerShell will initiate a backup process and wait for the process to finish before returning the results to screen. Don't get fooled; you might think that nothing is happening while the execution goes in, but, in reality, timer jobs related to the backup process are busy at work. Figure 8-5 shows the result of navigating to the Backup and Restore Job Status screen in the SharePoint Central Administration. This page will give you a live overview of what is actively going on with the backup process.

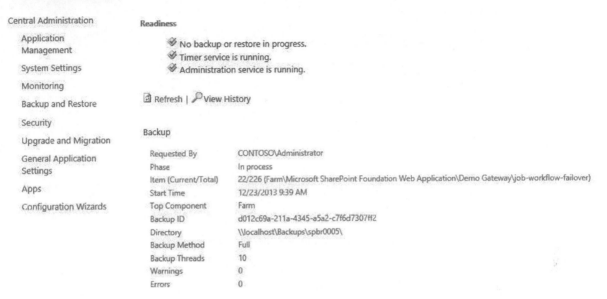

Figure 8-5. *Viewing an ongoing backup status through Central Administration*

Viewing Backup History

Once a SharePoint backup process is completed, it is inserted to the history list of its associated backup folder. A history list is nothing more than an XML file on disk that contains a record of all backup processes that have been sent to the folder. If you navigate to any backup folder, you should see a file named spbrtoc.xml. This is the file that keeps track of all backups. Using PowerShell, you can get a list of all completed backups for a specific folder using the Get-SPBackupHistory cmdlet. Figure 8-6 shows the execution of this cmdlet against a backup folder in which multiple backup processes were initiated. You pipe the resulting output into the generic PowerShell Format-List method in order to get more details out of the operation.

```
Get-SPBackupHistory -Directory \\localhost\Backups\ | Format-List
```

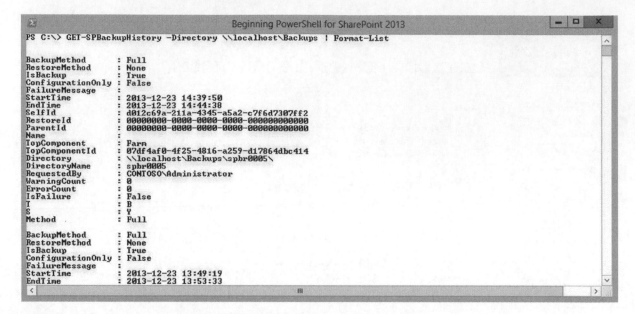

Figure 8-6. *Retrieving a list of all backups for a specific shared folder using PowerShell*

Automating a Site Collection Backup

The second flavor of backups we can do in SharePoint is what we call a site collection backup. As you've probably guessed by the name, this type of backup is aimed at a single specific site collection. The result of such an operation will be a single .bak file containing all information related to that site collection. Note that compared to a farm backup, site collection backups don't keep a history list of all completed processes. The PowerShell cmdlet for backing up SharePoint site collections is Backup-SPSite. All this method takes is a parameter that specifies into which shared folder to put the resulting .bak file.

The following code will initiate a site collection backup of the root site collection of your default Web Application. You specify to PowerShell that the name of the resulting .bak file should be RootSite.bak:

```
Backup-SPSite -Identity http://localhost -Path \\localhost\Backups\RootSite.bak
```

Restores

In the SharePoint context, a restore operation is the action of bringing back the content of backup files to life, either on the same server from which the backups are coming, or on a different, separate SharePoint environment. Just as with the backup operations, there are two types of SharePoint restores: a farm restore and a site collection restore. Both can be easily automated using PowerShell.

Restoring a Farm Backup

When restoring from a farm backup, you have the option to restore the content as a new environment, or to overwrite the existing one; these are called the restore methods. To initiate the restore process, you'll need to use the Restore-SPFarm PowerShell cmdlet. This cmdlet will expect you to pass it the location of the shared folder where the backup files are located, the restore method (new or overwrite), as well as the farm credentials.

The following PowerShell code will initiate a farm restore using the latest full backup files from our environment, and overwriting the current files and configuration. Note that this script will prompt you to enter the password for the farm account:

```
$farmAccount = Get-Credential Contoso\Administrator
Restore-SPFarm -Directory \\localhost\Backups\ -RestoreMethod Overwrite -FarmCredentials
$farmAccount
```

If you had wanted to restore the content to a new location, you would have needed to specify the value New to the -RestoreMethod parameter. Doing so will initiate PowerShell to prompt you to specify additional parameters such as a URL for the new web application and a new name for each of the databases (content, administration, and configuration). Figure 8-7 shows an example of trying to restore a farm backup to a new location.

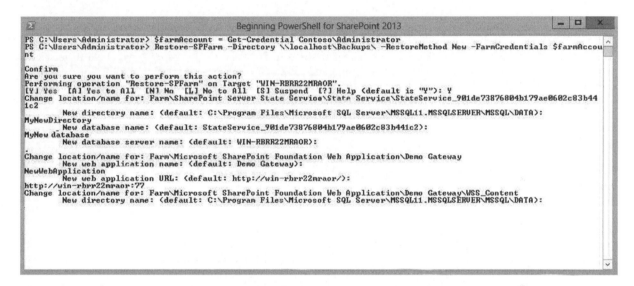

Figure 8-7. *Restoring a SharePoint farm backup to a new location using PowerShell*

Restoring a Site Collection Backup

The process of restoring content from a site collection backup file using PowerShell is very similar to the process of restoring a farm backup. The cmdlet used in this case is Restore-SPSite, and it requires you to specify the URL where you wish to restore the site collection's content to, as well as the path to the .bak file that contains the content. If you want to restore a site collection's backup to an existing location (e.g., overwrite a site collection), you'll need to pass the -Force parameter to the cmdlet.

The following PowerShell code example shows you how to restore the site collection backup file created earlier and overwrite its current location. This will replace the content that has changed since the moment we took the backup, and will revert it back to what it was. For those familiar with the concept of Virtual Machine snapshots in Hyper-V, this process is similar to rolling back a Virtual Machine's snapshot back to an earlier instance:

```
Restore-SPSite http://localhost -Path \\localhost\Backups\RootSite.bak -Force
```

Timer Jobs

Timer jobs in SharePoint are comparable to scheduled tasks in the context of the Windows operating system. They are, more often than not, repeatable activities set to execute at a specific time. The SharePoint object model allows for the development of custom timer jobs, which can help expand the set of default jobs we have to help maintain our SharePoint farm. Timer jobs are associated with schedules that determine the time lapse between two executions of its related activities. Schedules can be of any of the following types: Minutes, Hourly, Daily, Weekly, and Monthly.

The SharePoint timer jobs are responsible for activities such as the installation of SharePoint apps, the creation of variation pages in the context of publishing, the removal of deleted site collections, and so on. These are essentials to the well-being of your SharePoint environment. Using PowerShell, there are several ways for users to interact with these. We can use PowerShell to disable timer jobs completely, to enable them, set their schedule, or to force their immediate execution.

Getting a Reference to an Existing Timer Job

There are various reasons why you may want to get a reference to an existing timer job using PowerShell. To get a list of all the existing timer jobs in your SharePoint environment, you can use the Get-SPTimerJob cmdlet. The example shown in Figure 8-8 shows the result of obtaining a list of all timer jobs that have a schedule set to daily.

```
$dailyJobs = Get-SPTimerJob | Where{$_.Schedule -like "daily*"}
```

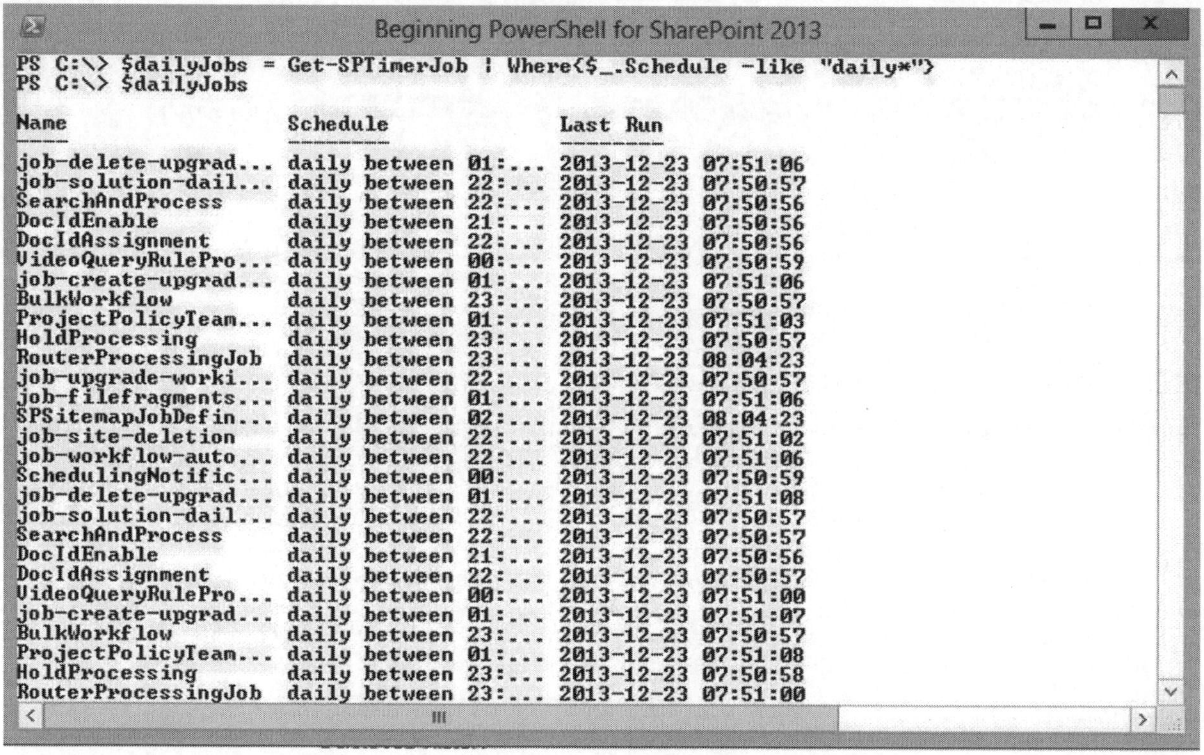

Figure 8-8. *Listing all timer jobs with a daily schedule using PowerShell*

Disabling a Timer Job

There might be some cases in which you wish to completely prevent a SharePoint timer job from running, for example, if you wish to prevent the app diagnostics timer job from running and gathering information because it can somehow affect the performance of your server. Using PowerShell, you can disable a timer job by calling the `Disable-SPTimerJob` cmdlet. This method expects to receive a reference to the timer job you wish to disable. The following PowerShell script will get a reference to a specific timer job (apps diagnostics), and disable its execution:

```
$appDiagnosticsJob = Get-SPTimerJob | Where{$_.DisplayName -eq "Diagnostic Data Provider: App Usage"}
Disable-SPTimerJob $appDiagnosticsJob
```

If you navigate to the Jobs Definition page in SharePoint Central Administration on the server, you should now see that the instance of the timer job specified in this script is now marked as disabled (see Figure 8-9).

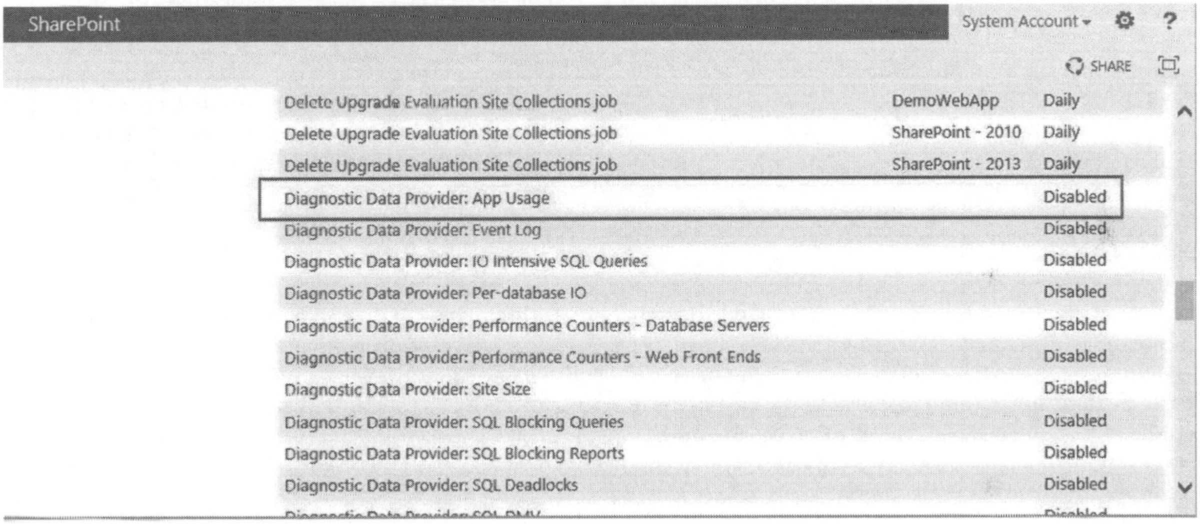

Figure 8-9. *Viewing a disabled timer job in Central Adminsitration*

Enabling a Timer Job

To enable a timer job in SharePoint using PowerShell, you'll need to use the `Enable-SPTimerjob` cmdlet. Just like the method for disabling a timer job, this method expects you to pass it a reference to the timer job object you wish to enable. The PowerShell code below will reenable the timer job you've disabled in the previous section:

```
$appDiagnosticsJob = Get-SPTimerJob | Where{$_.DisplayName -eq "Diagnostic Data Provider: App Usage"}
Enable-SPTimerJob $appDiagnosticsJob
```

Changing a Timer Job's Schedule

Another very common operation you may want to do is to change the schedule for your timer jobs. A very common scenario is to change the frequency of the timer job that automatically creates upgrade evaluation site collections for testing upgrades from SharePoint 2010 to SharePoint 2013 (more on this topic in Chapter 10). By default, this timer job is set to run once every day. During a migration project, you may want to bring this down to be an hourly process to allow your users to test their upgrades more rapidly. The PowerShell cmdlet to use to modify a timer job's schedule is the Set-SPTimerJob method. This cmdlet expects you to pass it the identity of the timer job to modify as well as its new schedule in the form of free text. The schedule parameter can be a little tricky to figure out. Table 8-1 gives you a list of all possible types of schedules as well as an example for each.

Table 8-1. *List of timer job schedules and descriptions of their uses*

Schedule Type	Example	Description
Minutes	Every 2 minutes between 0 and 59	Will execute every 2 minutes in the hour
Hourly	Hourly between 5 and 10	Will execute once every hour between the 5th and the 10th minute of the hour.
Daily	Daily at 23:00:00	Will execute every evening at 11 PM
Weekly	Weekly between Wed 07:00:00 and Fri 06:30:00	Will execute every week, any time between Wednesday 7 AM and Friday 6:30 AM
Monthly	Monthly at 17 20:00:00	Will execute at 20:00:00 the 17th of every month. Need to watch out to make sure the date exists in the month, otherwise the execution will be skipped (e.g., the 31st only exists for every 2 months)
Yearly	Yearly at Jan 17 12:30:00	Will execute once every year on January 17th at 12:30:00. Again, watch out for leap years

The following PowerShell code will change the schedule for the creation of upgrade evaluation site collection as discussed earlier. You will be using an hourly schedule to have the job execute every hour between the 5th and the 10th minutes of the hour. One thing to watch out here is that if you have multiple web applications created in your farm, the first line of script that gets a reference to the timer job instance will actually return one instance per web application. You need to make sure that you are modifying the instance that is associated with the web application you want to impact. Figure 8-10 shows the result of viewing the modified timer job's schedule through the SharePoint Central Administration web interface.

```
$upEvalCreation = Get-SPTimerJob | Where{$_.DisplayName -eq "Create Upgrade Evaluation Site
Collections job"}

Set-SPTimerJob -Identity $upEvalCreation[0] -Schedule "Hourly between 5 and 10"
```

Edit Timer Job ⓘ

Timer Links
Timer Job Status
Scheduled Jobs
Running Jobs
Job History
Job Definitions

Central Administration

  Application
  Management

  System Settings

  Monitoring

  Backup and Restore

  Security

  Upgrade and Migration

  General Application
  Settings

  Apps

  Configuration Wizards

Job Title

Create Upgrade Evaluation Site Collections job

Job Description

Creates upgrade evaluation site collections

Job Properties

This section lists the properties for this job.

Web application: Demo Gateway

Last run time: 1/3/2014 7:59 AM

Recurring Schedule

Use this section to modify the schedule specifying when the timer job will run. Daily, weekly, and monthly schedules also include a window of execution. The timer service will pick a random time within this interval to begin executing the job on each applicable server. This feature is appropriate for high-load jobs which run on multiple servers on the farm. Running this

This timer job is scheduled to run:

○ Minutes   Starting every hour between

◉ Hourly   [5] minutes past the hour

○ Daily   and no later than

○ Weekly   [10] minutes past the hour

○ Monthly

Figure 8-10. *Viewing a modified timer job's schedule through the SharePoint 2013 Central Administration web interface*

Starting a Timer Job

The last operation left for timer jobs that PowerShell lets you automate is the initiation of a timer job's execution. This lets you bypass a timer job's schedule and execute its associated actions right away. This is basically the equivalent of clicking on the "Run Now" button on the Edit Timer Job screen in Central Administration. The PowerShell cmdlet that lets you achieve this is `Start-SPTimerJob`. All this method expects is the identity of the timer job that you wish to execute.

    To illustrate the use of this method, we will use PowerShell to trigger the immediate execution of a SharePoint timer job, called "Delete Job History," which is set to execute on a weekly basis. The following code will automate this process. Figure 8-11 shows that the timer job executed properly.

```
$DeleteJobHistory = Get-SPTimerJob | Where{$_.DisplayName -eq "Delete Job History"}
Start-SPTimerJob -Identity $DeleteJobHistory
```

Figure 8-11. *Central Administration showing the execution of a timer job triggered by PowerShell*

Managing Services

In the SharePoint world there are over 30 associated services that run in parallel with the environment. These services control things like the search, the user profile synchronization, the sandboxed solutions, and so on. They can either run directly on one of the SharePoint web front-end servers or on a separate application server that is attached to the farm.

Many SharePoint service applications require that these services be started in the farm in order to execute properly. As an example, in order for you to be able to configure the user profile synchronization on your farm, the service application requires you to have both the User Profile Service as well as the User Profile Synchronization Service started in your farm. Using PowerShell, there are several operations you can automate that will interact with these SharePoint services. In this section, you will learn how you can automate operations to obtain references to these services, and how to start and stop them.

Getting a Reference to a Service Instance

A service instance represents the actual SharePoint service that you wish to interact with. Although there is only one entry for each service type in a farm (e.g., only one User Profile Service entry), there can exist various instances, running on different servers. For example, if you have three servers in your farm, say servers A, B, and C, you can have both server B and C run the Distributed Cache Service. There is, however, a maximum of one instance of a specific service running on each server at any given point. It is just that multiple servers can be used to run a service in a SharePoint farm.

To get a reference to a specific instance using PowerShell, we can use the Get-SPServiceInstance cmdlet. You will need to either pass it a GUID for your instance, or the name of the server you wish to retrieve the instances from. In the latter case, you will be getting a list of all services on a specific server. The following code example will show you how you can use PowerShell to retrieve a list of all services instances that have been started in your SharePoint farm, no matter the server on which they are running. Figure 8-12 shows the results of running this line of code in the PowerShell Console, in a tabular format to make sure we view all information on the screen.

```
Get-SPServiceInstance | Where{$_.Status -eq "Online"} | Format-Table
```

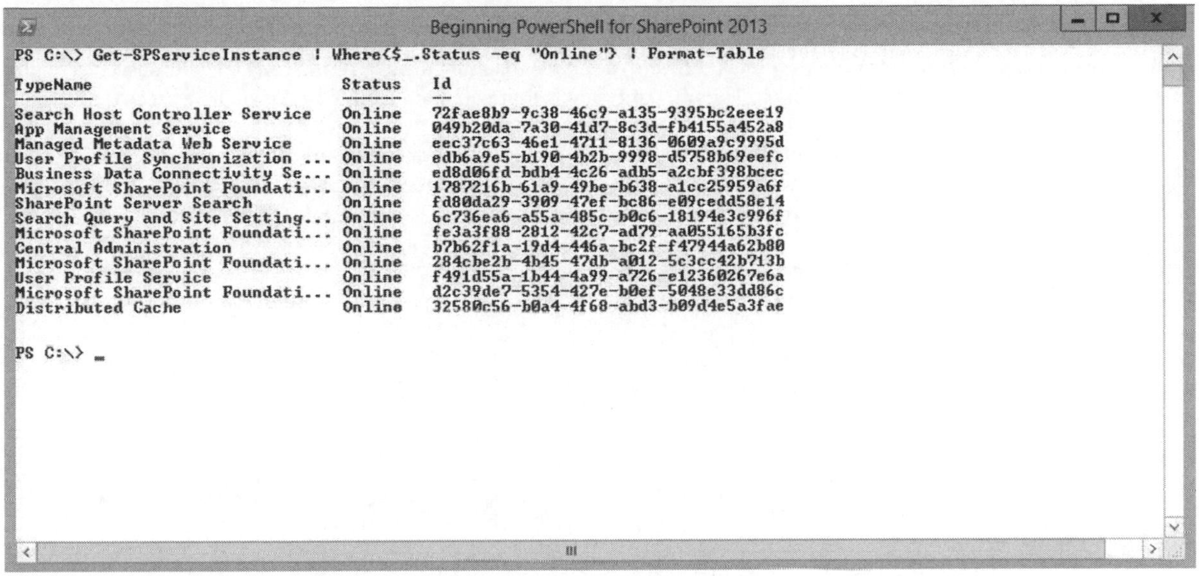

Figure 8-12. Listing all enabled timer jobs in the SharePoint farm using PowerShell

Starting a SharePoint Service Instance

Once you've obtained a reference to a service instance using PowerShell, there are really only two main operations that you can perform on them. You can either enable them, or disable them on a specific server. The PowerShell cmdlet used to enable a service instance on a SharePoint server is `Start-SPServiceInstance`. All this cmdlet expects as parameter is the identity of the instance to start. Remember that a service instance is unique to a server, meaning that the instance reference you obtain using the `Get-SPServiceInstance` already contains information about what server in the farm it's associated with. This means that there are no ways for you to specify to the `Start-SPServiceInstance` cmdlet what server to start a service on.

The following lines of PowerShell code will get a reference to the Visio Graphics Service on our main SharePoint Web Front-End (`WIN-RBRR22MRAOR`) and will start its instance. Figure 8-13 shows that the service instance has been properly started via the SharePoint 2013 Central Administration web interface.

```
$visioServiceInstance = Get-SPServiceInstance -Server "WIN-RBRR22MRAOR" |Where{$_.TypeName -Eq
"Visio Graphics Service"}

Start-SPServiceInstance $visioServiceInstance
```

Figure 8-13. Viewing the status of the Visio Graphics Services in Central Administration

Stopping a SharePoint Service Instance

The opposite process, the one in which you want to stop a service instance from running on a specific server, is in all fashions similar to the process of starting it. The only different is that you need to call the Stop-SPServiceInstance cmdlet instead.

The following code will stop the Visio Graphics Service instance you've started in the previous section. Figure 8-14 shows, through Central Administration, that the service instance is in the process of going back to its original stopped state after executing these PowerShell lines of code:

```
$visioServiceInstance = Get-SPServiceInstance -Server "WIN-RBRR22MRAOR" |
Where{$_.TypeName -Eq "Visio Graphics Service"}

Stop-SPServiceInstance $visioServiceInstance
```

User Profile Service	Started	Stop
User Profile Synchronization Service	Started	Stop
Visio Graphics Service	Stopping	
Word Automation Services	Stopped	Start
Work Management Service	Stopped	Start

Figure 8-14. *Viewing a service instance in the process of being stopped*

SharePoint Health Analyzer

The 2010 version of SharePoint has the concept of a health analyzer built into it. What this component does is run frequent checks on the farm's components to detect common issues that can impact the performance and the overall well-being of a SharePoint environment. These checks are called Health Analyzer rules, and they contain information about what to check in the SharePoint farm to detect anomalies and can even contain information about what corrective measures to automatically take if issues are detected. By default, SharePoint 2013 comes with 65 predefined Health Analyzer rules and they are all enabled. You can define your own custom rules if you wish, but this topic is outside the scope of this book.

Health Analyzer rules, just like timer jobs, have an associated schedule. For example, the rule that checks to see if the databases indexes' statistics are out of date runs on a daily basis. SharePoint 2013 has about twenty different timer jobs that are dedicated to executing and running the health checks specified in these rules. Depending on the type of schedule a Health Analyzer rule is given, it will get executed by a specific timer job. Figure 8-15 shows a list of all timer jobs that are dedicated to the Health Analyzer engine of SharePoint. In this section, you will learn how to use PowerShell to interact with the SharePoint 2013 Health Analyzer component.

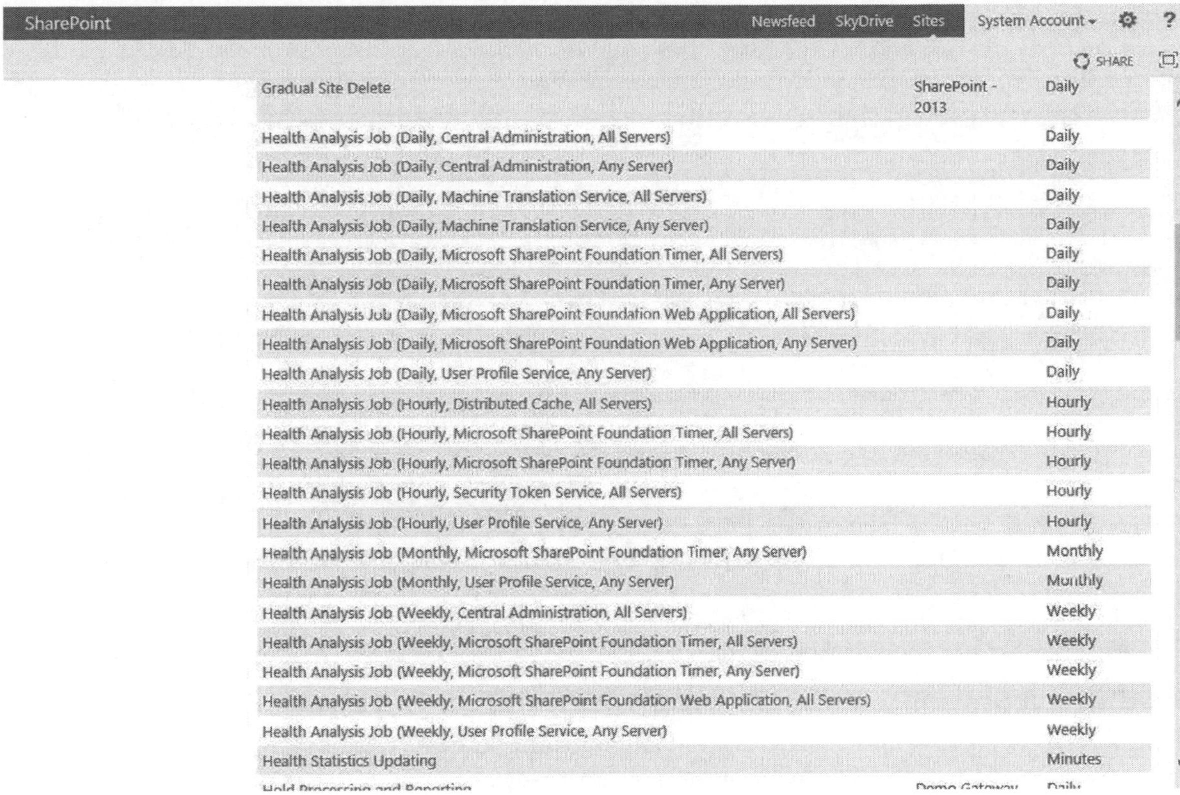

Figure 8-15. *A list of all Health Analyzer related timer jobs viewed in Central Administration*

Getting References to Health Analyzer Rules

You're probably starting to see a pattern here. The first topic I will cover in this section is how to get a reference to a Health Analyzer rule object so that you can extract information out of it. The PowerShell cmdlet you need to use to get such a reference is the `Get-SPHealthAnalysisRule` method. This cmdlet returns a list of all existing rules in your SharePoint farm.

The following PowerShell line of code will get that list and display the rule's name and its description in a tabular format on screen. Figure 8-16 shows a portion of the resulting table.

```
Get-SPHealthAnalysisRule | Format-Table -Property Name, Summary
```

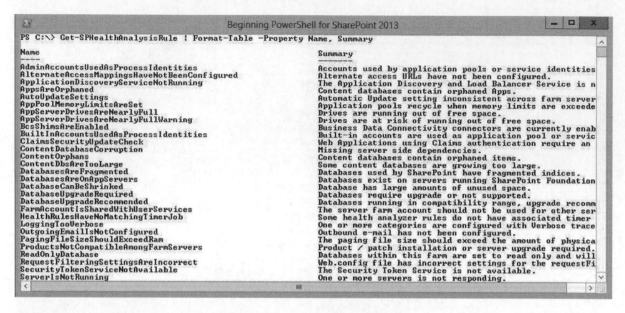

Figure 8-16. *A list of all SharePoint Health Analysis rules returned by PowerShell*

Disabling a SharePoint Health Analyzer Rule

To disable a Health Analyzer rule using PowerShell, you need to use the `Disable-SPHealthAnalysisRule` cmdlet. This method simply requires you to pass it a reference to the rule you wish to disable. Figure 8-17 shows the results of disabling the "Missing server side dependencies" rule.

```
# The code below uses the name of the rule, instead of the display name.
# These very often vary from one another.
$rule = Get-SPHealthAnalysisRule | Where{$_.Name -eq "ContentDatabaseCorruption"}

Disable-SPHealthAnalysisRule $rule
```

BROWSE	ITEMS	LIST				○ SHARE

Application pools recycle when memory limits are exceeded.	Weekly	Yes	No
Databases used by SharePoint have fragmented indices.	Daily	Yes	Yes
Databases exist on servers running SharePoint Foundation.	Weekly	Yes	No
The paging file size should exceed the amount of physical RAM in the system.	Weekly	Yes	No
Databases used by SharePoint have outdated index statistics.	Daily	Yes	Yes
The timer service failed to recycle.	Weekly	Yes	No
Search - One or more crawl databases may have fragmented indices.	Daily	Yes	Yes

◢ **Category : Configuration** (38)

Alternate access URLs have not been configured.	Daily	Yes	No
The Application Discovery and Load Balancer Service is not running in this farm.	Hourly	Yes	No
Automatic Update setting inconsistent across farm servers.	Daily	Yes	No
Built-in accounts are used as application pool or service identities.	Weekly	Yes	No
Missing server side dependencies.	Weekly	No	No
Databases require upgrade or not supported.	Daily	Yes	No
Databases running in compatibility range, upgrade recommended.	Daily	Yes	No
One or more categories are configured with Verbose trace logging.	Daily	Yes	No
Outbound e-mail has not been configured.	Weekly	Yes	No
Product / patch installation or server upgrade required.	Daily	Yes	No

Figure 8-17. *Viewing a disabled Health Analyzer rule in Central Administration*

Enabling a SharePoint Health Analyzer Rule

The opposite operation to enable a disabled rule is simple enough: use the Enable-SPHealthAnalysisRule PowerShell cmdlet and pass it a reference to the rule object as a parameter. The following code will reenable the "Missing server side dependencies" rule that you've disabled in the previous section:

```
$rule = Get-SPHealthAnalysisRule | Where{$_.Name -eq "ContentDatabaseCorruption"}
Enable-SPHealthAnalysisRule $rule
```

Summary

In this chapter, you have learned to interact with the administrative components of a SharePoint 2013 farm using PowerShell. You have learned how to use the scripting language to monitor certain aspects of your environment, and have learned how to perform backups of your content and configurations. You have now covered all aspects of on-premises SharePoint management using PowerShell. In the next chapter, you will learn how you can apply everything you've learned so far in this book to the cloud, by introducing new mechanisms that you can use to manage an Office 365 SharePoint Online environment hosted with Microsoft.

CHAPTER 9

■ ■ ■

Managing Office 365 SharePoint Online with PowerShell

As the title says, this chapter is about teaching you how you can use PowerShell to manage your SharePoint Online instance in Office 365. We will not be covering the Exchange and Lync aspect of the Office 365 story in this chapter. It is assumed that readers have already had some level of exposure to the maintenance of site collections in Office 365. In October 2010, Microsoft announced their new wave of online products that was going to be taking their Office suite to the clouds. This new service was going to let users manage their own SharePoint 2010 instances in a multitenant environment. For the sake of clarity, I will be using the term SharePoint Online to make reference to the SharePoint offering side of Office 365.

Microsoft had attempted in early 2009 to launch the ancestor of SharePoint Online, called Business Productivity Online Services (BPOS). This is my own opinion (one that I know is shared by all of my SharePoint colleagues), but BPOS was a disaster. The service offered highly restrictive SharePoint 2007 environments to users who could not do any significant level of customization to their site collection. Of course, Microsoft offered users the choice to buy a license for a dedicated online server instance, but the prices for those licenses were just ridiculous. Things got a lot better with Office 365. For barely $10 a month per user, you could create both a hosted collaborative SharePoint 2010 environment for your organization and also have a public site collection to expose to the outside world as your corporate web site. On top of this, for a few additional dollars monthly came all the Office client licenses benefits, which, for me, was simply icing on the cake.

Then, at the beginning of the year 2013, Microsoft announced that they were going to upgrade all SharePoint online farms to run SharePoint 2013, or to whatever their latest version of SharePoint was. I say this because even today, if you look at the configuration link files on the Office 365 servers, you see that they are running SharePoint version 16 dot something, and SharePoint 2013 was always labeled version 15. Anyway, we've sidetracked, but the important point to take out of this is that with this new cloud offering, Microsoft ensures that users will always be running the latest and greatest version of their platform.

In summer of 2012, Microsoft announced something they called the SharePoint Online Management Shell, which allowed users to remotely configure and interact with their SharePoint online instances using PowerShell. Of course, Microsoft could not make all the same cmdlets that you have on premises to interact with SharePoint available on the cloud. Remember that SharePoint Online is a multitenant environment and that there are several users on the same farm. Therefore, they needed to ensure that whatever cmdlets they made available were not able to go over the site collections boundaries. This chapter will be all about using this new SharePoint Online Management Shell tool to interact with your SharePoint Online environment.

Overview of the Environment

Throughout this chapter, I will be using an Office 365 trial account that I've created. The trial account is using Microsoft Office 365 E3 plan, which offers 30 days of free use. The account that I've created uses a custom subdomain that I registered when creating my trial registration. The domain that I will use in this chapter is PowerShellBook. onmicrosoft.com. The environment has been created from scratch, and only contains the default SharePoint site collections created by Microsoft on provision of a new Office 365 account. Figure 9-1 shows the default site collection made available by default using the SharePoint admin center of Office 365.

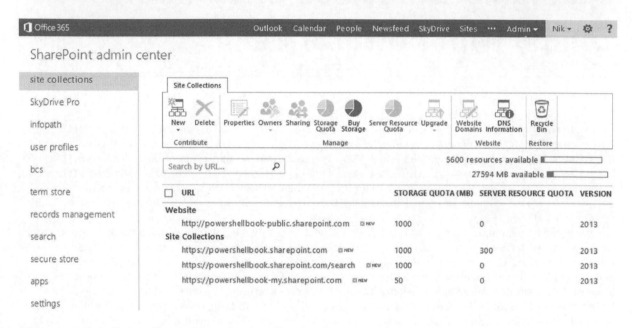

Figure 9-1. *Default site collections viewed in the Office 365 SharePoint admin center*

SharePoint Online Management Shell

As mentioned earlier in this chapter, Microsoft released a tool to help to manage SharePoint Online instances remotely using PowerShell. In order for you to be able to use it, you will need to go to Microsoft's site and download and install it locally. The tool can be downloaded from http://www.microsoft.com/en-us/download/details .aspx?id=35588. On the site, on trying to download the tool, you will be prompted to choose between the 32 -and 64-bit versions of the tool. Choose the appropriate version for your machine. The installation process is straight forward, and I won't be covering it in this book.

Once the tool is installed on your system, you can open a new instance of it. The SharePoint Online Management Shell looks in every aspect similar to the default PowerShell console. It uses the same profile, making it generic across all PowerShell consoles; the only difference is that you're not allowed to change the console's title. Figure 9-2 shows the default aspect of the SharePoint Online Management Shell.

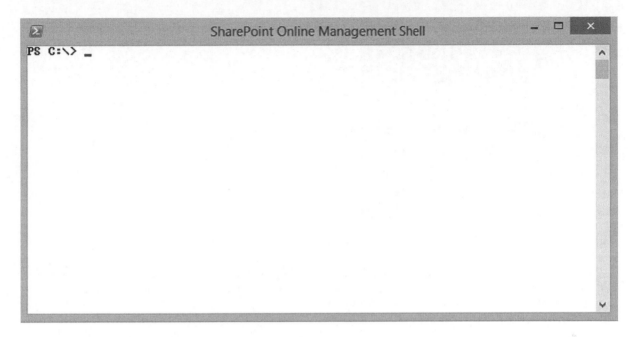

Figure 9-2. *SharePoint Online Mangement Shell console*

Connecting to the Office 365 Instance

The first thing to do once you have the management shell set up is, obviously, to connect to your remote Office 365 instance. The management shell offers a new cmdlet named Connect-SPOService that allows you to remotely connect to the Office 365 SharePoint Online service. Every PowerShell session that wants to interact with Office 365 needs to first authenticate using this method. In this example, you will use this cmdlet to connect to your environment using the following PowerShell line:

```
Connect-SPOService -URL https://powershellbook-admin.sharepoint.com -Credential
Nik@PowerShellBook.onmicrosoft.com
```

In this line, the URL parameter is the root of the SharePoint admin center for your Office 365 account, and in which the credentials used are the credentials of a user with administrator rights on the SharePoint Online instance. Calling this PowerShell line of code will automatically prompt the user for their credentials (see Figure 9-3).

Figure 9-3. *SharePoint Online Management Shell prompting for user's credentials upon authenticating*

Enter your credentials as requested, and click OK. It may take a few seconds for the management shell to properly authenticate you with Office 365. Once the authentication has been successful, you will simply be returned to the management shell and allowed to type in new commands.

Listing Available Commands

This is more of a refresher, but just like you did for the on-premises aspect of PowerShell, you can generate a list of all available cmdlets in the online shell by using the Get-Command cmdlet. However, simply calling this command without any filters will return a list of well over 1,000 items, including all the basic PowerShell cmdlets that are not specific to SharePoint. What you want to do is filter this list so that you only get the cmdlets that are pertaining to SharePoint back. The module that contains all of the SharePoint Online PowerShell cmdlet is named Microsoft.Online.SharePoint.PowerShell. Using this information, you can produce a query that will filter the list of all commands to only return the ones related to what you want. The following lines of PowerShell will allow us to achieve just that:

```
$spo = Get-Command |
Where{$_.ModuleName -eq "Microsoft.Online.SharePoint.PowerShell"}
```

With this command, you've captured all SharePoint Online related cmdlets into a PowerShell variable named $spo. Getting the Count property of this variable will tell you that there are currently 30 cmdlets available to manage SharePoint Online. Note that because this is a cloud environment, this number is subject to change at any time given that Microsoft has frequent releases for the online platform. The rest of this chapter will give you an overview of what each of these 30 online cmdlets are all about.

SharePoint Online Cmdlets

The following section will give details about the various cmdlets that are available to you in the cloud and will give some examples of real-life scenarios in which you may have to use them to manage your SharePoint Online instances. They are grouped by the type of SharePoint artifacts they interact with.

Site Collections

The current section will go over each PowerShell cmdlets that are available to interact with SharePoint Online site collections. There is a total of 11 cmdlets available to manage these. In the context of SharePoint Online, the PowerShell object that represents a site collection is called a SPOSite object.

Get-SPOSite

The Get-SPOSite cmdlet returns a reference to a SharePoint Online site collection. As mentioned earlier, the object returned by this method is a SPOSite object as opposed to a SPSite object for an on-premises site collection. Because this object exposes a different type of SharePoint artifact, the properties exposed by it are also different to the one exposed by the on-premises object. I've developed a short PowerShell script that allows you to loop through each property of a SPOSite object and prints its value on screen. The script will prompt the user to enter the URL to one of its SharePoint Online site collection, will get a reference to it, and will query its members to obtain the list of available properties. The script then loops through each of these properties obtained, and prints both its name and its value on screen. Figure 9-4 shows the execution of this PowerShell script against our public facing site collection.

```
$url = Read-Host "What is your Site's Url"
$site = Get-SPOSite $url

$members = $site | Get-Member | Where{$_.MemberType -eq "Property"}
for($i = 0; $i -lt $members.Count; $i++)
{
        $name = $members[$i].Name
        Write-Host $name":" $site.$name
}
```

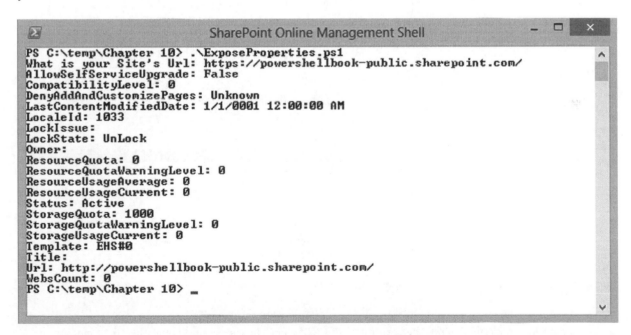

Figure 9-4. *SPOSite properties and their values for your SharePoint Online public facing site collection*

By default, Office 365 creates four site collections for each Enterprise level accounts. Table 9-1 shows the site collection template ID used for each of these four site collections for your demo account.

Table 9-1. *List of default SharePoint Online site collections and their associated site template id*

Site Collection	URL	Template ID
Public	`http://powershellbook-public.sharepoint.com`	EHS#0
Intranet	`https://powershellbook.sharepoint.com`	EHS#1
Search Center	`https://powershellbook.sharepoint.com/search`	SRCHCEN#0
My Site Host	`https://powershellbook-my.sharepoint.com`	SPSMSITEHOST#0

It is important to note that although the Search Center and My Site Host templates are also available on-premises, the two site collection templates used for the Public and the Intranet site collections are new templates that are exclusive to SharePoint Online in Office 365.

New-SPOSite

The `New-SPOSite` cmdlet lets you create a new SharePoint Online site collection. This PowerShell cmdlet takes three mandatory parameters to execute, a URL for the new site collection, the username of the Office 365 user that will be its owner, and a storage quota. You're probably wondering why you're not passing the site collection's template ID as a parameter. Actually, although this is not a mandatory parameter, you can still go ahead and pass it to the cmdlet. If you omit to mention it, your SharePoint Online will force you to select a template the first time that you try to access your new site collection. Figure 9-5 shows the prompt that a user gets the first time he or she accesses a site collection in SharePoint Online for which no default site collection template has been chosen.

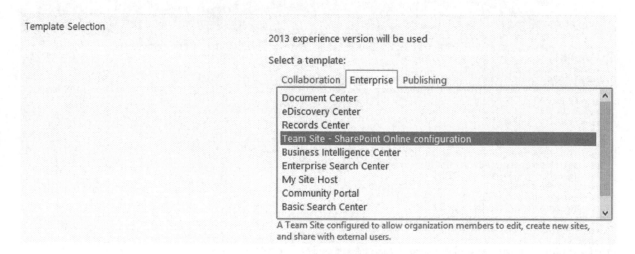

Figure 9-5. *SharePoint Online prompting user to select a site collection template*

Remember that I'm a developer at heart, and so, to me, something is always missing in the default offering of site collections in SharePoint Online. The beauty of Office 365 is that it lets developers create their own sandbox to develop custom business apps and test them out in the cloud. The online service offering gives the user the choice to create a developer's site collection, which is invaluable to any organization wanting to do testing for their

SharePoint 2013 apps. The first thing I always do when registering a new Office 365 account is to connect to its SharePoint Online portal and create such a site collection. The following few lines of PowerShell will show you how you can get started and automatically create such a site collection using PowerShell. The code shown here will automatically create a new developer site collection in your PowerShellBook SharePoint Online account. Figure 9-6 shows the new site collection being created in the SharePoint Online admin center. It normally takes a minute or two after the creation process has been initiated by PowerShell for the SharePoint Online site collection to be entirely created.

```
New-SPOSite -URL https://powershellbook.sharepoint.com/sites/dev -Owner Nik@PowerShellBook
.OnMicrosoft.com -StorageQuota 500 -Template DEV#0
```

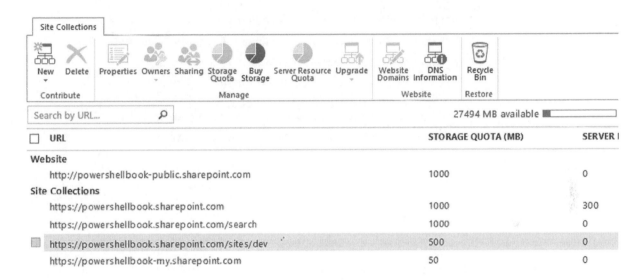

Figure 9-6. *Developer site collection being created in SharePoint Online admin center*

Remove-SPOSite

The Remove-SPOSite cmdlet is to be used when you wish to delete an existing SharePoint Online site collection. The only parameter required for this PowerShell cmdlet is the URL to the site collection that you wish to delete. The following line of PowerShell code will delete the developer site collection that you've created in the previous section of this chapter:

```
Remove-SPOSite https://powershellbook.sharepoint.com/sites/dev
```

Repair-SPOSite

This SharePoint Online cmdlet is a special one. You can call Repair-SPOSite against a single or a group of site collections in your SharePoint Online account, and it will run all health analyzer rules against them. If it encounters any errors, it automatically attempts to fix them. This operation is not available through the web interface of the SharePoint Online admin center; you must use the SharePoint Online Management Shell to use it. Although there is no real need for Office 365 clients to use this cmdlet at the moment, it was probably one of the most widely used cmdlets by the Microsoft team when they had to upgrade millions of tenants from SharePoint 2010 to SharePoint 2013 back in the spring of 2013. Assuming that Microsoft ever releases another version of their SharePoint Online offering, there may be some future need for this cmdlet. Figure 9-7 shows the result of running this cmdlet against your demo intranet site.

```
Repair-SPOSite https://powershellbook.sharepoint.com
```

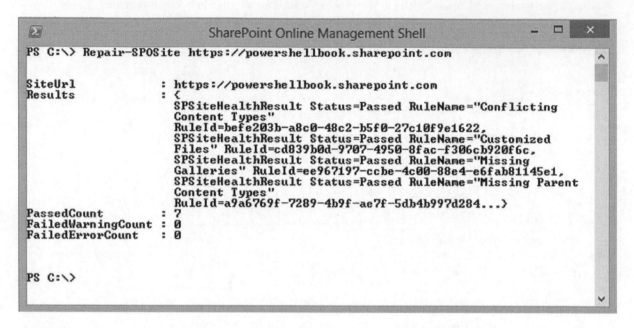

Figure 9-7. *Running the repair site collection PowerShell cmdlet against a SharePoint Online site collection*

Set-SPOSite

Imagine that you wish to use PowerShell to modify a property of an existing site collection, say, its title. Your normal reaction may be to use the `Get-SPOSite` PowerShell cmdlet to get a reference to the site collection, and then to set its `Title` property to whatever you wish. The big problem with this approach using SharePoint Online is that a SPOSite object does not expose the `Update` method that is normally used to commit changes on SharePoint artifacts back to the database. Therefore, simply getting a reference to the site collection and setting the value of one of its property is not going to work. This is where the `Set-SPOSite` cmdlet comes to the rescue. This cmdlet lets you specify what property of a SPOSite object you wish to set, and in the background it secretly calls the `Update` method on the object. The PowerShell code below shows you how you could use PowerShell to set the title of your internal SharePoint Online site. Figure 9-8 shows the result of executing this line of PowerShell code:

```
Set-SPOSite https://powershellbook.sharepoint.com -Title "This is me showing the Set-SPOSite cmdlet"
```

Figure 9-8. *Internal SharePoint Online site collection's root web title changed using PowerShell*

There are several other properties that can be modified using this method. Table 9-2 gives a list of all of the properties of a SharePoint Online site collection that can be set using this PowerShell cmdlet.

Table 9-2. *List of SharePoint Online site collection properties that can be modified using PowerShell*

Property Name	Description
AllowSelfServiceUpgrade	True or false to specify if a site collection administrator is allowed to upgrade its site collection or not
LocaleId	Specifies the locale ID of the language to use for the site collection
LockState	Sets a lock on a site collection. Available values are: NoAccess—Redirects user to a specific URL Unlock—Users access the site normally
Owner	Sets the owner of the specified site collection
ResourceQuota	Specifies a resource quota in megabytes for the site collection
ResourceQuotaWarningLevel	Specifies the warning level in megabytes that, when reached, notifies the site collection administrator that the site collection is approaching its maximum resource quota
StorageQuota	Specifies a storage quota in megabytes for the site collection
StorageQuotaWarningLevel	Specifies the warning level in megabytes that, when reached, notifies the site collection administrator that the site collection is approaching its maximum storage quota
Title	Specifies the title of the site collection

Test-SPOSite

The Test-SPOSite cmdlet does the same thing as the Repair-SPOSite cmdlet, but it doesn't actually commit the changes. Using it results in the same thing as calling the Repair-SPOSite using the -WhatIf switch, which also won't commit the results of the operation.

Upgrade-SPOSite

Just as was the case for the test and repair functions, the upgrade cmdlet for SharePoint Online site collections has already served its purpose, and tenants won't have to use it anymore. It was heavily used by the Microsoft team when upgrading tenant site collections from SharePoint 2010 to SharePoint 2013. If you try to call this PowerShell cmdlet against any of your existing site collections, you will simply get a notification message saying that the site has already been updated and that it does not need to be updated (see Figure 9-9).

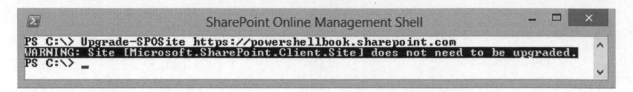

Figure 9-9. *SharePoint Online Management Shell printing notification on screen that site collection is not upgradable*

Request-SPOUpgradeEvaluationSite

The Request-SPOUpgradeEvaluationSite PowerShell cmdlet lets a user request a temporary Upgrade Evaluation site collection in Office 365. This method was mostly used when Office 365 tenants were given the option to upgrade from their original SharePoint 2010 site collections over to the new SharePoint 2013 ones. Now that every new tenant is automatically given a 2013 environment, the use for this cmdlet is slowing disappearing. Making calls to this cmdlet doesn't do anything anymore. No upgrade evaluation sites will ever be triggered for site collections that are already running in compatibility mode.

Get-SPODeletedSite

Just as was the case for SharePoint on-premises, site collections that have been deleted through the web interface are given a second shot at life. One major difference in the online world, however, is that in Office 365, even SharePoint site collections that have been deleted through PowerShell are sent to the recycle bin. The SharePoint Online admin center offers the option to view deleted site collections by clicking on the Recycle Bin button in the management ribbon (see Figure 9-10).

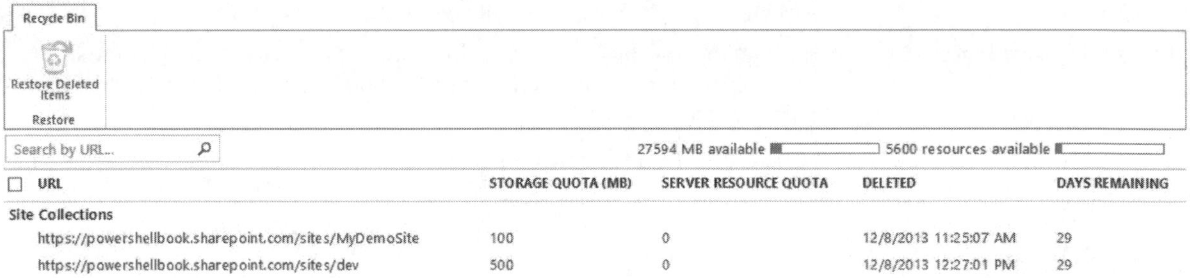

URL	STORAGE QUOTA (MB)	SERVER RESOURCE QUOTA	DELETED	DAYS REMAINING
Site Collections				
https://powershellbook.sharepoint.com/sites/MyDemoSite	100	0	12/8/2013 11:25:07 AM	29
https://powershellbook.sharepoint.com/sites/dev	500	0	12/8/2013 12:27:01 PM	29

Figure 9-10. *Recycle bin in the SharePoint Online admin center*

The Get-SPODeletedSite PowerShell cmdlet takes in a unique parameter, the URL of the deleted site collection to which you wish to obtain a reference. A deleted site collection in SharePoint Online is represented by the SPODeletedSite object. Figure 9-11 shows how you can obtain a reference to the deleted developer site collection that you've deleted previously, and shows you all the methods and properties exposed by this object.

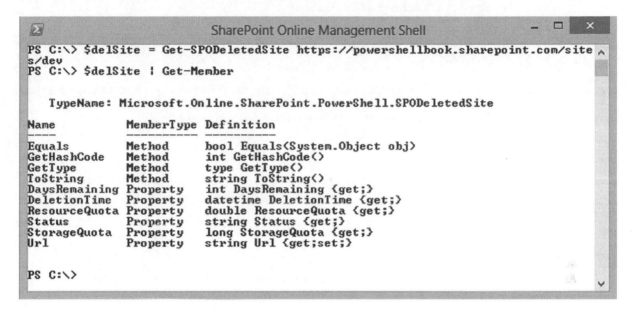

Figure 9-11. *Getting a reference to a deleted site collection in SharePoint Online and listing its available properties and methods using PowerShell*

Restore-SPODeletedSite

The Restore-SPODeletedSite PowerShell cmdlet restores a deleted site collection back to life. While they are in the recycle bin, site collections are no longer accessible through the browser. Restoring a deleted site collection puts it back in the list of available site collections in the SharePoint Online admin center. The Restore-SPODeletedSite cmdlet simply takes the URL of the site collection that you wish to restore from the recycle bin. The process of restoring a deleted site collection converts the SPODeletedSite object back to a SPOSite object.

Remove-SPODeletedSite

Remove-SPODeletedSite is like the "Grim". It takes a site collection that has been previously deleted and that is patiently waiting in the recycle bin, and permanently makes it disappear. Once a site collection has been removed from the recycle bin, it is no longer restorable; it's gone. One very interesting fact is that in SharePoint 2013, there is no way for an administrator using the web interface to force the deletion of a site collection from the recycle bin. Site collections that have been deleted in Office 365 are given a 30-day grace period during which administrators can reverse their decision and restore them. If after these 30 days the site collections are still in the recycle bin, then SharePoint Online will automatically remove them permanently. Using PowerShell is the only way for an administrator to force an immediate permanent deletion of a site collection. The following line of PowerShell will take the developer site that you've deleted previously and permanently delete it from this world. Figure 9-12 shows the permanent removal of your developer site using PowerShell.

```
Remove-SPODeletedSite https://powershellbook.sharepoint.com/sites/dev
```

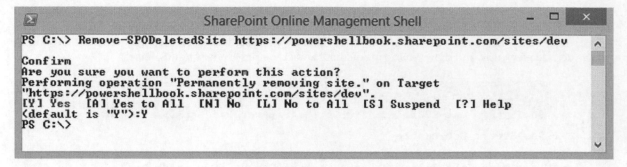

Figure 9-12. *Permanently deleting a site collection from SharePoint Online using PowerShell*

SPOSiteGroup

In this section, I will cover the various PowerShell cmdlets that are made available to you in the SharePoint Online Management Shell console to manage site collection security groups. SharePoint Online includes default security groups that vary from the default ones that you have on-premises.

Get-SPOSiteGroup

The Get-SPOSiteGroup PowerShell cmdlet allows you to get a list of all existing security groups for a specific site collection. The default security groups in each site collection vary. Table 9-3 lists the various default security groups in each, and lists their default permissions.

Table 9-3. *List of default security groups and their permissions in Office 365*

Site Collection	Security Group	Permissions
Public Facing	Approvers	Approve
	Designers	Design
	Hierarchy Managers	Manage Hierarchy
	Home Members	Contribute
	Home Owners	Full Control
	Home Visitors	Read
	Restricted Readers	Restricted Read
	Translation Managers	Restricted Interfaces for Translation
Intranet	Excel services Viewers	View Only
	Members	Edit
	Owners	Full Control
	Visitors	Read
My Site	Members	Contribute
	Owners	Full Control
	Visitors	Read

(continued)

Table 9-3. (*continued*)

Site Collection	Security Group	Permissions
Search Center	Approvers	Approve
	Designers	Design
	Excel Services Viewer	View Only
	Hierarchy Managers	Manage Hierarchy
	Members	Contribute
	Owners	Full Control
	Restricted Readers	Restricted Read
	Translation Managers	Restricted Interfaces for Translation
	Visitors	Read

You can obtain the permission level associated with each site collection security group by accessing the Roles property of a group. The following example shows how you can determine the permission level associated with the *Translation Managers* group of our default Search Center site collection (see Figure 9-13).

```
$groups = Get-SPOSiteGroup https://powershellbook.sharepoint.com/search
$translationMgr = $groups | Where{$_.Title -eq "Translation Managers"}
$translationMgr.Roles
```

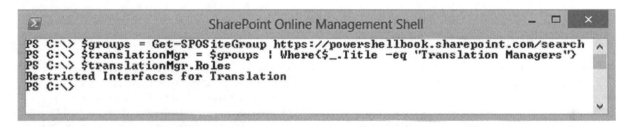

Figure 9-13. *Getting the permission level of a site collection security group in Office 365 using PowerShell*

New-SPOSiteGroup

The New-SPOSiteGroup PowerShell cmdlet lets you create a new SharePoint Online site collection security group. It requires you to pass in the site collection's URL where you wish to create this new security group, the name of the new group, as well as the permission level that you want to assign to it. Figure 9-14 shows you how you could use this cmdlet to create a new security group on your public site called *MyNewGroup* having both *Contribute* and *Design* rights.

```
New-SPOSiteGroup https://powershellbook-public.sharepoint.com
-Group "MyNewGroup" -PermissionLevels "Contribute", "Design"
```

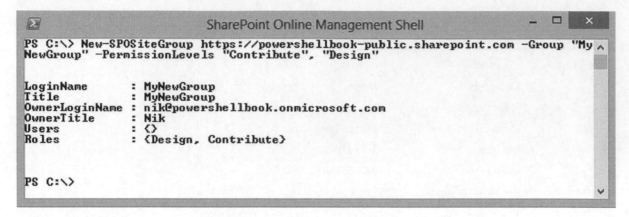

Figure 9-14. *Creating a new site collection security group in Office 365 using PowerShell*

Remove-SPOSiteGroup

Starting to figure out a pattern in the available methods? Yes, you've guessed it; the Remove-SPOSiteGroup cmdlet lets you delete an existing site collection security group. It simply requires you to pass it the URL of the site collection, as well as the name of the security group to delete. For example, to delete the security group that you've created in the previous section, you could run the following line of PowerShell:

```
Remove-SPOSiteGroup https://powershellbook-public.sharepoint.com
-Identity "MyNewGroup"
```

Set-SPOSiteGroup

Just as was the case when we dealt with SharePoint Online site collections, the Set-SPOSiteGroup cmdlet lets you modify properties related to existing site collections' security groups. For example, if you wish to modify the permission levels of a specific group, you'll need to use this cmdlet to do it. Assume that you want to modify the permissions level of a custom security group called "Partners" that exists on your public-facing instance. Assuming that this group currently has Design permission, if you wish to bring this down a notch and simply grant contributor access, you could use the following line of PowerShell code to make the change shown in Figure 9-15:

```
Set-SPOSiteGroup https://powershellbook-public.sharepoint.com -Identity "Partners"
-PermissionLevelsToRemove "Design" -PermissionLevelsToAdd "Contribute"
```

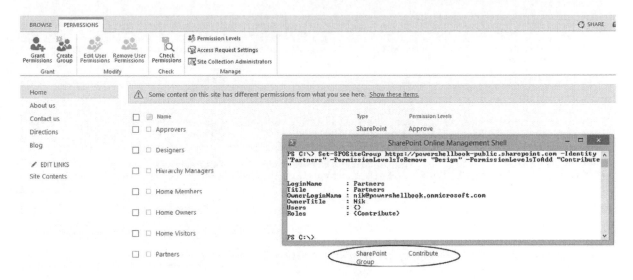

Figure 9-15. *Custom site collection security group's permission level modified by PowerShell*

Users

In this section, I will cover the various PowerShell cmdlets that are available to us to interact with SharePoint user objects. In Office 365, there are two types of users with whom you can interact. The first type, internal users, typically works for your company. They have been assigned an Office 365 license and have a user name on the company's domain in the cloud. The second type, external users, are users that are not employees of the company but that need to be granted some level of access to SharePoint sites in order to consult or contribute on documents or items store in SharePoint Online. These users are identified by their personal or external organization's email (e.g., @gmail.com, @hotmail.com, @contoso.com, etc.). In this section you will learn how to use PowerShell to interact with both types of users in the SharePoint Online context.

Get-SPOUser

The Get-SPOUser cmdlet lets you obtain a list of all users (internal and external) on a specific SharePoint Online site collection. The only required parameter is the site collection's URL. Figure 9-16 shows the result of executing this PowerShell cmdlet against our internal site collection.

```
$users = Get-SPOUser https://powershellbook.sharepoint.com
```

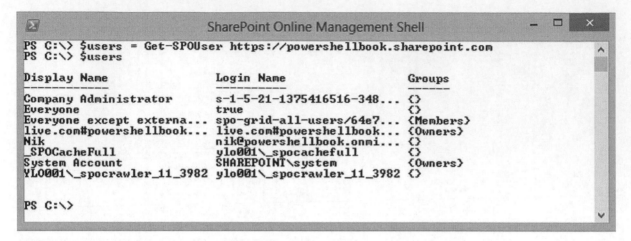

Figure 9-16. *Listing all users on an internal SharePoint Online site collection using PowerShell*

You can see from this example that there are some abstract users being returned. Those are simply what I would consider "maintenance" accounts. They are required accounts that the SharePoint farm needs in order to operate properly. What I'm really interested in are the two accounts right in the middle of the list. You can easily see my personal account on my domain (nik@powershellbook.onmicrosoft.com), but what about the live.com#powershellbook@outlook.com user? This is an external user I invited to join my SharePoint site. I put him in the Owners group, giving him complete access over the site collection. This user can login to my Office 365 environment by using its personal @Outlook.com email account, and interact with the environment as if he was a company's user.

Get-SPOExternalUser

The Get-SPOExternalUser cmdlet lets you get a list of all external users specified in your current Office 365 tenant account. The last part of my previous sentence is key to understanding how external users are managed in SharePoint Online. They are not managed at the site collections level directly but are, rather, generic to all of your SharePoint environments. Just like the internal users, these are stored at the account level. When you add an external user to a site collection, however, it gets registered against it, and the site collection keeps a footprint of its login name. This makes sense when you think that even external users a My Site page created in your environment; SharePoint needs to know who they are, no matter what site collection you are in. Get-SPOExternalUser doesn't require any parameters. It simply connects to your tenant store and returns all of the external users it finds, no matter where in the site collection architecture they were granted access. Figure 9-17 shows the result of executing this cmdlet against our demo Office 365 tenant account:

```
Get-SPOExternalUser
```

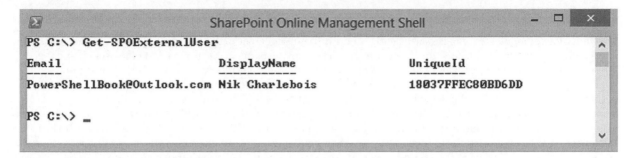

Figure 9-17. *Getting a list of all external users for an Office 365 tenant account using PowerShell*

Note that there is no way for you, with this cmdlet, to identify where in the site collections' architecture a specific external user has been granted access. You would have to loop through each one and check for their presence in the list of users. The following PowerShell script allows you to enter the user name of a specific external user and to figure out what site collections he's been granted access to (see Figure 9-18):

```
# Prompts for the external user's login name;
$extUserName = Read-Host "External User Name?"

# Gets a list of all available site collections in the current tenant;
$sites = Get-SPOSite

# Loops through all site collections
for($i = 0; $i -lt $sites.Count; $i++)
{
    # Query the list of users for the current site collection to see if external user is in
    # there;
    $user = Get-SPOUser $sites[$i].Url | Where{$_.LoginName -like "*$extUserName"}
    if($user -ne $null)
    {
        # If the user has been found, print the site's Url he has been found in;
        Write-Host $sites[$i].Url
    }
}
```

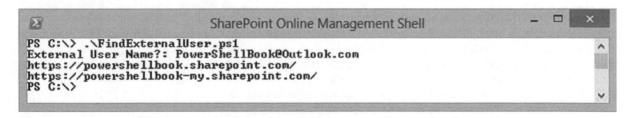

Figure 9-18. *Finding site collections in which a specific external user has access to using PowerShell*

Add-SPOUser

The Add-SPOUser cmdlet lets you add an existing user to a SharePoint Online security group. This PowerShell method takes in three required parameters: the URL of the site collection, the name of the group to add the user in, and the login name for the user to add. This cmdlet allows you to add both internal and external users to security group. For example, you could try to add an internal user by passing its user name in the form Domain\Username or add an external user using the default user id provided with Office 365 that includes its email address (e.g., live.com#powershellbook@outlook.com). However, an external user name needs to have been registered against the site collection before attempting to add it to a security group; otherwise, Office 365 won't recognize its login name. For example, Figure 9-19 shows the use of this cmdlet to try to add the same external user to two different site collections. In the first case, the external user had not been registered with the site collection, whereas, in the second case, the user had properly been registered. Note that there is currently no way to use the SharePoint Online Management Shell to automatically register an external user against a site collection.

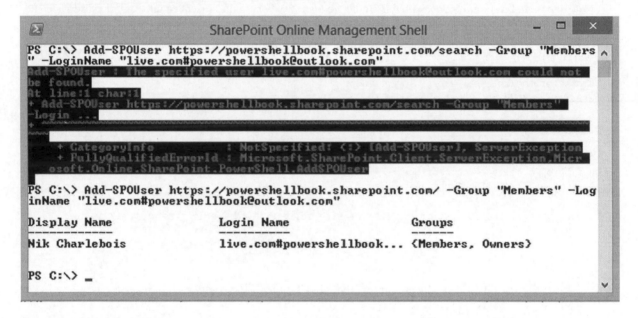

Figure 9-19. *Trying to add an external user against two different site collections using PowerShell*

Remove-SPOUser

The Remove-SPOUser cmdlet lets you remove both an internal, and an external user from a SharePoint site collection. It requires you to pass it both the site collection's URL and the login name for the user to remove. Remember that when dealing with external users, when you are at the site collection level, login names take the form of *<Authorization Provider>#<User Email>* (e.g., Live.com#PowerShellBook@Outlook.com). The following line of PowerShell will remove the external user you've added to our internal site collection:

```
Remove-SPOUser https://powershellbook.sharepoint.com
-LoginName live.com#powershellbook@outlook.com
```

Remove-SPOExternalUser

You are probably wondering why it is that you need a separate remove method to get rid of external users, when the method I've just covered takes care of both internal and external users. You need to remember that when I talk about external users, you must think of this in the tenant context, meaning external users are registered against your entire Office 365 account. When an external user is registered against a specific site collection, it becomes what I'd call a "semi-internal" user, meaning that you can interact with it as if it was just a regular internal SharePoint user. The concept of external user only really makes sense when you're talking about the higher level of SharePoint management: the entire SharePoint environment. This method deals exactly with this. It gets rid of an external user at the tenant level, meaning that it will no longer be registered at the account level.

In order to use the Remove-SPOExternalUser cmdlet, you'll need to obtain the external user's unique id. An important thing to note as well is that by simply removing the entry to the external user at the tenant's level, you are not revoking the user's access to the site collections to which he has been granted access previously. The following PowerShell script will come in handy if you ever need to get rid of an external user and want to ensure all registered instances are also removed from the site collections. Therefore, the script makes sure that the specified external user is no longer able to access any SharePoint site collection in your Office 365 environment:

```
# Get the external user login name;
$extUser = Read-Host "External User Login Name?"

# Get a list of all site collection;
$sites = Get-SPOSite

for($i = 0; $i -lt $sites.Count; $i++)
{
    $user = Get-SPOUser $sites[$i].Url | Where{$_.LoginName -like "*$extUser"}
    if($user -ne $null)
    {
        # Remove the user from the site collection;
        Remove-SPOUser $sites[$i] -LoginName $user.LoginName
    }
}

# Gets the external user's unique id and remove it from the tenant account;
$userRec = Get-SPOExternalUser | Where{$_.LoginName -eq $extUser}
Remove-SPOExternalUser $userRec.UniqueId -Confirm:$false
```

Set-SPOUser

The Set-SPOUser cmdlet lets you specify if a specific user should be granted site collection administrator rights or not. For example, the following line of PowerShell code could be used to revoke my SharePoint site collection administrator rights from your internal SharePoint environment. Just make sure that you don't accidentally remove administrative rights from your unique administrator account when using this cmdlet:

```
Set-SPOUser https://powershellbook.sharepoint.com -LoginName Nik@PowerShellBook.OnMicrosoft.com
-IsSiteCollectionAdmin $false
```

Apps

Just like the on-premises story, SharePoint in the cloud on Office 365 also lets you install and develop custom SharePoint 2013 apps. You can create a developer's site collection and let your developers publish apps in testing to it. Once the apps get approved, they can be pushed in your organization's store and be consumed by all your site collections. The current section will give you an overview of what can be achieved with PowerShell to maintain and monitor your apps in an Office 365 SharePoint Online environment.

Get-SPOAppInfo

Assume that you have installed a custom app from the Office marketplace on one of your sites. The Get-SPOAppInfo cmdlet lets you get a reference to this app instance by simply passing it the name of the app you've installed somewhere in any of your site collections. Because this is tough to explain, I'll show you a concrete example. Assume that a user went in the Office app marketplace and installed an app, called Timer Clock, on my internal SharePoint Online site collection. I now want to go and get a reference to this app instance. By using the Get-SPOAppInfo cmdlet and passing it the name of my app instance, I can get easily get a reference to that object. Notice that in this example, I'm simply passing it part of the actual app's name. This works fine because PowerShell treats this parameter as a wildcard and gets any app that has the word "timer" in its name. Using this method gives you an overview of all of the apps that have been installed throughout the SharePoint Online environment as well as telling you important information about them, such as the source from which they were installed (organizational catalog, marketplace, etc.). Figure 9-20 shows the results of running this line of PowerShell code:

```
$timerClockApp = Get-SPOAppInfo -Name "Timer"
```

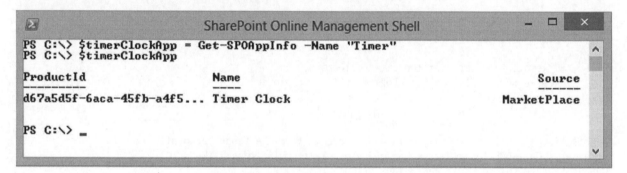

Figure 9-20. *Getting information related to installed apps in an Office 365 environment using PowerShell*

Get-SPOAppErrors

In Office 365, you are given the option to create an App Catalog for your tenant account. An app catalog site collection is created by using the Apps management section in the Office 365 SharePoint Online admin center (see Figure 9-21). This type of site collection allows you to make custom apps developed by your organization available to all site collections, and lets end users install and use them as they wish.

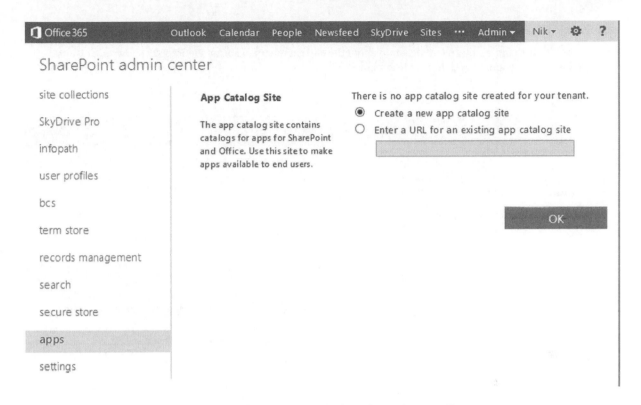

Figure 9-21. *Creating a new App Catalog site collection using the web interface in Office 365*

The question now becomes, how do you monitor errors related to these custom apps your development team produces? The Get-SPOAppErrors cmdlet lets you access information related to errors due to installation, upgrade, and execution errors. It requires you to pass the app's product ID as a parameter. This data is only being updated every 24 hours by Office 365 timer jobs, so don't worry if you don't see stats appear right after your users start calling you about errors. The following example shows a scenario in which a faulty app has been deployed to the organization. Users trying to access the app in question are getting an error page. Calling the following lines of PowerShell code would return a list of all errors associated with the MyCrashingapp instance:

```
$myCrashingApp = Get-SPOAppInfo -Name "MyCrashingApp"
Get-SPOAppErrors $myCrashingApp.ProductId
```

Tenant

As mentioned previously, SharePoint Online in Office 365 runs in a multitenant mode, meaning that there are multiple users/organizations on the same SharePoint farm. PowerShell provides you with various ways of viewing information about the tenant's account. This section will give an overview of what the various options are available to you with the SharePoint Online Management Shell.

Get-SPOTenant

The Get-SPOTenant cmdlet returns information about the current tenant account. Figure 9-22 shows the results of running this cmdlet against our demo environment:

```
Get-SPOTenant
```

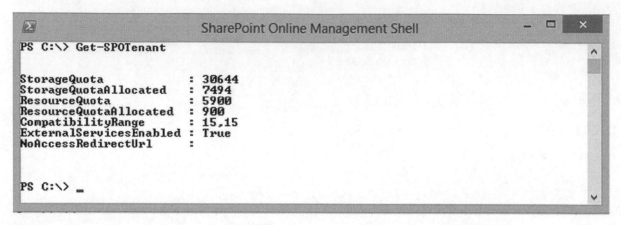

Figure 9-22. Getting information about the current Office 365 tenant account using PowerShell

Set-SPOTenant

You can use this cmdlet to set properties of the current tenant account. One example of properties you can set is the NoAccessRedirectUrl, which specifies a URL to redirect a user if the site they are trying to access has been locked. A locked site means it can't be access by users. In real life, you want to lock a site while it is in development or while it is undergoing maintenance. It is a temporary state that freezes a site collection into its current state. To illustrate this, assume the following scenario. Pretend that you need to lock down the developer's site collection in your environment because you want to prevent users from submitting new apps in testing (harsh example). You want users trying to access the developer site while it is locked down to be redirected to a user-friendly page that will explain to them what is going on, and tell them when to expect that the site will be back up. This PowerShell script will start off by locking the developer site, and then will set the NoAccessRedirectUrl property of your tenant account to contain the URL of the temporary page to which you want to redirect users:

```
Set-SPOSite https://powershellbook.sharepoint.com/sites/dev -LockState NoAccess
Set-SPOTenant -NoAccessRedirectUrl https://powershellbook-public.sharepoint.com
```

Get-SPOTenantLogEntry

You probably got very excited when you first read the name of this PowerShell cmdlet. Let me burst your bubble right away; it doesn't do what you think it does, at least not exactly. The biggest downside of SharePoint Online is that we don't have direct access to our servers and therefore can't directly get access to the SharePoint logs. The cmdlet lets you get access to certain information pertaining to your tenant account logged in the SharePoint logs. It will contain information about component failures if there are any (BCS, User Profile Service, etc.). It also contains information related to important events that happened on the environment. Figure 9-23 shows you what the results of running the method against our demo environment are. By looking at it, you can see that two events have been logged, one for every developer's site that I created. This could be important information for you to monitor, because developer sites allow users to side-load SharePoint apps. You probably don't want anybody creating such sites and loading their own applications in them.

```
$logs = Get-SPOTenantLogEntry
$logs[0].Message
```

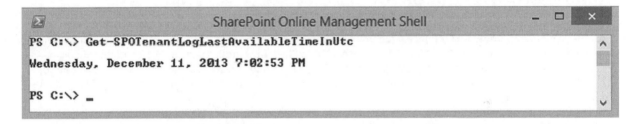

Figure 9-23. Displays the latest log entry from our SharePoint Online environment using PowerShell

Get-SPOTenantLogLastAvailableTimeInUtc

Yes, somebody at Microsoft ought to be fired for coming up with such a long name for this PowerShell cmdlet. On the good side, the `Get-SPOTenantLogLastAvailableTimeInUtc` cmdlet does exactly what its 10-foot-long name says it does: it returns the date of the latest log entry in UTC time. This cmdlet could prove useful if you are automating a script that regularly checks on the cloud server to see if any new errors have been logged, and then notify the user. Figure 9-24 shows the results of running this cmdlet against our demo environment.

```
PS C:\> Get-SPOTenantLogLastAvailableTimeInUtc

Wednesday, December 11, 2013 7:02:53 PM

PS C:\> _
```

Figure 9-24. Getting the last log entry time from SharePoint Online using PowerShell

Web

I have mentioned previously that there is no way through the SharePoint Online Management Shell to create new webs in SharePoint Online. However, when creating a new site collection, you are also creating a root Web, which is assigned a web template type. There is only one PowerShell cmdlet in SharePoint Online that interacts with web objects. However, as you'll learn in the next section, there are many more options available to you to deal with webs in Office 365.

Get-SPOWebTemplate

The `Get-SPOWebTemplate` cmdlet returns a list of all available web templates in SharePoint Online. Figure 9-25 shows the resulting list produced by this cmdlet.

```
SharePoint Online Management Shell                    –  □  ×

PS C:\> Get-SPOWebTemplate

Name                  Title              LocaleId    CompatibilityLevel
----                  -----              --------    ------------------
STS#0                 Team Site             1033                     15
BLOG#0                Blog                  1033                     15
BDR#0                 Document Center       1033                     15
DEV#0                 Developer Site        1033                     15
DOCMARKETPLACESI...   Academic Library      1033                     15
OFFILE#1              Records Center        1033                     15
EHS#1                 Team Site - Shar...   1033                     15
BICenterSite#0        Business Intelli...   1033                     15
SRCHCEN#0             Enterprise Searc...   1033                     15
BLANKINTERNETCON...   Publishing Portal     1033                     15
ENTERWIKI#0           Enterprise Wiki       1033                     15
PROJECTSITE#0         Project Site          1033                     15
COMMUNITY#0           Community Site        1033                     15
COMMUNITYPORTAL#0     Community Portal      1033                     15
SRCHCENTERLITE#0      Basic Search Center   1033                     15
visprus#0             Visio Process Re...   1033                     15


PS C:\>
```

Figure 9-25. Listing all available web templates in SharePoint Online using PowerShell

Doing More with the Client Context

I'm sure that a lot of people were disappointed when they learned that there were only 30 PowerShell cmdlets made available to manage SharePoint Online. Let me bring up some good news: there are other ways than by using the default cmdlets to interact with SharePoint Online using PowerShell. In SharePoint 2010, Microsoft introduced a new development model called the *Client Side Object Model,* often referred to as *CSOM.* This new model allows developers to build applications running remotely outside of the SharePoint server and allows them to interact with the remote SharePoint environment.

Microsoft released three flavors of this new model: the JavaScript model, the Silverlight model, and the .NET model. If you've never heard of Silverlight, don't worry about it; it was never good enough to get two capitalized letters like the other good Microsoft products (just joking). We will not be covering this topic in this book, due to the technical aspect of it. This book is intended for PowerShell beginners, and I feel that developing PowerShell scripts with CSOM is really an advanced development topic. Just know that whatever you are able to do using this model, it is possible to automate with PowerShell; for example, creating webs and subwebs under a site collection and dynamically changing themes for sites are now possible with this new approach.

Summary

In this chapter, you've learned that you can use PowerShell for more than just managing SharePoint on-premises environments. With the SharePoint Online Management Shell, you now have the option to automate operations on your Cloud environments residing in Office 365. In the next chapter, I will discuss how you can use PowerShell to help you in the process of upgrading SharePoint 2010 environments to SharePoint 2013.

CHAPTER 10

■ ■ ■

Upgrading from SharePoint 2010 to 2013 Using PowerShell

In this last chapter of the book, I will take a step back and look at the scenario in which your organization already has a SharePoint 2010 environment deployed and is looking at upgrading it to SharePoint 2013. The upgrade story has been a changing one between versions of SharePoint for the last decade. If you take a look back at SharePoint Portal Server 2003, you had three options when it came to upgrading to SharePoint 2007. The first option was to do an *in-place upgrade*, which simply required you to put in the installation media, start the upgrade wizard, and pray for the best. Unfortunately, this didn't work well for customized SharePoint environments. The second option, called the *gradual update*, allowed you to run both SharePoint 2003 and 2007 side by side. The third and last option was to do what Microsoft calls a *database attach*. This basically involved you to start by creating a new SharePoint farm running the desired version of SharePoint, in this case 2007, and to attach copies of your previous environment's content databases. In many cases, the third option was the preferred one. People often decided that while upgrading the software that they might as well upgrade the hardware as well. From SharePoint 2007 to 2010, Microsoft dropped the option to do gradual upgrades, and decided to only stick with database attach, and in-place upgrades. With SharePoint 2013, the only option left to upgrade from a previous version is to attach a database to a new SharePoint 2013 server and upgrade it from their using PowerShell.

Of course, there is no way for you to automate the upgrade process from beginning to end using PowerShell; however, you can use several cmdlets provided to us by SharePoint to help us achieve your goal. This chapter is intended to be used as a quick reference guide for automating portions of your upgrade's process. With the use of PowerShell, you will learn how to detect missing features in the new SharePoint 2013 farm, convert content databases to SharePoint 2013, create evaluation site collections to preview what the upgrade will look like, and, finally, upgrade a site collection.

At the end of this chapter you will have learned how to create a PowerShell script to automate as much as possible the upgrade process of a SharePoint 2010 farm to SharePoint 2013.

Throughout this chapter I will use a demo environment that you will build especially for demonstrating the upgrade process of a highly customized SharePoint farm.

Overview of the Source Environment

For demonstration purposes, the SharePoint 2010 environment you used had a lot of customized solutions. The 2010 farm contains two content databases and only has Search service applications instantiated within it. In almost any real-life scenario, your source 2010 environment will have various types of service applications.

You should note that only six types of service applications in SharePoint 2010 have an upgrade option for 2013. Those are:

- Business Data Connectivity service application

- Managed Metadata service application

- PerformancePoint Services service application

- Secure Store service application

- User Profile service application

- Search service application

To get more information on how to upgrade existing service applications to SharePoint 2013, please refer to the following TechNet article: http://technet.microsoft.com/en-us/library/jj839719.aspx.

The Database Detach/Attach Process

The simplest way for you to attach a content database from an existing SharePoint 2010 environment to a new one is to detach the database from the 2010 environment, to copy its associated .mdf file over to the new server, and then reattach it. In this section, I will give you a high-level view of how you can detach your SharePoint 2010 content databases and reattach them over to your new SharePoint 2013 environment.

Detaching and Copying a Database

Again, let's start with detaching your existing SharePoint 2010 content databases from the database server. The reason that you have to detach the content database is that you will get an error if you try to copy an attached SQL Server database. Figure 10-1 shows the error you will see if you try to copy a database to another location without first detaching it from its current SQL Server instance.

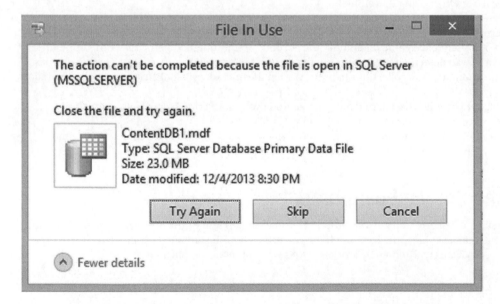

Figure 10-1. Error from trying to copy a SQL Server database that is still attached

There are several options available to you to detach a SQL database. The most common way of doing it is probably to open SQL Server Management Studio (SSMS), to navigate to your database, to right-click the instance, and to choose Tasks ➤ Detach (see Figure 10-2).

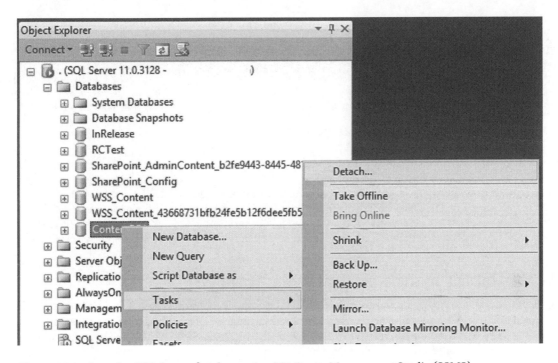

Figure 10-2. *Detach a SQL Server database using SQL Server Management Studio (SSMS)*

However, now that you're a PowerShell superhero, you'll want to spice up things a bit and automate the detach process via a script. To add to the fun, Microsoft has now made available a built-in SQL Server PowerShell module that allows you to directly interact with SQL Server using the PowerShell console. The SQLPS module can be imported into your PowerShell session by calling the Import-Module SQLPS cmdlet. It is important for you to note that this module is only available in SQL Server 2012. With this module imported onto your PowerShell session, you now have access to the extremely useful Invoke-SQLCmd PowerShell cmdlet that lets you execute SQL commands against our local SQL Server and databases.

In order for you to be able to detach the database, you need to first close all existing connections to it. In the Transact-SQL world, the SQL query to execute to achieve this is the following:

```
ALTER DATABASE <Database Name> SET SINGLE_USER WITH ROLLBACK IMMEDIATE
```

Once called, this query will tell your SQL database to close all existing clients' connection. The way is now open for you to detach the database using PowerShell. The SQL query to use to detach a database is:

```
EXEC sp_detach_db '<Database Name>', 'true'
```

This query executed the sp_detach_db stored procedure that is responsible for detaching SQL databases. Putting it all together, your PowerShell script to detach your ContentDB1 database will look like the following. Figure 10-3 shows the execution of this script on your SQL Server hosting the SharePoint 2010 databases.

```
Import-Module SQLPS
Invoke-SQLCmd "ALTER DATABASE ContentDB1 SET SINGLE_USER WITH ROLLBACK IMMEDIATE"
Invoke-SQLCmd "EXEC sp_detach_db 'ContentDB1', 'true'"
```

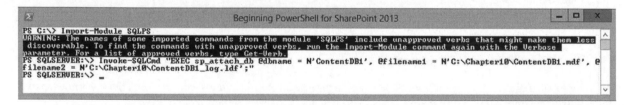

Figure 10-3. *Detaching a SQL Server database using PowerShell*

Detaching a database simply means that it is no longer associated with any SQL Server, and that its .mdf file, which contains all the actual data, is no longer used by any process. The next step is to copy the .mdf file for our ContentDB1, along with its associated log file (.ldf), over to your new SharePoint 2013 SQL server. To keep things simple, we will do this manually. The database files are by default located under the installation directory of SQL Server. In my case, the files were located in C:\Program Files\Microsoft SQL Server\MSSQL11.MSSQLSERVER\MSSQL\DATA. For the purpose of this demo, copy the database files under folder C:\Chapter10\ on the destination SQL Server.

Attaching a Database to the New SharePoint Farm

Now that both files have been copied over, you are now ready to do the opposite process of what you just did, which is to attach the copied database onto your new SQL Server. The process to attach SQL databases is in every way similar to the one that you used to detach them. Import the SQLPS module in your PowerShell session, and then directly call the Invoke-SQLCmd cmdlet, passing it the following SQL query:

```
Invoke-SQLCmd "EXEC sp_attach_db @dbname = N'ContentDB1',
@filename1 = N'C:\Chapter10\ContentDB1.mdf',
@filename2 = N'C:\Chapter10\ContentDB1_log.ldf';"
```

This SQL query will execute the sp_attach_db stored procedure, telling it to name your newly attached database "ContentDB1", and passing it the physical path to both the .mdf and the .ldf files. Figure 10-4 shows the execution of your PowerShell script that automates the attach process of your ContentDB1 database.

```
PS C:\> Import-Module SQLPS
WARNING: The names of some imported commands from the module 'SQLPS' include unapproved verbs that might make them less
  discoverable. To find the commands with unapproved verbs, run the Import-Module command again with the Verbose
  parameter. For a list of approved verbs, type Get-Verb.
PS SQLSERVER:\> Invoke-SQLCmd "EXEC sp_attach_db @dbname = N'ContentDB1', @filename1 = N'C:\Chapter10\ContentDB1.mdf', @
filename2 = N'C:\Chapter10\ContentDB1_log.ldf';"
PS SQLSERVER:\> _
```

Figure 10-4. *Attach a SQL Server database using PowerShell*

Now that you've learned how to detach a database from one server to another one, you are ready to proceed and mount your SharePoint 2010 databases onto your new SharePoint 2013 environment. In this case, before proceeding with the next section, you will have to repeat the steps learned in the current section for your ContentDB2 database.

Mounting and Testing Content Databases

In this section, you will learn how you can validate that a content database is ready to be upgraded to SharePoint 2013. Assume that the SharePoint 2010 content databases have been already attached to a newly built SharePoint 2013 farm. As mentioned in the previous example, you had a SharePoint 2010 farm that contained two content databases. The first database, ContentDB1, contained three site collections, and the second one, ContentDB2, contained a single one. Figure 10-5 represents the two content applications and the site collections that they each contain.

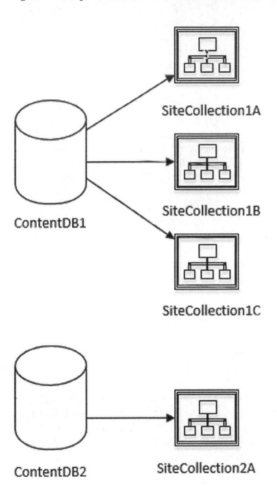

Figure 10-5. *SharePoint 2010 content databases and their associated site collections*

The SharePoint environment in your example contains several custom solutions developed by developers in your organization. These solutions contain various features that are activated at different levels in the site collections. Each solution has been globally deployed in your farm, meaning that it has been made available to all web applications. Figure 10-6 lists the different custom applications that have been globally deployed in our SharePoint 2010 source farm.

Name	Status	Deployed To
chapter7solution.wsp	Deployed	Globally deployed.
mybigdumbsolution.wsp	Deployed	Globally deployed.
nikblogdemo.wsp	Deployed	Globally deployed.
noneedforarealsolution.wsp	Deployed	Globally deployed.

SharePoint 2010   Central Administration ▸ Solution Management
This page has a list of the Solutions in the farm.

Central Administration
Application Management
System Settings
Monitoring
Backup and Restore
Security
Upgrade and Migration
General Application Settings
Configuration Wizards

Figure 10-6. *Globally deployed solutions in our farm*

Pretend that you've completed the database detach process, and that the two content databases (ContentDB1 & ContentDB2) have both been copied over and attached to the new SharePoint 2013 farm. You now need to tell your new SharePoint 2013 about the fact that these two new databases are actually SharePoint content databases. To do so, call the Mount-SPContentDatabase PowerShell cmdlet. This cmdlet requires you to pass in the URL of a web application to link the content databases. For the purpose of the demonstration, create a new SharePoint web application on port 8333 (port number chosen randomly) using PowerShell, and attach the content databases to it. The following PowerShell script will automate this process:

```
$ap = New-SPAuthenticationProvider
$admin = Get-SPManagedAccount contoso\administrator

$webApp = New-SPWebApplication -Name "DemoWebApp" -URL "http://localhost:8333"
-ApplicationPool"DemoAppPool" -ApplicationPoolAccount $admin –AuthenticationProvider $ap

Mount-SPContentDatabase "ContentDB1" -ebApplication "http://localhost:8333"
Mount-SPContentDatabase "ContentDB2" -ebApplication "http://localhost:8333"
```

The process of mounting a database can take several minutes. During the process, PowerShell will update the percentage completed for the mount operation. Now, remember that our SharePoint 2010 farm had these four custom solutions deployed onto it; but what about the 2013 environment? If you execute this code before you've correctly deployed these four solutions in your new environment, you may get errors on databases that contain site collections on which these features have been enabled. Figure 10-7 shows the errors thrown by PowerShell when trying to upgrade ContentDB1.

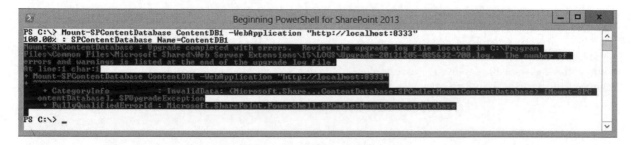

Figure 10-7. *Errors mounting a SharePoint 2010 Content Database in a SharePoint 2013 farm*

As indicated in the error message, to obtain more information related to what the actual error really is, you can have a look at the log file generated in the 15 hive. Another option is to use the Test-SPContentDatabase PowerShell cmdlet that will take a look at your partially mounted database and write the associated upgrade errors on screen. Figure 10-8 shows some of the errors that are being generated by calling this cmdlet on your ContentDB1 database.

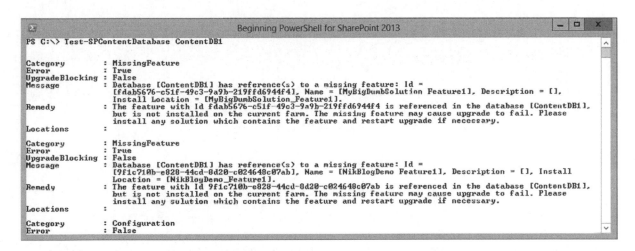

Figure 10-8. *Upgrade errors using the Test-SPContentDatabae PowerShell cmdlet*

You can clearly identify that your ContentDB1 database contains at least one site collection that requires the "MyBigDumbSolution" solution deployed, as well as another site collection requiring the "NikBlogDemo" solution. In a real-world scenario, when you upgrade a SharePoint 2010 environment to a new SharePoint 2013 one, you'll want to make sure that all of the solutions deployed on the source farm are also deployed on the destination one. This will ensure that you don't get any errors about missing features. However, if you are unsure if some solutions on the source farm are still being used or not, then it may be a good idea to do a brute force approach and only deploy the features reported as missing on the destination farm. You may as well do a cleanup while you are upgrading. In my case, I'll go ahead and deploy all of the four SharePoint 2010 custom solutions identified in Figure 10-6. Using the techniques that you learned in Chapter 7, deploy the custom SharePoint 2010 features over to your new SharePoint 2013 environment. Figure 10-9 shows that the same four solutions that you identified earlier have been successfully deployed onto your new SharePoint 2013 farm.

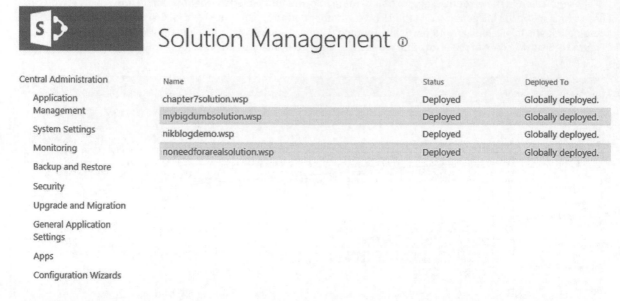

Figure 10-9. Our four custom SharePoint 2010 solutions deployed onto the new SharePoint 2013 environment

With all the custom solutions brought over, you are now ready to analyze your content database for errors. Before you move forward, however, take a look at what would have happened if you had tried mounting the content databases after the four custom solutions had been properly deployed onto your environment. To test this out, you will need to undo the mounting process that you have already done on your content databases. This process is called dismounting a content database from a SharePoint farm. Using PowerShell, you can call the Dismount-SPContentDatabase cmdlet passing it the name of the database to detach. Figure 10-10 shows the execution of the following script to detach both your ContentDB1 and ContentDB2 databases from your SharePoint 2013 environment:

```
Dismount-SPContentDatabase ContentDB1 -Confirm:$false
Dismount-SPContentDatabase ContentDB2 -Confirm:$false
```

```
Beginning PowerShell for SharePoint 2013                 _  □  X

PS C:\> Dismount-SPContentDatabase ContentDB1 -Confirm:$false
PS C:\> Dismount-SPContentDatabase ContentDB2 -Confirm:$false
PS C:\>
```

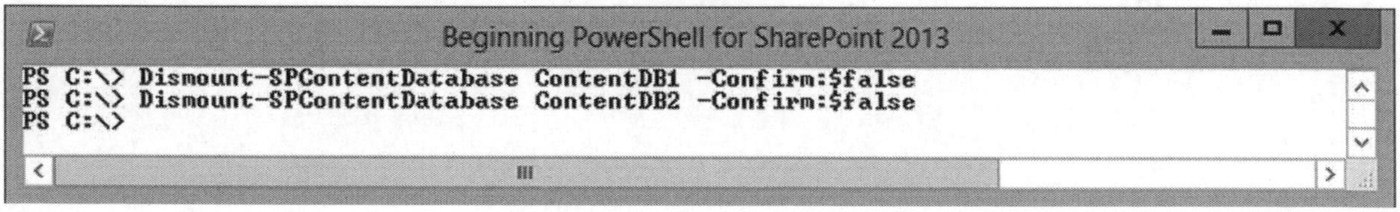

Figure 10-10. Dismounting SharePoint content databases from a farm using PowerShell

Note that you are only doing this for the purpose of explaining to you how the process would have worked from beginning to end, assuming no upgrade errors were encountered along the way. You don't normally have to dismount the databases after the missing features have been added to the farm. If you now try to remount the two content databases, no errors will be thrown in the PowerShell console. There may be warnings in the background, but these won't be shown on screen, unless you rerun the Test-SPContentDatabase cmdlet. Figure 10-11 shows the results of mounting your two content databases in a scenario in which no errors were encountered.

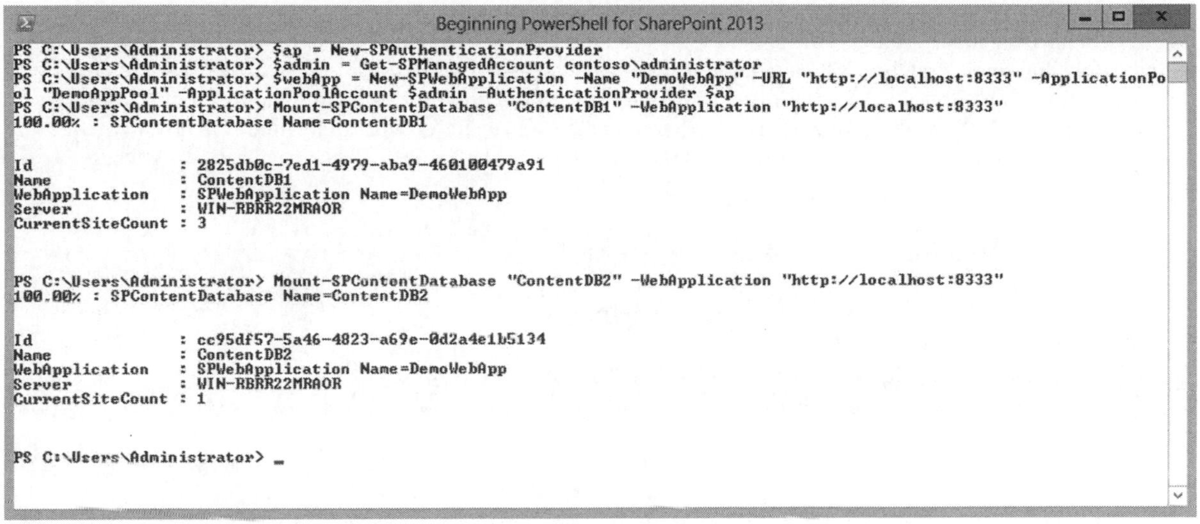

Figure 10-11. *Mounting SharePoint databases with no errors using PowerShell*

SharePoint 2010 Compatibility Mode

You are now done with your migration—at least, almost done. Now that your two content databases have been attached to the SharePoint 2013 farm, SharePoint will recognize the site collections they contain and make them its own. If you look in Central Administration, you will see that the four content databases (three contained in ContentDB1, and one contained in ContentDB2) are not shown under the web application that you created on port 8333 earlier. Figure 10-12 shows the listing of site collections for your web application in Central Administration.

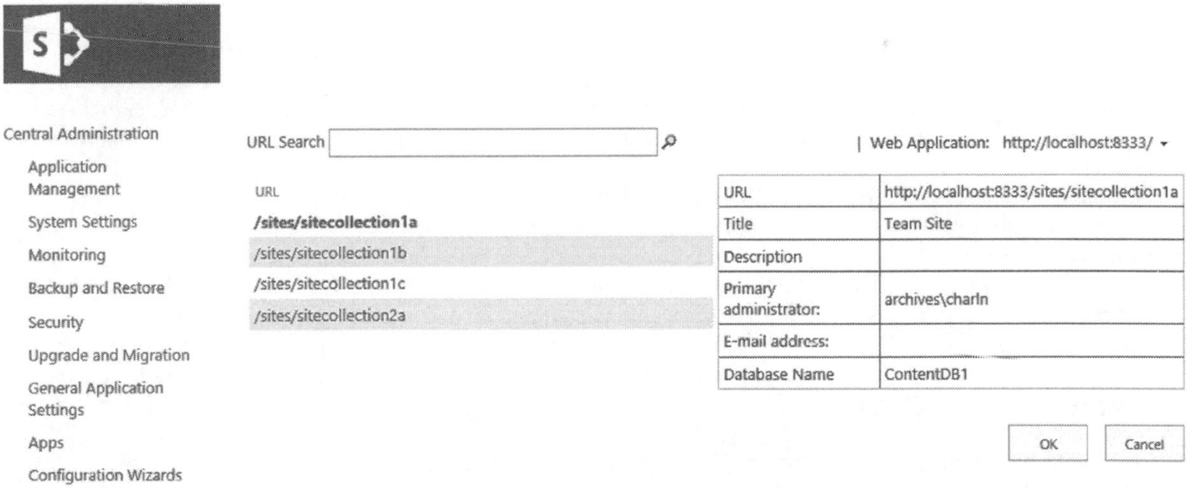

Figure 10-12. *Site collections from the imported SharePoint 2010 content databases view in Central Administration*

This means that the site collections listed here are registered with SharePoint and accessible via the browser. If you try to navigate to any of them, you should see something that looks exactly like SharePoint 2010 site collections, with the only difference that they will have a notification bar at the top. This notification bar is only there to notify the administrators that the site that they are viewing is running in a SharePoint 2010 compatibility mode, and that they should probably think about upgrading it to SharePoint 2013. Even in "compatibility mode," nearly all of the SharePoint 2010 features are still made available to the users. Figure 10-13 shows your site collection 1A access through the browser.

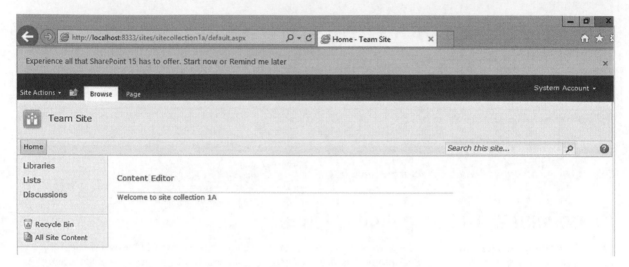

Figure 10-13. *Site collection 1A viewed in SharePoint 2010 compatibility mode*

Upgrade Evaluation Site Collection

One of the nicest new additions to the SharePoint 2013 upgrade story is the introduction of this new concept of creating an evaluation site collection that lets users preview their existing site collection that are in compatibility mode as if they had been permanently upgraded to SharePoint 2013. An evaluation site collection is a temporary, exact copy of a site collection that lets users test out how certain features or portion of their sites will react to the new 2013 components. Evaluation site collections are created under the same parent URL, but an -eval is appended to the site collections' names.

Evaluation site collections are created by a timer job that runs on a daily basis by default. When requesting a new evaluation site collection, users are simply putting the request in a queue, and this request is later picked up by the timer job that then processes the request and creates the new site collection. Using PowerShell, it is possible for an administrator to put such a request in the timer job's queue by calling the Request-SPUpgradeEvaluationSite. Remember that this simply puts the request in the waiting list; it doesn't automatically create the evaluation site. If you wish to accelerate the process, you can simply force the "*Create Upgrade Evaluation Site Collections job*" to run now. The following PowerShell lines will automate and initiate the creation of the upgrade evaluation site collection for your SiteCollection1A site collection.

```
Request-SPUpgradeEvaluationSite http://localhost:8333/sites/sitecollection1a

$webApp = Get-SPWebApplication http://localhost:8333
```

```
$evalJob = Get-SPTimerJob | ?{$_.Title -match "Create Upgrade Evaluation Site Collections job"}
| ?{$_.Parent -eq $webApp}

Start-SPTimerJob $evalJob
```

Once executed, you should be able to navigate to your upgrade evaluation site collection by adding -eval to the URL. In this case, the upgrade evaluation site collection for the SiteCollection1A site collection has been created at http://localhost:8333/sites/sitecollection1a-eval. It is important to note that the upgrade process can take several minutes to complete. Don't worry if the first time you try to access your evaluation site is still looks like 2010, or worst, like a mix of both 2010 to 2013. Once the upgrade process has completed, you should be able to view and interact with your site collection in its temporary 2013 shape. Figure 10-14 shows the upgrade evaluation site collection for site collection 1A.

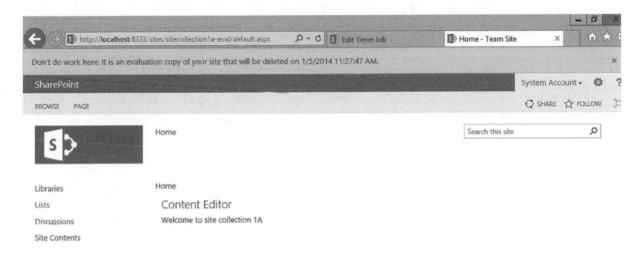

Figure 10-14. *Upgrade Evaluation site collection for SiteCollection1A*

■ **Note** Running the Request-SPUpgradeEvaluationSite PowerShell cmdlet against the root site collection creates the upgrade evaluation site collection under: /sites/root-eval and it is not assigned any expiry date.

Note that this upgrade evaluation site collection is only temporary and that it will be automatically deleted after a period of time. By default, SharePoint 2013 sets the expiry date of such site collections to 30 days after their creation. You can modify this date using the ExpirationDate property of the site collection. For example, in this case, you can change the expiration date of your evaluation site collection to tomorrow, using the following lines of PowerShell. Figure 10-15 shows the notification bar of your upgrade evaluation site collection after updating the expiration date to tomorrow.

```
$now = ([System.DateTime])::Now
$tomorrow = $now.AddDays(1)
$evalSite = Get-SPSite http://localhost:8333/sites/sitecollection1a-eval
$evalSite.ExpirationDate = $tomorrow
```

Don't do work here. It is an evaluation copy of your site that will be deleted on 12/6/2013 11:47:21 AM.

Figure 10-15. *New expiration date set by PowerShell*

Upgrading Site Collections

After you are done testing your upgrade using the upgrade evaluation site collection, you can initiate the official upgrade process for your site collections. Using PowerShell, you can initiate the upgrade process by calling the Upgrade-SPSite cmdlet passing it the URL of the site we wish to upgrade. In this example, the following lines of PowerShell will call the upgrade process on your SiteCollection1A site collection:

```
Upgrade-SPSite http://localhost:8333/sites/sitecollection1a -VersionUpgrade
```

Unlike the process of creating the upgrade evaluation site collection, the official upgrade process is instantaneous. Just as with the mounting operation, PowerShell will initiate the upgrade sequence and display the percentage completed on screen. Remember that upgrading a site collection does not automatically remove its associated upgrade evaluation site collection. You'll either need to remove it manually or wait for it to fade out and be picked up by the deletion timer job after its expiration date is passed.

Summary

This is it: you are now qualified to upgrade your organization's SharePoint 2010 environment to a brand new shiny SharePoint 2013 one. You are now a PowerShell rock star! In this chapter, you learned how the new upgrade evaluation site collection process works in SharePoint 2013, and you have automated its creation using PowerShell. It is important to remember that by using these, your users testing the upgraded environment should not put any business critical information in them. When the official upgrade process will be initiated, only data contained in the original site collection will be brought over.

APPENDIX A

PowerShell Cmdlets

This appendix gives a brief overview of the various PowerShell cmdlets we covered in this book and gives examples of how to use them.

Add-SPSolution

Adds a SharePoint solution to the farm. Need to reference the local .wsp solution file (see Chapter 7).

```
Add-SPSolution [UNCPath to the local .wsp file]
```

Backup-SPFarm

Creates a backup of a specific database, of a web application, or of the entire SharePoint farm (see Chapter 8).

```
Backup-SPFarm -Directory [Path to the backup directory] -BackupMethod Full
```

Backup-SPSite

Creates a backup of a specific site collection (see Chapter 8).

```
Backup-SPSite -Identity [URL of the site collection to backup]
-Path [Path to where to store the resulting .bak file]
```

Copy-SPSite

Creates a copy of an existing site collection at a different location inside the same SharePoint web application (see Chapter 6).

```
Copy-SPSite [URL of the site collection to copy]
[URL of the destination where to copy the site collection]
```

Disable-SPTimerJob

Disables a specific timer job, preventing its execution (see Chapter 8).

```
Disable-SPTimerJob [Reference to the timer job instance]
```

Enable-SPTimerJob

Enables a specific timer job, allowing it to execute based on its established schedule (see Chapter 8).

```
Enable-SPTimerJob [Reference to the timer job instance]
```

Export-SPAppPackage

Exports a specific app instance into a local .app package (see Chapter 7).

```
Export-SPAppPackage -App [Reference to the app instance]
-Path [Local path to the .app file to store]
```

Export-SPWeb

Exports a SharePoint web into a local file (see Chapter 8).

```
Export-SPWeb [URL of the web to export] -Path [Local path of the .cmp export file where to store
the exported web]
```

Get-SPSppInstance

Returns a collection of app instances installed on a specific web (see Chapter 7).

```
Get-SPAppInstance -Web [URL of the web to get the app instances from]
```

Get-SPBackupHistory

Returns the history of all backup and restore operations that took place in a specific folder (see Chapter 8).

```
Get-SPBackupHistory -Directory [Path to backup folder]
```

Get-SPFarm

Gets a reference to the local SharePoint farm (see Chapter 8).

```
Get-SPFarm
```

Get-SPServiceApplication

Returns a collection of all instances of service applications in the SharePoint farm (see Chapter 8).

```
Get-SPServiceApplication
```

Get-SPServiceApplicationPool

Returns a collection of all IIS application pools (see Chapter 8).

```
Get-SPServiceApplicationPool
```

Get-SPServiceInstance

Returns a collection of all services instances for a specific server or for the entire SharePoint farm (see Chapter 8).

```
Get-SPServiceInstance
```

Get-SPSite

Returns a collection of all site collections in the SharePoint farm (see Chapter 6).

```
Get-SPSite
```

Get-SPTimerJob

Returns a collection of all timer jobs registered in the SharePoint farm (see Chapter 8).

```
Get-SPTimerJob
```

Get-SPUser

Returns a collection of all users associated with a specific SharePoint web (see Chapter 6).

```
Get-SPUser -Web [URL of the web to get the user list from]
```

Get-SPWeb

Returns a reference to a specific SharePoint web (see Chapter 6).

```
Get-SPWeb [URL of the web to get a reference to]
```

Get-SPWebApplication

Returns a collection of all SharePoint web applications contained in the local farm (see Chapter 8).

```
Get-SPWebApplication
```

Get-SPWebTemplate

Returns a collection of all web templates contained in the local SharePoint farm (see Chapter 6).

```
Get-SPWebTemplate
```

Import-SPAppPackage

Imports a local app package into a specified site collection. It requires users to specify the source origin of the package. This value can be Marketplace, CorporateCatalog, DeveloperSite, ObjectModel, or RemoteObjectModel (see Chapter 7).

```
Import-SPAppPackage
-Path [Local path to the .app package to import]
-Site [URL of the site collection in which to import the app package]
-Source ([Microsoft.SharePoint.Administration.SPAppSource]::ObjectModel)
```

Import-SPWeb

Imports a SharePoint web, a list, or a library based on an exported .cmp SharePoint artifact from a local file (see Chapter 6).

```
Import-SPWeb [URL of where to restore the web]
-Path [Local path to the .cmp exported web file]
```

Install-SPApp

Installs an app on a specific SharePoint web (see Chapter 7).

```
Install-SPApp
-Web [URL of the web on which to install the app instance]
-Identity [Reference to app instance]
```

Install-SPSolution

Installs a SharePoint farm solution that has been previously added to the farm (see Chapter 7).

```
Install-SPSolution [Name of the solution]
```

Mount-SPContentDatabase

Attaches a SharePoint database to the current farm (see Chapter 10).

```
Mount-SPContentDatabase [Name of the content database on the SQL Server]
-WebApplication [URL of the web application to link the database to]
```

Move-SPSite

Moves a site collection from one content database to another (see Chapter 6).

```
Move-SPSite [URL of the site collection to move]
-DestinationDatabase [Name of the destination database on the SQL Server]
```

New-SPAppManagementServiceApplication

Creates a new instance of the App Management Service application (see Chapter 7).

```
New-SPAppManagementServiceApplication
-ApplicationPool [Reference to the associated application pool]
-Name [Name to give to the service application instance]
-DatabaseName [Name to give to the associated SQL Server database]
```

New-SPAppManagementServiceApplicationProxy

Creates an App Management Service application proxy and associates it with its service application instance (see Chapter 7).

```
New-SPAppManagementServiceApplicationProxy
-ServiceApplication [Reference to the service application instance]
-Name [Name you wish to give to the service application proxy]
```

New-SPConfigurationDatabase

Creates a new SharePoint configuration database for the local farm (see Chapter 5).

```
New-SPConfigurationDatabase
-DatabaseServer [Name of the SQL Server]
-DatabaseName [Name you wish to give to the new database]
-AdministrationContentDatabaseName [Reference to the SharePoint Administrative Database]
-Passphrase [Secret passphrase to configure the farm]
-FarmCredentials [Secure credentials to run the farm account]
```

New-SPContentDatabase

Creates a new SharePoint content database in the farm's SQL Server (see Chapter 5).

```
New-SPContentDatbase [Name of the new content database]
-DatabaseServer [Name of the farm's SQL Server]
-WebApplication [URL of the SharePoint web application to associate the content database with]
```

New-SPServiceApplicationPool

Creates a new IIS application pool (see Chapter 5).

```
New-SPServiceApplicationPool [Name to give]
-Account [Username of the account to use to run this application pool]
```

New-SPSite

Creates a new site collection (see Chapter 6).

```
New-SPSite [URL of the new site collection]
-OwnerAlias [Username of the account to use as farm administrator]
```

New-SPSubscriptionSettingsServiceApplication

Creates a new instance of the Subscription Settings Service application (see Chapter 7).

```
New-SPSubscriptionSettingsServiceApplication
-Name [Name to give the service application instance]
-DatabaseName [Name of the database associated to the service application instance]
-ApplicationPool [Reference to the application pool to use to run the service application]
```

New-SPSubscriptionSettingsServiceApplicationProxy

Creates a new service application proxy for a Subscription Settings Service application instance (see Chapter 7).

```
New-SPSubscriptionSettingsServiceApplicationProxy
-ServiceApplication [Reference to the associated service application]
```

New-SPWeb

Creates a new SharePoint web (see Chapter 6).

```
New-SPWeb [URL of the new web]
```

New-SPWebApplication

Creates a new SharePoint web application (see Chapter 5).

```
New-SPWebApplication
-Name [Name of the new Web Application]
-ApplicationPool [Name of an existing application pool to associate the web application with]
```

Remove-SPConfigurationDatabase

Permanently deletes the SharePoint farm's configuration database that has been previously dismounted (see Chapter 10).

```
Remove-SPConfigurationDatabase
```

Remove-SPContentDatabase

Permanently deletes an instance of a SharePoint content database from SQL Server (see Chapter 10).

```
Remove-SPContentDatabase [Reference to the SharePoint content database]
```

Remove-SPServiceApplication

Permanently deletes and instance of a SharePoint service application (see Chapter 8).

```
Remove-SPServiceApplication [GUID of the service application to delete]
```

Remove-SPServiceApplicationPool

Permanently deletes an IIS web service application pool (see Chapter 8).

```
Remove-SPServiceApplicationPool [Reference to the IIS web service application pool to delete]
```

Remove-SPSite

Deletes a SharePoint site collection (see Chapter 6).

```
Remove-SPSite -Identity [URL of the site collection to delete]
```

Remove-SPSolution

Deletes a SharePoint farm solution from the farm (see Chapter 7).

```
Remove-SPSolution [Name of the .wsp package to remove]
```

Remove-SPWeb

Deletes a SharePoint web (see Chapter 6).

```
Remove-SPWeb [URL to the web to delete]
```

Remove-SPWebApplication

Deletes a SharePoint web application (see Chapter 8).

```
Remove-SPWebApplication [URL or name of the web application to delete]
```

Request-SPUpgradeEvaluationSite

Puts a request to have an upgrade evaluation site collection created in a queue. Daily timer job will then take care of creating it (see Chapter 10).

```
Request-SPUpgradeEvaluationSite [Reference to the original site collection]
```

Set-SPServiceApplicationPool

Changes the account used to run a SharePoint IIS web service application pool (see Chapter 5).

```
et-SPServiceApplicationPool [Reference to the IIS web service application pool]
-Account [Username to use to run the application pool]
```

Set-SPTimerJob

Sets a new schedule for a running SharePoint timer job (see Chapter 8).

```
Set-SPTimerJob
-Identity [Reference to the timer job]
-Schedule "Hourly between 5 and 10"
```

Set-SPWeb

Configures various properties of a specific SharePoint web (see Chapter 6).

```
Set-SPWeb [URL to the SharePoint Web]
-RelativeUrl [New relative URL of SharePoint web]
```

Start-SPServiceInstance

Enables a specific SharePoint service instance on a specific server or on the entire farm (see Chapter 8).

```
Start-SPServiceInstance [GUID of the service instance to start]
```

Start-SPTimerJob

Immediately executes a specific SharePoint timer job, then its normal execution schedule resumes (see Chapter 8).

```
Start-SPTimerJob [Reference to the timer job to execute]
```

Stop-SPServiceInstance

Stops a service instance for a specific SharePoint service (see Chapter 8).

```
Stop-SPServiceInstance [GUID of the service instance to stop]
```

Test-SPContentDatabase

Tests a SharePoint content database against its associated web application to ensure all customized components are installed (see Chapter 10).

```
Test-SPContentDatabase [Name of the content database to test]
-WebApplication [URL of the web application to test the database against]
```

Uninstall-SPAppInstance

Uninstall a specific SharePoint app instance (see Chapter 7).

```
Uninstall-SPAppInstance [Reference to the app instance to uninstall]
```

Uninstall-SPSolution

Uninstalls a specific SharePoint farm solution from the environment. Uninstalling it doesn't remove the .wsp from the server. You will need to use the Remove-SPSolution cmdlet to do so (see Chapter 7).

```
Uninstall-SPSolution [Name of the wsp solution to remove with its .wsp extension]
```

Update-SPAppCatalogConfiguration

Updates the location of the app catalog (see Chapter 7).

```
Update-SPAppCatalogConfiguration [URL of the new location of the app catalog]
```

Update-SPAppInstance

Updates an app instance to a greater version (see Chapter 7).

```
Update-SPAppInstance [Reference to the old version of the app instance]
-App [Reference to the newest app instance]
```

Update-SPSolution

Updates an already deployed SharePoint farm solution to its newest version (see Chapter 7).

```
Update-SPSolution [Name of the farm solution to update including the .wsp extension]
-LiteralPath [Local path to the newest .wsp solution package]
-GACDeploy
```

Index

Get the eBook for only $10!

Now you can take the weightless companion with you anywhere, anytime. Your purchase of this book entitles you to 3 electronic versions for only $10.

This Apress title will prove so indispensible that you'll want to carry it with you everywhere, which is why we are offering the eBook in 3 formats for only $10 if you have already purchased the print book.

Convenient and fully searchable, the PDF version enables you to easily find and copy code—or perform examples by quickly toggling between instructions and applications. The MOBI format is ideal for your Kindle, while the ePUB can be utilized on a variety of mobile devices.

Go to www.apress.com/promo/tendollars to purchase your companion eBook.

Printed by Publishers' Graphics LLC USA
DBT140311.15.16.2